The **Strength** and **Resilience** ... ırch

BUILDING BRIDGES
of grace

TREVOR GRIFFITHS
With a Foreword by Mark Stibbe

Building Bridges of Grace:
The Strength and Resilience of an Emotionally Intelligent Church

Copyright © 2015 by Trevor Griffiths.

First paperback edition printed 2015 in the United Kingdom.

Unless otherwise stated, Bible quotations are from the New International Version.

No part of this book shall be reproduced or transmitted in any form or by any means, electronic or mechanical, including photocopying, recording, or by any information retrieval system without written permission from the publisher.

Published by Trevor Griffiths using KWS services: www.kingdomwritingsolutions.org

Further copies of the book printed with colour diagrams, and related study materials, can be purchased from www.emotionallogicshop.com and https://www.eltcollege.com

ISBN 978-0-9931920-0-5

The **Strength** and **Resilience** of an **Emotionally Intelligent Church**

BUILDING BRIDGES
of grace

Dedication

For Marian, my wife, so strong in forgiveness.

Contents

Foreword by Mark Stibbe 11

Part 1: Discovering the emotional intelligence of grace

1. **Walking with a living God** 19
   Cure and healing, focus and context

2. **How does emotion fit with spiritual healing?** 39
   Our spiritual and physical natures meet in emotion

3. **Climbing to the high platform** 57
   Grace is shown in both the joy and grief of love

4. **Stepping into a Bible hologram** 91
   The chosen unity and mutual understanding of grace

5. **Unearthing the roots of conflict** 113
   Triune principles organise life among diversity

6. **The grace to reconcile** 131
   The emotional chaos of division

Part 2: Emotional intelligence in the challenge of unity

7. **Our Father in heaven** 175
   The source of life, seen differently

8. **God's kingdom on earth, as in heaven** 195
   Justice, mercy and humility in the land

9. **Give us this day our daily bread** 209
   Feeding together on the living Word to grow as a person

10. **Forgiveness** 221
    Grace to forgive is a pre-condition for reconciliation

11. **Temptation and evil** 233
    Evil choice magnifies others' grief in order to control them

12. **Kingdom living** 249
    Living diversity in unity fulfils God's Promise to Abraham

    Appendix—A simple look at triune neuroscience 261

    Glossary of triune terms 271

    Bibliography 283

Figures

Fig. 1	Three example Stepping Stone card patterns	74
Fig. 2	An Example Loss Reaction Worksheet	79
Fig. 3	The triquetra—an image of dynamics	118
Fig. 4	Networks of triquetra	119
Fig. 5	One living God as a Holy Trinity of Persons	121
Fig. 6	Humankind as an image and likeness of God	124
Fig. 7	Three association areas of the brain	126
Fig. 8	The conversational orientation of personhood	128
Fig. 9	The Structuralist analytical perspective	149
Fig. 10	The Individualist analytical perspective	152
Fig. 11	The Collectivist analytical perspective	155
Fig. 12	Communion	161
Fig. 13	Restricted group identity—a preference for structure	162
Fig. 14	Restricted group identity—a preference for change	163
Fig. 15	Restricted group identity—a preference for relatedness	164
Fig. 16	A triune person with heart and mind	165
Fig. 17	Ethical categories map onto triune principles	166
Fig. 18	A Loss Reaction Worksheet—developing triune prayer	167

Plate 1	Presentation to Pope John Paul II	168

Electronic download copies of this book and 'print on demand' copies will have greyscale pictures and diagrams. To download the colour diagrams free of charge, go to:

https://www.eltcollege.com/grace-diagrams

Foreword by Mark Stibbe

I'm delighted and honoured to provide a foreword for this ground-breaking, thoughtful and (for me) timely book.

In recent months I've been struck by how emotionally unintelligent I have been over the course of my life. I have had little grasp of what I'm truly feeling, why I'm feeling these feelings, and how I'm meant to manage them in a godly and creative way. For much of my life I have been living with a deep sense of grief about my abandonment as a baby by my biological mother, and then my subsequent abandonment by my adoptive parents on the steps of my boarding school on my eighth birthday (an event I refer to as my second orphaning). I have repressed these 'great sadnesses' as part of my survival strategy, dissociating myself from the pain. The effects have not been good in some of my most important relationships.

And they have not been positive in my working life either. As a Vicar in the Church of England for nearly a quarter of a century I can now say, with the benefit of hindsight, that much of my working life was lived not only in a state of repressed mourning but also with unresolved anger over my separation from my parents (both sets). Starved of my true parent's love, I lived with an unhealthy need for attachment and affection from those I served as a leader. This was not a strong centre from which to live my life, relate to others or do my work.

In the end, the only thing that began to displace this pain has been the ongoing experience of the perfect love of our Father in heaven, found in Jesus, and ministered through the Spirit of adoption. Slowly, over the years, this experience of the love of Father God has begun to put me more and more in touch with my true feelings and in the process disentangled me from the roots and the fruits of my abandonments.

For me then, and I know for countless others too, emotional intelligence has become a matter of life and death. I have simply had to understand what I feel, how I feel and why I feel—not only the human feelings of separation (the ultimate agony) but also the divine feelings of embrace (the ultimate ecstasy) in Abba Father's love.

However, for many Westerners (especially Brits), this emphasis on feelings is discomforting. Brought up in a culture where Stoicism has been a key to survival and rationalism has been apotheosised to the level of a deity, this is all too subjective—dangerously so. Add to the mix the fact that the Western churches have historically bought into Enlightenment rationalism and you have all the ingredients for a cocktail of trenchant anti-emotional rhetoric.

At the same time, however, counter-currents have been growing, morphing into culture-changing megatrends.

For example, the mustard seed of clinical psychology in the twentieth century—which has now burgeoned into a veritable tree of many psychoanalytical and counselling branches—has brought us closer and closer to the relatively uncharted world of understanding and managing our human emotions.

Within the churches, the advent of the Pentecostal and then the Charismatic movements in the twentieth century has not only spawned the most impressive growth in churches worldwide (both numerically and organically), it has also brought a fresh wind of experiential, living faith into believers' lives, giving them not only light in the head but heat in the heart (and we all know that light and heat makes fire!).

This has dramatically changed the landscape.

In the non-church context, particularly in the corporate world, there is now an acknowledgment that leaders need to be not only socially intelligent (able to relate to and influence others in a positive, healthy way). They need also to be emotionally intelligent (able to monitor their emotions well, and those of the people they're influencing). Dan Goleman has been especially significant in this regard. Although he wasn't the first to propose this, his book Emotional Intelligence was the first to show leaders in a popular, non-academic way how EQ was every bit as important as IQ, perhaps more so.

Meanwhile, in the church, the dramatic expansion of the Pentecostal movement worldwide meant that sooner or later the experience of the life-enhancing, re-invigorating work of the Holy Spirit of God would need to be underpinned by a robust theology. So in the 1980s Pentecostal theology was formally born and nurtured by Sheffield Academic Press's Journal of Pentecostal Theology and its series of book length, scholarly studies of the work of the Spirit. One of the first of these was Steven Land's pioneering book, Pentecostal Spirituality: A Passion for the Kingdom. This is quite simply one of the most important books I had read until then.

I remember the fresh breeze of the Spirit blowing on my heart as I opened Pentecostal Spirituality and read Land's impassioned plea for a third, vital element in Christian theology. We had orthodoxy (right teaching) and orthopraxy (right believing), Land said. But what about orthopathy (right feeling)? Why have we been so reticent about discussing authentic, Spirit-ual experiences? Why is it that such subjects are only really brought up in seasons of revival, as in the Great Awakening, when Jonathan Edwards wrote his magisterial work, The Religious Affections?

In highlighting this neglect of experiential discourse, Land proposed that in light of the breathtaking new encounters with the Spirit of Pentecost on the worldwide stage there should be a proper place given to orthopathy in theological studies. In other words, Land proposed that the churches globally now needed to become emotionally intelligent—able to understand what constitutes legitimate, Biblical experience and what does not. Put in the language of John Wesley, he argued that we should work with the quadrilateral of Scripture, tradition, reason and experience, reinstating that broken fourth leg of the table which is experience.

All of this I welcomed at the time and I welcome now.

However the Church has been waiting several decades for a rigorous theological examination of how to manage human emotions and spiritual experiences in a way that is healthy and healing.

That day has now dawned with the publication of Dr Trevor Griffiths' book that you're about to read.

This is quite simply the deepest, most eloquent and stretching study of emotional intelligence in the life of Jesus and in the contemporary churches—Protestant, Catholic and Orthodox—that you'll have read.

It is a passionate, sometimes poetic, plea for emotional intelligence in and between churches today.

Born from considerable experience in his role as a medical doctor, as well as his equally impressive experiences of living in community and exploring Christian traditions beyond his own, *Building Bridges of Grace* is a remarkable book. It is a book to be read slowly and certainly more than once.

Here Trevor takes us on a sometimes arduous journey of exploration in which we learn how to manage our emotions well and in the process climb on to the high platform of grace where we are welcomed and embraced by the triune God through the Spirit of adoption. From that elevated vantage point, we see things far more clearly (through divine eyes) and become far better equipped to confront in a productive way the divisions that have marred and disempowered the Church. From this high platform of grace, we are able to understand the emotions of grief and anger that so often disable the process of peace-making, asking 'what am I grieving about losing in this act of building bridges?' Asking that kind of honest question then proves to be the springboard for unity in and among churches—a unity that formally would have been inconceivable.

There is so much more I could say about this book, in praise of its subtle balance of personal narrative and universal truth-telling, and in particular its extraordinarily daring and insightful use of the Lord's Prayer as a hook on which to hang some of the most radiant insights about reconciliation that I've read anywhere.

But you need to read it for yourself.

As you do, have a handkerchief ready.

You may find that tears start to fall as the healing begins.

Dr Mark Stibbe
Published Author, Writing Coach and Business Leader

Part 1

Discovering the emotional intelligence of grace

For God so loved the world that he gave...

Chapter 1

Walking with a living God

Have you ever had an experience where the shock waves compelled you to look at life from a completely new perspective? For Marian and I, it was a shocking incident about churches that changed life's direction.

We were both National Health Service General Practitioners at the time, husband and wife in the medical practice I had started a few years before. By God's grace we are still active Christians now, twenty five years later, and can tell the story of how this incident has turned to God's glory. It is a story in the making still, as if continuing the biblical book of Acts into the future.

Marian and I were exploring how the models of healing we used in our secular medical work related to, and differed from, the Christian ministry of healing at our church and in other Christian settings. We were part of a group of like-minded Christian healthcare professionals meeting regularly in Plymouth, linked into two national movements that were looking at the same. One was a charismatic professional development movement called 'Christians in Caring Professions'. In the other Marian and I had been appointed jointly as observers for the 'Pentecostal Churches of the British Isles' on 'The Churches' Council for Health and Healing' in London. This was chaired by Bishop Morris Maddocks, running trans-denominational work groups that produced reports on different aspects of healing. I had a somewhat scholarly thread running through my approach, having started my training as a doctor at Oxford University. Marian's presence was more practical and 'earthed', which became more important later.

With this background, Marian and I were developing patient-centred ways to take a 'spiritual history' in the GP consulting room without commenting on beliefs. This extends the way doctors talk about any sensitive areas of life with their patients, such as smoking habits, sexual preferences, alcohol use, relationship strengths, and so on. A spiritual history might highlight the wider relational context in which we could agree sustainable health plans with patients.

We took the view that a person's spirituality reflects his or her sense of belonging in the widest context of life that they are able to imagine. That broad view of spirituality, as the fact of connection in movement, makes it easy to talk in the doctor's office about how this unique person sees love in relation to healthy living, qualifying that term by saying, "…in love's widest sense of connection". When appropriate for someone searching, Marian and I might say that the Church is the power of love to heal available for anyone in a community.

Then, one day, a patient booked in to see me and told me this. He said, "You know, you told me that the Church is the power of love to heal. Well, I started going to that church up the road, and do you know what I discovered? The way they run down the people who go to the other churches in this area deeply upset me. It was so hurtful. I thought, 'How can this be a source of love for me, if they hate each other so?'"

I had no answer for him. I tried making allowance for human weakness and failings, but it sounded hollow. He was right. I was cornered and defeated. I took it back to the focus group for supervision.

He had stopped going to church, and he withdrew from associating with Christians. Marian and I had to accept that this lament is heard frequently and pervasively among those who avoid churches. As a direct consequence, we simply had to stop saying to people, in the total privacy of a doctor's consulting room, that the Church is the power of love to heal. The attitudes among people gathering in their little churches had impacted in a destructive way what could be said in a totally private conversation somewhere else.

That distant impact is true spirituality. It is equivalent to the effect of a strong blast of wind, the force of which was generated somewhere distant and out of sight, but which was felt locally. In this instance, however, human spirit, human spirituality, was speaking words of deathliness, not words of life.

The churched people concerned could have no idea of the consequences of their choice to speak in this way. The Church Family, when seen from above, as if from a high viewing platform, is thus killing itself, self-harming at least, and denying the world the love that God wants to share. Sibling rivalry, self-interest, has taken over. Cain still slays Abel in the background of the present moment in many Christian hearts. Brothers still sell Joseph into slavery and act as if he is dead.

The time has come it seems to me, now that this story has worked its way through to something constructive, to help the Church locally and world-wide to explore some new ways to relate. The era we are now entering, 2,000 years after our Teacher arrived, is tipping out of its fourth five-hundred year cycle (more about that later) into an uncertain future. I see the signs in my travels that a new and life-giving pattern is emerging, just as it did during the splits at roughly 500, 1000 and 1500 CE. This book is to help you prepare for your arrival there, at the Third Millennium re-gathering of the Church into true unity among personal diversity, even in the midst of troubled times.

Moving on from disappointment to God's way

Marian and I decided to shift our energies. Our supervision and support group encouraged us that defeat in a skirmish did not mean we had all lost the war. If you find a wound, dress it and carry on. If you find a body beaten and unconscious, care for it and trust in God's healing. That was our attitude towards God's Church. If the local churches were too sick to offer the power of love to heal the wider community, then we needed to become doctors to the Church.

We decided to start working to improve understanding and to promote a loving attitude between the different churches in our community. Many people, both in and out of the consulting rooms, had found our view of the Church helpful, as having a loving purpose to heal communities. It had enabled them to see beyond 'it', the Church, as a hothouse in which to grow religious *beliefs* in people, or prune their exuberant behaviour. The apparent need to believe in certain dogmas or to conform to unexplained moral rules could be an insurmountable barrier to 'outsiders' who longed to explore Christian spirituality. By seeing the Church as a source of love freely given, new movement may become more possible, with more hope for change.

We had become highly motivated for change by this setback from an invisible source. This individual's disconnected choice to speak in that way had been a spiritual reality, known only by its effects at a distance. There was something about the invisible source of that spoken deathliness that called forth an urge in us to respond. It was an emotional urge. We *felt* the movement caused by our valued connection with both the Church, and with our medical patient. But how could Marian and I, within our group, be sure to respond in mutual support and not out of a vengeful human desire to return hurt without hope? We had to find a way to respond in God's way, for healing of the Church towards spiritually renewed life.

From each unique person's point of view, their spirit *is* the patterned movement emanating from *their self* as a focal point in the interconnected universe and thus influencing others. If we say someone is 'spirited' we usually mean something like 'they create many patterns of movement that influence others and enrich *their* personal experience'. I suppose we could say likewise that God is spirited. Biblically, God is Spirit; but that may not emphasize the sense of movement sufficiently. So when we think about God as Holy Spirit, we need to think about patterned movement spoken into life, like the gentle power of the wind. It was in that gentle power of Holy Spirit that Marian and I in our responsive group chose to respond.

Initially our approaches led to some glorious relationship-building between equally hopeful and envisioned individuals from different churches. Times of shared worship and relationship building by testimony encouraged a joyful personal energy among us. However, we found that it could not be sustained in the face of competing church events. Each church seemed reluctant to advertise shared events in their newsletters. As a medic I wondered why the treatment was failing. What was the resistance? The patient was dying again, turning inwards, distracted, weak and disengaging from the life of the community. Why?

It was through this that I realised the vital impact of how leadership in church settings inspires a sense of belonging in those who attend. Without a vision for the world God so loves, Christian leaders have difficulty seeing why their church families should put time to seek unity of spirited movement with people in other church families. Perhaps it also seems too risky for their 'belief agenda'. Perhaps they were worried that people would put their energies into dubious practices and behaviours that others would not understand. St Paul urged people to love the diversity of active church ministries before agreeing to believe precisely the same. His call to the Church, recorded in Ephesians 4:1-13, is for disciples to seek unity of Spirit *before* unity of faith. Even more directly, in Ephesians 3:17-19, Paul urges,

'And I pray that you, being rooted and established in love,
may have power together with all the Lord's holy people, to

grasp how wide and long and high and deep is the love of Christ, and to know this love that surpasses knowledge.'

Perhaps one style of leadership that equates faith and knowledge with belief would encourage people to gain a sense of belonging in a church first by rubbing shoulders with those who profess the same beliefs, rather than with those who can move together in and for the world? That might cause what we had experienced.

This was in the 1980's. The Charismatic Movement was beginning to spread into the Anglican and Roman churches (to some people's surprise and horror, and to our delight). The free churches were simultaneously breaking up, sadly, into smaller and smaller 'fellowships', usually over disagreements about doctrine that concealed underlying personality clashes among aspiring leaders. Something was opening doors in leaders' minds to practice aggressive, possessive, mutually critical power-mongering. I can say this because, for a year, I became the part-time Director of 'Crossline' in Plymouth, a trans-denominational, volunteer, 24-hour telephone crisis and counselling service. I met most of the church leaders during that time, and concluded that apart from a few notable exceptions this was the most aggressive, resistant and ambitious bunch of men I had ever come across! Most that I met each seemed to be proudly holding up his own ladder to heaven and, pointing upwards to the small corner he could see, directing people *this* way.

This failure on a larger scale served only to motivate Marian and I further. So many unusual things had happened in our walk with the One living God (I'll tell you more about that later) that we could not doubt God as the source of ever-renewed life. My enquiring mind and spirit took me deeper and deeper to unearth the roots of the destructive and deathly attitudes I was encountering. It led me further and further back, where I saw the same tensions in the history of the Early Church, and how churches had developed and diversified through centuries of political pressure and turmoil. It took me also on a path to understand the modern mind-sciences, which I have discovered do not conflict with Christian thinking, but support it; more of that later, too.

I was beginning my work towards a model of how people with similar brains can so completely misunderstand each other at times! Perhaps seeing a reasonable and integrating mental *structure behind the causes of that misunderstanding* might automatically give people the insight needed to overcome those misunderstandings. Then the emotional tensions that come with them might be turned instead into the energy to build a life together.

With that developing insight emerged some new ways to think about leadership, and about 'church'. From now on when I use Church with a capital 'C' I shall mean the Church Universal called out from the sea of people to be the mystical Body of Christ (a married Bride) in and for the world God so loves. I shall also use a capital for the major branches of the Universal Church, the Orthodox, Oriental, Roman and Protestant Churches, to distinguish these large-scale exploratory 'movements' from their local worshipping fellowships, for which I shall use the lower case 'church'. Becoming church is not the same as becoming Church. Local church can war against Church. It's all about where we believe we belong.

To recognise this is not bad news! New ways of being 'church' locally are appearing all across the world, and in all the major branches or movements of the Church. It seems timely to be writing about this model of misunderstanding, to support this emerging new movement for reintegration with others who differ from us with a greater insight into the mystical immanence of God among us all.

I had discovered also something more glorious, lying deeper than the roots of misunderstanding and destructive attitudes. I discovered there the bedrock of God. The transcendent, patient God made immanent is there, at the very source of our thinking and action. I discovered a way to describe God's image in human being, in the way humankind's minds are able to *illuminate* their present moment. With that, there comes the potential for our growth more into the likeness of God. I believe I have found the Apostle John's starting point (John 1:4-5): "In Him (the Word) was life, and that life was the light of men. The light shines in the darkness, but the darkness has not understood it." I gained a clearer picture of mind; and of heart, and spirit, of the need for human diversity to reflect the fullness of God, and of how the salvation of souls is obscured now, its meaning wrapped up and tied in knots by ancient language. I felt a call to explain how 'ever renewed life', eternal life, is found through joining the Family of God now as 'Church in the community', which extends beyond death. This is personal salvation.

To explain that discovery and its impact, I need to tell you more about Marian's practical approach to problems, which so constructively complements my head in the clouds, as she calls it!

Keeping spirituality practical and earthed

It happened like this.

About two or three years before the incident I have just described, Marian and I had met as junior hospital doctors in Plymouth and become engaged to be married. We were exploring together how church life and worship might form part of our renewed way of living, having both come from broken first marriages that failed under the pressures of those early years as hospital doctors, working 90 hours a week and more. Exceptionally in that profession, I was at home sick one day when a lady from our Pentecostal church called round to leave a message about a meeting she had heard of that evening to do with Christianity and healthcare. I was in one of those short, sharp food poisonings from which I recovered, as men do, remarkably rapidly when the prospect of some other activity looms. Marian and I arrived there late, but in time to hear the speaker tell a story that turned our world upside-down.

He was Dr Peter Quinton, a General Practitioner from Shrewsbury, who had decided that it was entirely reasonable, if you saw a human being as a spiritual creature, to offer to pray with patients alongside all the other interventions a medic can offer, if that gives the patient no offence. His experience was that most patients welcomed the offer of prayer as a sign of personal concern, not as any imposition.

This GP said he always felt confident to pray against fear, because fear could not come from a loving God but was born of a lie of some sort. I'm not sure that I entirely agree with that point, as I shall explain later, but do hear where this goes next. He told us of a young woman who was ill from a congenital heart problem, which had been fully investigated at Bristol, and who had been booked to have open heart surgery. She was very fearful of the operative risks, and prior to travelling to Bristol she accepted the GP's offer of prayer against the fear. The GP said that, as he prayed, the words just *slipped* out that she would go to Bristol 'wholeheartedly'. The pre-operative chest X-ray, when she arrived there, showed a normal heart. Cardiac catheterisation was repeated, with a completely different result to before—a normal heart! She did not have the operation, having been mysteriously healed. The lady said afterwards that when the GP had prayed with her all she had felt was a gentle 'frizzle' run through her.

Now, at the time, I would say I was exploring Christianity and not *fully* committed. Marian had previously been a very committed Christian, but had drifted away under the weight of disappointments from her marriage. I was genuinely a 'seeker after truth', having had deeply moving religious experiences in the past, but finding myself unable to get on with churches. I had tried, but they seemed to be missing the point. I went through my medical training with a completely secular mind-frame, learning about human beings as if they were test-tubes of chemicals into which we could tip other chemical correctives, or surgically re-align the tubing. As a good scientist, however, I knew that a scientific theory is never *proven* by experimental evidence. It remains a hypothesis, to be tested in other settings and by different teams to see if supportive results strengthen its *predictive value*. If ever an experimental finding is totally *inconsistent* with the theory, then the theory is partially wrong (non-predictive); and it must be developed further to account for the finding. Bad science is where you reject the finding (and the researchers who observed it) because it does not fit your pet theory!

To a good scientist, an unusual event that does not fit the prevailing dominant theory is an exciting opportunity to develop new ways to understand life. That was the attitude with which I heard Dr. Quinton's story. I was pleased to discover that Marian felt the same. Of course, we could reject the observation and slander the GP's good name, but where is the progress in that? If this were true, and if it had any predictive value, then the whole edifice of scientific materialism had crumbled in that GP's consulting room! Human being would have to be something infinitely, beautifully more than scientific material.

Full of curiosity, at the end of the meeting we met three other people who were likewise interested to explore the implications of this, two GPs and a Health Visitor. We decided to meet fortnightly, to work out how to proceed. And that's where the fun began.

It was a launch pad. A year or so later, Marian and I had been involved, much to our surprise, in 'speaking' physical healing into a person, in spiritual deliverance ministry, and in transfiguring a person's life through sharing revealed knowledge and wisdom. We were, and are, convinced that something unique happens when people open their hearts and minds to the bigger system of God (however you understand that to be, or not to be) in which we all participate unknowingly. This is as true as all the physical chemistry of bodily life with which scientific medicine works. Somehow these two approaches to humanity co-exist.

I wanted to find out how they relate to each other; and Marian wanted to live it.

We had also seen that the value of prayer ministry in our church, now not strictly a Pentecostal Church but a renewed charismatic fellowship, could be sapped away when people return to those *environments* that stress or undermine them. Did this mean that, for these people, the change had been all imagination, or mental illusion? Or, did it mean that a *social* reality can be as powerful in the human physical condition as is the chemistry of medication, pills and nutrition?

An idea had formed in our minds, and this was where Marian's practical approach came to the fore. We needed a sort of spiritual intensive care unit; a place, an environment, where people could stay for a few days or maybe a couple of weeks, where they could receive more rounded ministry designed to help them make *sustainable* changes in their lives that would then support the benefits of their prayerful relationships and connections.

The elders of the charismatic church into which we were now securely rooted were supportive of the idea, but they could think of no way to bring this about. Gradually the realisation dawned on Marian and me, now that we were married and life had moved on, that we could be the answer to our own prayer. Although junior hospital doctor and trainee GP salaries were not huge, we earned more than most people in the church, and perhaps we could buy a larger property than our own comfort required, and provide that home as a prayer ministry base for others to use.

And so began the story of how South Highlands came to be a kingdom home. Marian may get around to writing a book about the miracles of timing and guidance we experienced during the year and more that it took to complete the purchase. She is a bit busy at the moment with full-time medicine and other commitments, including Street Pastoring. Basically, having survived what felt like a year-long tribulation of personal preparation, we started to call the miraculous timings that lead to break-through 'God-incidences'. It is more honest than calling them 'co-incidences' once we recognised how those moments in time emerge from our 'place of belonging', rooted into a broader and universal picture of ever-renewing life. People do not just rattle around in a scientifically-imagined vacuum flask. Order emerges from inter-connected chaos by consistent, loving feedback.

An old Jewish joke is relevant here. "How do you make God laugh? Answer... Tell Him your plans!" This year of preparation made us let go of our plans and start listening to God's. I mean that literally. At one point, our disappointments were building up so much that Marian and I were questioning if we should even leave the church. We had just finished some supermarket shopping, and were sitting in the car talking about what we might do. Suddenly and simultaneously we stopped, mid-sentence, and looked at each other. The shock-doubt-awe on her face must have matched mine; I had just heard a man's voice, as if from near the windscreen, saying, "Stay. You will be giving to the church." From the look on her face I knew that Marian must have heard the same. It was a deeply emotional moment, being stopped in our tracks like that. We continued to look at each other, then Marian simply said, "Well that's decided that, then!" And we drove home and put the shopping away.

That year of preparation left us in a state of total dependence on God's inspirational guidance. Whenever in subsequent years we forgot this tensioning distance between 'the still, quiet voice within' (or without) and our plans, and when we lived instead from our own understanding of situations, life would edge towards a random, chaotic, confusing disorder until we noticed what we were doing, or not doing. It was as if on those occasions of forgetfulness we re-entered a massive, uncontrolled, worldwide *social experiment*. Life separated from God (however you understand God to be, or not to be) is an uncontrolled social experiment in which individuals all over the place are guessing their way into an unknown future 'just to see what happens'. Meanwhile, in the depths of their hearts, silently in the formation of their present moments, the immanent

God is whispering, "The kingdom of heaven is at hand! Just look!"

The evidence of God-incidences (and there were many others) now surrounds us in the very stones that hold together as this solid home that we eventually bought. South Highlands is the middle third of a late Georgian mansion, set in 2 ¾ acres of gardens and paddock just off the centre of a medium-size town of 12,000 people. We bought and furnished this home even though it was on the market at a price impossibly far beyond our price range. Whenever we doubt—and we do doubt at times—we look around at the walls and stones and land and we are reminded by them that eternally we belong in something greater. The physical home took shape and became a living form *as a homely expression of* a higher order personal life, of God.

When we moved in, just to give you another example of the way it was, the people buying our semi-detached suburban house insisted that all our furniture and contents had to be out by midday. However, South Highlands had to be treated for woodworm throughout that same whole day, floorboards up! Having no money left to pay for professional removers, our loving church became prime movers. While one man in a van collected donated furniture from peoples' lofts, others cleared everything from our former home onto the drive and street. Items were taken by a convoy of cars, and carried into South Highlands across a few floorboards replaced in the hall immediately after that bit of treatment had been completed. The fumes encouraged people to move fast. Everything was stored in a single downstairs room that did not need treating. I remember and honour Antonio, an Italian crippled by polio who, with his enormous limp, carried items in one hand out from our former house and up to the cars, a big smile on his face as he lived fully to his limits the place where he belonged, in this kingdom fellowship and on the move. I remember as he looked up to the sky while carrying the very last of the items in his hand. A severe storm had been forecast (I hadn't mentioned that, had I?), and it was proving accurate. The first drops of rain started to fall just as the last of the items went into a vehicle. It built up into a Force 9 gale that night, and two ships went down at sea.

We stayed with hospitable friends for three days while the woodworm fumes cleared, a little bit like the flood waters for Noah, I suppose. We returned to camp in the lounge and slowly distributed the furniture around the house. These friends, Jenny and Graham with their three young boys, were our 'link family'. Together we made a team, sharing decisions with them, praying and working together to make South Highlands into a home. Two helpers, unrelated to each other, Ian and Joanna, also moved in to be the 'frontline workers'. We had a clear vision of how it would run. Marian and I, being busy, would earn the money to keep the place running in the background, being available occasionally for prayerful support or ministry. There would be one or two residents staying for short periods of time while they received ministry, counsel, prayer and supportive guidance from Ian and Joanna. We would all be prayerfully and practically backed up by our link family and the church elders. The residents, we had decided, would leave smiling and waving after a week or two, healed, restored and hopeful.

It never happened like that. Life with God is unpredictable, thank God! We are not automatons. Sometimes, I think a clear vision is the way God guides people like us around a blind corner, from where we join in the real action picture!

After we had furnished and decorated the place, two residents did move in for a period of ministry and re-building of their lives. Each had very different sorts of life problems and backgrounds, which meant that all of us in the house had to learn to become sensitive to each other's ways of saying things, listening to each other's 'language' to understand each other. That became a guiding principle, which lasted throughout the next twenty years for the hundred or so other people who came to stay. Not only did we thus avoid becoming labelled as a specialist unit in one sort of issue or another, but we also lived 'listening for' the uniting nature of human values in amongst behavioural diversity. We did not want South Highlands to become institutionalised. It remained a home in which the Holy Spirit was invited to live among us, and in which we dwelt among God.

Within a fairly short period of time it became clear that both of our live-in helpers had their own life problems, which were as significant as those of the residents there for ministry, but different from theirs. I am sure they will not mind me saying this, because they know that Marian and I also developed problems adjusting to living in a totally new way. Community challenged each of us uniquely. We needed to give as much attention to our own personal development as we did to each other's. The spiritual environment became intensely emotional, which I have come to recognise is not a bad thing when emotions are understood God's way, which I shall return to later.

We were not working to any therapeutic model. The residents had moved in knowing that this was an exploration of sustainable spiritual healing. So, the fact that they stayed for very much longer than we had imagined was not seen by anyone as a failure. It was more a lesson about re-building lives. Marian and I became drawn into the day-to-day practicalities far more than we felt able or prepared. People looked to us to fulfil quasi-parental roles, for which we felt ill-equipped, not having brought up children of our own. Our external link family became an essential component of the community, a sanctuary and refuge, a safe place for residents, workers and ourselves equally, where we could share our hearts as the whole edged towards chaos—out of which began to emerge something quite remarkable and beautiful.

We found that the most unexpected person would have an answer to someone else's dilemma or difficulty. These were moments of 'connection'. They enhanced everybody's self-respect, and made us all the more aware of each other as whole people.

People's confidence improved to explore new ways to develop

their lives. They knew that there was a responsive network in which they belonged, and where they could be honest, although not always without difficulty. Marian rose brilliantly to the practical challenges of running an extended household alongside Joanna, while carrying on with her work in General Practice. She was 'present', even while absent, guiding and encouraging everyone to participate in daily household activities, teaching them by example. This 'earthed' their personal development into practical life skills, which are important if people are to sustain self-respect while organising a home of their own later. My role increasingly was to bring a routine of prayer to the house, to make it a spiritually aware environment with a rhythm into which people could connect if they wished, and co-ordinate with others as they explored opportunities for renewing their lives. For example, we all shared an evening meal. I reasoned that 'Humanity does not live on bread alone, but on every word that comes from God', and so we inserted a 'middle course' after the main, during which anyone could share a bible reading or insight they had gained during the day. It finished with a time for prayerfully seeking guidance; and then we enjoyed dessert.

In this way we discovered that our home was made by a woman's touch and a man's word. Emotions were less chaotic. The Holy Spirit drew to our attention different aspects of life at a pace that was manageable for change and reflection; and the home was held in unity in Christ in the hearts of its lead couple.

Of course gender roles can be reversed in home-making, but a man's touch and a woman's word may carry different qualities, may they not? Diversity and difference are vital for a community to be living creatively. Flexibility of diverse roles in responsive relationships is life-giving and healthy when it enables people to explore different ways of living. However, when problems arise among a community of people, and the emotions reveal hidden values in conflict, we discovered that creative solutions are most likely to be found if the genders can also 'revert to type' for a time, name the losses, and then diversify again from there.

Marian and I continued to feel that our role was not to offer specific ministry prayer. Some sorts of 'prayer ministry' are like a surgeon's knife in medical healthcare, focused on the problem rather than the person. For that sort of ministry by intervention residents could, and should, take the initiative to go outside the home. Our role in the home was to create an environment, a context in which the Holy Spirit was welcomed, where people could experiment interacting with others while integrating the effects of interventions elsewhere. We did not become an old-fashioned, paternalistic priesthood, dispensing our answers to peoples' problems. One resident once commented, for example, that he was learning much about how to develop his own capacities by observing the way Marian and I resolved our disagreements. We had been led to create an open order of emotional worlds interacting, where we could see personal growth in steps towards maturity. It emerged through conversational interactions in a social system, not dependent on the ministry intervention that we had imagined when we first set out.

Healing and cure, context and focus

We stopped calling ourselves a healing community and started saying that the household of South Highlands was an extended Christian family. Personal development occurred in a family-shaped community where diversity was encouraged to flourish. Specific ministry found its place, its limits and its meaning within this wider context. Healing was taking longer than we had imagined, but it was running deeper, turning individuals into adult sons and daughters in a Family of God.

The aim was *mature mutual inter-dependence*. By responding to the call we had felt from God, Marian and I had unexpectedly found how the Church's healing ministry and the secular 'medical model' relate.

In the medical model, people are seeking cure *from* a condition, or to be cured of a condition. The condition is considered, in a way, to be separate from the person. *It* affects the person, who remains unchanged once it has gone. In the Christian model of healing, people are not healed 'from', but are healed into a creative system of relational connections. A person is healed into wholeness, and is thoroughly changed in this maturing process.

Cure from, and healing into, are totally and completely *compatible* with each other.

This 'unified distinction' of cure and healing needs to be kept clearly in mind. Various other confusions and misunderstandings can then fall into a creative order. For example, this distinction is made within the whole medical healthcare system, although post-modern developments within that system have tended to obscure it, unhelpfully I believe. The medical model does recognise that it is the person who is healed, and that this *healing* may or may not include cure of the disease or condition that is troubling him or her. Traditionally, doctoring is work that diagnoses and cures the disease; while nursing creates the relational and environmental conditions in which the person (the patient) can optimally heal, both internally, and by re-making his or her socially-connected life. That renewed life may or may not have residual limitations from the disease, injury or degeneration. A good healthcare team will integrate both, and include the follow-up social and pastoral work relevant to sustain the cure within that person's unique life context.

These distinctions have broken down in recent years in UK medicine. Gender associations have changed. Male leaders in the nursing professions have introduced a focus on tasks performed by nurses, rather than on the way nurses must create a relational and environmental *quality* that is important to foster healing. In some settings even the notion of 'healing' has become task-orientated, with special 'healers' being invited in to lay hands on patients. I shall say nothing more than to sound the GP's thought-invoking, "Hmmm…"

So does Christian healing differ? I would like to place this idea before you, for you to think about. I believe it differs in only one simple respect—the social network into which Christian healing brings personal wholeness is a radically different Family of God, in which God's loving presence mingles to re-create life eternally through word and action.

Without that presence, Christianity has *nothing* unique to offer people, other than perhaps the smug criticism of lifestyles and the moral codes of rules that have so plagued the Church's divisive human history for over a thousand years.

Many people are looking for miraculous cures for their conditions and disease. They look to the Church to take it away. Does that sound familiar now? They turn to the Church as if they are turning to a doctor, looking for cures, so that they can then just walk away but unchanged within.

Jesus saw this characteristic in people—their longing for a quick and easy fix. I believe that is why St John, the specialist in divine love, records in more detail than the other Gospel writers what happened *after* the miraculous feeding of the five thousand. In John 6, from verse 22 to 71 at the end of the chapter, the disciple whom Jesus loved reports how Jesus spoke in ways that turned away vast numbers of his followers, using words that John could not know would eventually cause intense persecution of the early Church in the following two centuries. Read them. I do not want to quote them. The risk of a nasty death for the early Christians became a test of character for any follower who believed in *him*. A disciple in those days, and perhaps in our future, must be willing to risk his or her comfortable life to be adopted into the Family of God. (There are compensations, we know!) Going back to the story John told, the day after that amazing miracle (that event when matter somehow behaved unpredictably) people had followed in search of Jesus. He had crossed the lake earlier. When they found him, Jesus began all that he had to say to them with these words (v26), "I tell you the truth, you are looking for me not because you saw miraculous signs, but because you ate the loaves and had your fill."

Jesus knew peoples' hearts. He knew what moved them. These days that capacity goes by the name of emotional intelligence. E-motion = energy in motion. Emotional intelligence is *knowing* what moves people from within. Having insight into what moves people can be learned, especially when a method of 'taking note of the important things' is assimilated into normal conversations. Therefore, when you next consider Jesus' greatness as a Teacher, think not only about the idea he is sharing to believe in, but also about the way he spoke knowing how his words would impact the lives of those who heard them. Growing in emotional intelligence to the fullness that Jesus has is vital to becoming a healing community for others. That crowd that followed Jesus around the lake... was it a healing community for others? That church at the end of your road... is it a healing community for others?

We can become emotionally intelligent *in Christ*. From that perspective we too might see that a hope for cure, or for being fed, is not the healing that God earnestly desires for His People. Miraculous and mysterious cures truly are signs of the higher order of Life, when God's presence and Word are allowed to bring movement within our spiritually-blind human systems. But, "Please take it away!" is not the goal of *healing*. Even Lazarus died again. The goal of healing is to create a character mature and strong enough to endure through suffering and change and even death with a living hope that life shared with others is ever-renewed. Having once been miraculously resurrected, that man Lazarus is not still physically here today. Nevertheless, his story is a lesson to us all of the power present in the connection made when you hear your name called by one who loves you. That is true spirituality.

Chapter 2

How does emotion fit with spiritual healing?

Building a healing community is a deeply emotional process

We had re-discovered in South Highlands the early Celtic Christian tradition of hospitality. Celtic monasteries were usually simple collections of huts with a prayer rhythm based on the inspiration of St Anthony and the early Desert Fathers. There was a strong sense of connection to the whole process of creation, with participation in its rhythms of life. We might call it an earthed view of spirituality. This view had slipped into decline after the greater influence of Roman ways, following the Council of Whitby in 664 CE, which brought a greater reliance on *sacramental* intervention—on tasks for cure. We might call it an interventionist view of spirituality.

Now, to develop a full picture of spiritual healing it is important for us to remember that, in 664 CE, Papal unity was not then exercised as the dreaded Papal 'authority' as we now know it. It was an 'authority of love' in which the Papal *office* represented the *unity of the whole Church*. A duty was placed on others to come to a place of agreement around that office, or at least to agree to differ peacefully with each other in order to maintain the unity of the Spirit represented by that 'office'. Papal authority (the power to make others obey the words of the man who currently occupied the office as Pope) only became *that* sort of authority towards the end of the first Millennium, during the split between the Eastern churches and Rome over a number of issues. A Pope's dominance, for which both the Eastern Orthodox and Western Protestant Churches now criticise Rome, was not the reason why at Whitby the Celtic Church submitted to Rome. The Church leaders submitted out of love, to maintain unity, while accepting that certain doctrines they commonly held could be taken to an unhelpful extreme—specifically, the Pelagian belief that Man is intrinsically good as part of God's good Creation. This belief had been taken by some to an extreme by suggesting that humanity has a God-given *in-built capacity* to behave with full moral responsibility.

There *is* a problem with that Pelagian view, called sin, but now 1300 years later a better way has re-opened than only to cure individual souls of the problem. It is to heal into wider community the gathering of people who have previously believed in their own righteousness (and any other extreme views). What do I mean by this statement?

Both parts of the now-divided Western Church (Roman and Protestant) share the mind-set that favours cure of souls, the one by sacrament and the other by declarations of faith (hence competition between Protestant leaders to make the *right* declaration). Such is the interventionist view of spirituality for cure of souls. Marian's practical approach to lived spirituality in building community, however, had led us to re-discover the other mind-set. Our story will go on to show how we discovered that this mind-set is held still by the Celtic and the Eastern Orthodox Church, and also by the global, boundary-breaking Charismatic Movement. All of these see *healing* of souls to include movement into community, into fellowship, koinonia, family. The problem now is this: movement into community, people discover, is emotionally painful and demanding *before* the benefits are felt.

Humankind is built for fellowship, however. For a full healthcare system, cure by tasks and healing by context to re-adjust in communal life are completely complementary. Both are needed also for a full Church, which means that everybody in the Churches needs to reflect on how his or her mind set about spiritual healing, earthed or interventionist, might limit Godly healing *if it excludes the other.*

Holy Spirit gives life to the Church not just for the benefit of its individuals, but to share that life for the healing of the world. Having started out from our Protestant roots to heal the source of sickness and conflict in the local churches, we discovered the solution lies in another phase of whole Church development that is on the go already world-wide. In this global phase of renewal I believe God might be asking his growing Family to mature beyond playing 'doctors and nurses'. I believe that, and shall be explaining how, God wants his Church to become a loving, teaching presence in and for the wider community, *showing* as light the fullness of Godly humanity in the image and likeness of Christ. Others will see this light when they see people's grief being turned to joy as those who differ are reconciled to each other. If we are to become that sort of right-teaching, radiant community, however, we shall need to become more emotionally intelligent, as Jesus was, to live in grace.

Having the grace to reconcile

I was invited to speak at an evening service in a prominent charismatic church in Plymouth on the subject of emotion and spiritual healing. After the service a disorderly queue gathered to give their personal response, or to ask a question. One woman said it was the first time she had ever heard anything affirmative or positive said about emotions in a church. She thanked me sincerely.

Then a man in his late twenties took his opportunity, stepped forward and said, "I am not a Christian, and I have no interest in churches, but this evening I was driving home after work, and as I went around that roundabout outside I felt this irresistible urge to look at this church and to come inside. I arrived half way through your talk, and what you said was *exactly* what I needed to hear about a situation I feel stuck in. I want to thank you. I don't know what all this is about, but now at least I do know what to do next." We shook hands. No words were needed as we looked at each other, but a personal exchange took place. The spiritual healing that this man was in the process of receiving, by the Holy Spirit at work already in his heart, only needed my heart-felt and physical handshake connection to become real and living in his world. It was an emotional moment. I did then think it reasonable to say, "Let the Holy Spirit continue to inspire you."

Was the emotional exchange in silence just a side effect of thinking? No. Did that emotion complicate or interfere with pure reason? No. Was that emotion a vital part of the spiritual connection being made? Yes. He was taking away the grace to reconcile.

Turning emotional turmoil into the energy to move on with others

That man had been in emotional turmoil about a situation he felt stuck in. He would have heard me talk about how to turn the unpleasant emotions of loss and grieving for accumulating disappointments into the energy and wisdom to make relationships deeper, rather than choose to break them.

Where in Scripture can we find an example of something similar? Fortunately there is one as our Patriarch Abraham enters the Promised Land to settle there *peacefully* among the Philistines, even in the face of trouble and fear.

In Genesis 21:22-34 we read that Abraham had been 'sojourning' as a nomad in the Negev among the Philistines. He had dug a well, but the locals had claimed it was theirs. Abraham could have turned his emotional response about this lie into a potentially destructive confrontation with the Philistines, which was probably exactly what the locals wanted as an excuse for trouble. However, he did not. He gave. He had the grace to give, and the will to forgive. And out of that emotional wisdom, he lived and thrived in peace with others in the stretch of earth to which God had called him. His son Isaac continued there also, in the Promised Land, despite continuing trouble, which he similarly managed.

> *Abraham said to Abimelech, "These seven ewe lambs you will take from my hand, that you may be a witness for me that I dug this well." Therefore the place was called Beer-Sheba; because there both of them swore an oath. So they made a covenant at Beer-Sheba. And Abraham stayed in the earth of the Philistines for a long time.*
> (Genesis 21:30-31,34)

There is a variety of Tamarisk tree that grows very tall with a strong trunk, and provides good, spreading shade. It grows well in dry conditions such as the Negev. Even today these can be found at the Ein Gedi oasis by the Dead Sea. Abraham planted a Tamarisk tree at Beer-Sheba. There he called upon the Lord. The Tamarisk tree is a growing sign of *grace and covenant,* in the shade of which different peoples may rest together.

Abraham had had to learn this maturity of 'covenant agreement' as a way to manage fear. He had nearly lost his wife because of a previous mis-judgement about how to appease people seen as powerful, like Abimelech, King of the Philistines. Having deceived people that Sara was his sister, Abimelech decided to marry her, which would have spoiled God's plan for blessing the whole world! God, of course, could redeem that emotionally charged situation, and Abraham learnt through this to be truthful with people, and full of grace. Someone other than a maturing Abraham might have felt stuck when confronted with a lie, and reacted desperately to save face and pride. Abraham had learnt, however, to stand in the strength of a covenant relationship with God to face the turmoil of this world. Spiritual healing into community with diversity needs emotion and 'reasoning from experience' to work in partnership. Many people feel that the only way to handle emotional turmoil is to get rid of emotion. But our exploration of spiritual healing by building community with people who are different has suggested otherwise. It suggests that when emotion is seen as a vital part of relationship building, of maintaining covenant relationship, it gains a meaning and a useful purpose that simply cannot be seen when people think in a purely self-centred way. That may present a deep challenge to some churches. Should they break away in the face of this? No.

Bringing reason and emotion into a creative partnership

For nearly three thousand years an ancient Greek Stoic 'wisdom' has dominated character development for individuals in many societies and religious traditions. It elevates reason to a higher level of humanity than emotion, and this 'wisdom' teaches people to use *classical logic* to justify keeping their emotion 'under control'. However, this view of a strong character is now deeply challenged by evidence both from the modern neuroscience of brain scanning, and from the New Science of *'adaptive living systems'*. When combined, these create a new 'wisdom' about inter-active living, in particular about organisations or gatherings of people in which several individuals contribute socially. In an interactive system, a new order of logic emerges in which emotion finds a new *informative* value. The new wisdom is that, by consistent feedback and responsiveness within a system, order emerges out of chaos. Emotional honesty and clarity of emotional communication have vital parts to play in this process.

Out of these developments at the turn of the 20th Century has emerged also a new 'bio-psycho-social' model of personal health and wholeness. This is a non-individualistic view of humanity. Emotion has a vital place for full humanity *in equal partnership with reason* to steer or 'weight' decisions that affect well-being and healing among communities of people. Classical *linear* logic is entirely satisfactory for assessing the unreasonable claims of individuals. However, the New Science as it appears in the bio-psycho-social model of personhood adds to linear logic another dynamic logic, of how life outcomes for individuals are affected by extended *patterns of ongoing communication.*

These patterns of communication among people can bring order out of chaos at several levels of life simultaneously—for example in improved local environments, physical health of the body, mental stability, family dynamics, social inclusion in societies, and so on. For this 'constructive' effect to occur, consistent feedback in conversations becomes a 'principle of organisation', in which emotional messaging has a vital part to play. When this principle of organisation is not present, relationships may fracture, producing mistrust and separation into factions of 'them' and 'us'.

These same principles of organisation can relate to healthy spirituality also. Remember, in our medical work, Marian and I had developed a view that spirituality may be understood as the way a person makes sense of his or her utter relatedness within the widest 'wholeness' in which they feel a sense of *belonging*. This sort of spirituality can be true whether in a religiously structured or in a person-centred view of life. Conflict between monotheists of different religions, when seen in this New Science light of emergent living order, is not so much about converting or resisting other people's beliefs (the diversity of which will always remain). The conflict is moved more by people's sense of *belonging* or rejection among 'others' in the wider emotive patterning of life. It has a similar psychological root to sibling rivalry. The way forward, I shall be proposing to you, is to explore together how *Holy Spirit* emerges within people to bring *Godly order* in their communications. Emotion, properly understood, has a vital role in this. It is no less than the domain of life where our physical and our spiritual natures meet to move us on together.

New conversational solutions to cultural and social conflict are now opened by making a significant shift in attitude towards emotional information. No longer is reason used just to *control* emotion, or to 'get rid of it', or conceal it, as promoted by some communally unwise approaches to life. Emotion naturally comes under self-control when the person knows that he or she is being *heard* within a system, because then the emotion has fulfilled its useful bio-psycho-social and *spiritual* purpose.

Emotional Logic is an innovative, teachable, mental framework for conversations that is based in the constructive principles of organisation by safe feedback. Distress, tension, confusion and social turmoil can now be explained not only in individualistic terms (such as mental illness that 'affects' a person, or as that person's behaviour problem), but also in humane relational terms with grace as 'the emotional chaos of a broken heart when grieving for multiple disappointments unheard'. Emotional Logic provides the consistent feedback needed for constructive social and personal order to emerge from chaos by communication. *Resilient emotional honesty* can thus be a firmer foundation than emotional repression (with spasmodic venting in conflict) on which to build a future shared alongside others.

Three essential mind-shifts about emotion

To grasp hold of this new wisdom and make it active daily in your conversations and decisions, you may need to make three mind shifts about emotion.

1 Emotions are physical preparation states for social action or withdrawal

Emotion is not just some vague vapour that gets in the way of clear thinking. Emotion is your real-time body chemistry re-organising from one state of preparation to another for a different sort of physical action or withdrawal. This re-organisation is your inner reaction responding to your ongoing social setting. It arises automatically as a reflex in your body when some change challenges your life values for survival or thriving. The preparations are co-ordinated by hormones released into the blood stream.

Your emotional preparations also give out social messages—a fact that those who are individualistically minded will find inexplicable. These subtle messages move others also to prepare for *their* action or withdrawal in response to yours. The messages are in facial expressions, body posture, chemical pheromones released in your sweat, and in your tone of voice (your para-verbal language). Emotion thus makes more sense when it is seen to belong *in a system of human inter-actions.* Only an individualistic mentality can interpret 'my emotion' as private and uniquely precious, or 'what makes me special', or as just a side-effect of thoughts that gets in the way and may spoil life. On the contrary, your emotion is the evidence that you are a socially connected person. When thus understood, your emotion has *useful purposes* within your social and spiritual systems. E-motion = energy in motion.

The *feeling of an emotion* is different. The feeling is an 'extract' sample of the physical preparations ongoing, which enters your brain processing as *information* that some internal change is happening. The feeling arises 0.2-0.9 seconds after the emotional preparation has started. By that time, in that time-frame, you may have already begun to react, and so may others.

Over time, people learn to *interpret* their feelings of emotion. They are like a person's radar, sensing movements around. Just as the blips on a screen need interpreting, so too do our feelings of emotion. The ideas people develop about their feelings of emotion—their understanding—then *modifies* their reflex behavioural reactions. However, the cycle starts that way round, not with thoughts first that lead to emotions. Certainly there is feed-back from ideas and beliefs that modifies emotional feelings, sometimes out of all proportion to ongoing situations, but the reality of emotion is in the domain of the physical systems of life that people *share.*

As people make choices based on their interpretation of feelings, a sense of personal identity develops. The evidence for personal identity is seen in the impact those choices have on others. In a socially and spiritually healthy system, this feedback will generate diversity as constructive movement among unity. In an unhealthy system, feedback from personal choices will generate doubt, mistrust, separation and brokenness. This is the non-religious spirituality of human nature. We are not human bodies with a spiritual part; we are spiritual, connected creatures learning to become more humane.

Emotional Logic works at this deep level, at which personal identity is being formed out of physical interactions between people. Feedback learning enables people to reasonably *re-interpret the feelings* of their inner preparations, which are ongoing in real-time pre-consciously. When people learn where their unpleasant feelings of emotion fit within an overall process of adjustment, they can choose how to get constructive movement back into life instead of feeling stuck. Emotional Logic is thus solution-focused. People learn to make a *rational action plan* based on the named values that have generated their emotional preparations. Such a plan turns the emotions into constructive personal energy, making the person feel more effective and hopeful, growing confident that he or she belongs in wider and wider systems of life.

2 Love is made known as both joy, and grief

Love in its widest sense of connection with someone or something beyond oneself is made known as both joy, on 'gathering together', and equally as grief, on separation, brokenness or misunderstanding. Grief is the price that people pay for loving. Grief's unpleasant emotions are there, however, for a constructive, life-promoting reason. They move people in unusual ways to explore new ways to *re-connect with others,* and so to discover the joy of love again when change has pushed them out of a comfort zone.

Grief is not one emotion among many, but a range of emotional preparations for action or withdrawal—shock, fear, anxiety, brittleness, anger, guilt, yearning, wanting, emptiness, despair, sadness, and so on. Bereavement, when someone close has died, is the most intense form of grieving; however the identical range of emotional preparations is triggered by disappointments and setbacks, when anything valued is seen to be at risk of being lost. During times of change, several different loss reactions can accumulate one on another, generating an emotional turmoil or chaos in which people are feeling angry about one loss, guilty about another, shocked about a third, depressed about yet another, all at the same time so that the person does not know *what* he or she feels. That is when emotion can seem like a problem rather than the energy to find a solution.

If these unpleasant emotional preparations were not built into our survival mechanisms, however, there would be no hope for joy, and no energy to adjust to change. God cannot simply 'take the unpleasant emotions away', as some people pray, because that would remove the possibility of God's love from a changing world. The important thing to learn instead is how to co-operate with God's love, so that we do not get *stuck* with these unpleasant emotions, or display them simply to inflict them on others without mutuality or understanding. Learning Emotional Logic's mental framework achieves that. Some people try to avoid grief by never feeling connected to anyone beyond their self, but this strategy brings its own further set of losses. Having a mental framework that makes sense of unpleasant emotion enables rational decisions to be made about how to *turn the personal energy* into appropriate action, basing those decisions on naming the underlying values that the grief is trying to preserve.

3 Grief includes the potential for personal growth

Grief emotions thus have solution-focused useful purposes. There is a process of adjusting that is logical, so that people can choose where they want to be in it. Can I recognise and name the potential losses hidden within this change? Can I prevent any of those losses I have named? If not, can I do something reasonable to get back a valued feature of life that I have already lost? If not, or if I have tried and failed, what does life look like if I have to let go of this in order to move on? The unpleasant loss emotions (grieving) are genetically in-built preparation states organising personal energy to achieve this logical process phase-by-phase constructively with others. We shall look at this in more detail in the next chapter, but for now the important point is to see the overview of this process for healthy social (systemic) adjustment.

It starts with *doubt* about my ability to handle some new or unexpected change, and works through to develop a better ability to *explore* new resources and skills that move life on constructively with others. Doubt first emerges as feelings of shock, perhaps then shelving the issue in denial. Shock and denial both have useful purposes, however, that we shall look at in the next chapter. We encourage people to not tell themselves off for having these reactions, but to learn to harness the unpleasant feelings for useful purposes. The exploratory phase we then call a *growth cycle*, because through it people can emerge from change stronger. Between these two phases, however, people may feel urged to prevent losses that are connected with the change. The anger and guilty self-questioning associated with preventing loss may cause problems.

The emotional preparation states that are used to bring about movement, from doubt to personal growth, may be called 'emotional Stepping Stones'. Each is a firm, inner place of personal organisation on which people 'balance' ready to leap on to the next, and so make a path across a river or swamp in life. Seven such firm preparation states are genetically in-built, all with useful purposes: shock, denial, anger, guilty self-questioning, bargaining to recover things where there is risk, depressive emptiness, and a sadness that can mix with hope to explore new opportunities for growth. Balancing on each of the Stepping Stones brings a range of *feelings* associated with the underlying emotion, uniquely for each individual, so that each person has to learn to interpret their feelings to makes sense of their emotional and social world—the inscape and the landscape of their life to navigate.

The logic of Emotional Logic refers to how one emotional preparation *can evolve into another* to energise the reasonable process of adjusting to changing circumstances. Emotion and reasoning do not need to war against each other, sapping personal energy. All the unpleasant emotions of grieving have a rational place within this constructive overview of adjusting.

We say there are no negative emotions, only unpleasant ones that have useful purposes. They can be harnessed and turned to build resilient *patterns of communication*. These are 'living words', on which people can stand to make shared life adaptive and sustainable as their families and neighbourhoods grow.

God-given emotion

We learnt at South Highlands that all these unpleasant emotions have useful purposes *within the kingdom of God* for renewing life. They provide information not only about how values affect the way individuals relate to each other, but also about how our values are challenged on hearing the living Word of God. In our home, people engaged emotionally not only with the small microcosm there of the extended family system, but also with the macrocosm of eternity through the Word of God and the inspiration of prayer. The kingdom of heaven is not a place of pure reason. It is an opening of many unpredictable ways just beyond our fingertips that can restore joy through reconnecting with others. Grief reactions are in-built to entering the kingdom, until joy is fully restored. The Orthodox say that the first gift of the Holy Spirit is tears. The aim of many creative conversations in South Highlands had been to ensure that grief reactions were understood not in a destructive or distracting way, or just by acting out their tensions, but in a constructive and sustainable way that led to the grace to reconcile.

I shall be telling more of that story over the next few chapters, and of how developing an organised approach to those conversations took me out from Ivybridge to share the method with the worldwide family of the Church, and through the Church to anyone. It is all about 'becoming familiar with grief', not in a morbid way of ruminating on problems, but becoming familiar in ways that turn the energy of unpleasant emotions into the energy to rebuild relationships during times of change. That's grace.

When we choose to recall God's living words into the movement of our physical life shared with others, our emotions bring together these two great systems in which we participate. Our emotional feelings can even, in partnership with grace-filled thought, become *sacred information* about how our relationship with God is impacting the world in which we are earthed. Our emotions are not merely soulish, or only self-centred. When we remind ourselves of God's presence, our emotions give us *even more* information about how life is being tensioned here and now among humanity that has fallen from perfect relatedness. That information is vital to advance God's kingdom. This awareness is Godly emotional intelligence.

The kingdom of God has something to do with people planting seeds of life, which survive and thrive against all odds and reproduce to make more seeds, and on and on as life is forever renewed. Godly emotion, when I am moved in loving relationship with the Persons of God, can guide intelligent kingdom seed-planting and gardening.

Finding balance in the Church's healing ministry

God grieves about fallen humankind. God so loved the world that God gave... God so loved the world that God gave to restore us. That image of a loving God turning grief into peaceful hope *does* dwell within humanity. It is there as our potential for responsiveness, giving our feedback conversationally to God, and to each other, turning grief into peaceful hope. In this there is healing, whether by intervention, or by being more earthed in God's inter-active Creation.

What does 'connection with a living, loving God' mean? Each of us can somehow know God as an echo conversationally within —otherwise human beings could have no way to understand God's living words when we do listen for them. In our South Highlands extended Christian Family we saw this 'echo within' in the way people recognised Godly order emerging in those 'moments of connection' between unexpected people. From such moments we subsequently saw growth arise unpredictably out of human chaos. That 'knowing echo' from an indwelling image of God in humankind is not an intrinsic goodness. In fact, the model of misunderstanding I shall introduce to you later readily separates our human nature from that image, so much so that I would say that it is impossible to save ourselves by our own moral choices alone.

We need to be in a conversation with the *diverse* Church Family if we are to understand those 'echoes within from God's call' constructively. We also need to be in a conversation with God if we are to live our salvation. Fundamentally we humans are too easily able to ignore that image of God within, and to focus our attention instead on more worldly affairs. But the optimistic view is also true in our experience. When people do ask, and listen, they are able to know that strange, still voice of God echoing within *in their own language*, and to know that here is guidance.

The Charismatic Movement through the Western Churches has emphasised the importance for Christian living of both fellowship (koinonia), and of inspirational prayer ministry. Marian and I started our exploration of this from seeing some people return repeatedly for prayer ministry, discovering its counterpart in family-building. Over the years we have found that emotional intelligence among those involved in prayer ministry can improve the insight and discernment with which they identify and name features of life to bring before God for inspirational prayer. Also the after-care of people who have received ministry could include helping them to learn that same emotional intelligence, so to improve their relationship-building by growing an inner resilience that would prevent recurrence of the original problem.

Emotional intelligence is a vital part of the Church becoming stronger and more resilient as a source of light and guidance for the wider community.

Stepping up to the high viewing platform of grace

The place where Marian and I have found rest, among the expressions of unpleasant emotional tensions that sometimes filled South Highlands, is in God's grace. Imagine grace is a high viewing platform, somewhere along a mountainous, populated coast bordering an ocean. From here, holding the rail safely, we can look into life, both as nature close by, and to the far distance in perspective. The vista from this firm, high platform is magnificent, certainly. The heavens, sky and mountain peaks above, and deep, deeply down, zooming in to see into the valleys of the human heart and mind, where, in distant miniature in villages and towns, the woes and dreams of people interact, and where communities can be seen gathering into changing forms, or tearing apart through misunderstandings and doubts.

From here we can invite you to look, with us, even more deeply into the previously un-seen groundswell of God's grace. Grace, as the unity of God, moves behind every interaction people have with each other, even as waves of misunderstanding roll across seas of humanity, scattering back to chaos and spraying the waters of grace into which God had spoken order.

When a doorway first opens before you into this high viewing platform of grace, it will reveal for you the Holy Trinity seated there at an iconic table, welcoming you and adopting you into the Family of God, if you so choose to accept the invitation. After spending some time with them, becoming familiar with them—well, Family if you like—I hope you will feel able to learn a little of the language by which the dynamics within *human* families and communities is explained. This language of emotions, this emotional intelligence, will empower you, unexpectedly perhaps among other benefits, to explain Holy Spirit to others in more constructive language than before. It will enhance your spiritual and physical resilience together, a bit like family therapy on a church-wide scale. Then grace will remain as the measure of all our inter-actions and prayers.

Stepping into ever-renewed life, or eternal life if you prefer that translation, is like stepping onto that platform of grace, with its ongoing consequence that God's love is all around you in a renewed Creation, spiritually healed.

Chapter 3
Climbing to the high platform

From the valley, we look to the hills from where our salvation comes (Psalm 121). Somewhere up there is that high viewing platform.

From there we could see grace everywhere. From here, we must search for it among the phenomena of daily living, and in the stories we hear. Where, for example, among the Gospel accounts of miracles, sermons and parables can we see emotional intelligence in the grace of Jesus? He came from our Father full of grace and truth (John 1:14), so it should be there. If we are to model on our teacher, our Rabbi, this feature of his life needs to be brought into clear focus.

Sometimes it appears obviously in scripture. Is there anyone who thinks that Jesus was not emotional when he wept at Lazarus' tomb? Jesus wept. It is the shortest and perhaps the most telling verse in the Holy Bible (John 11:35). Verse 36 continues, 'Then the Jews said, "See how he loved him!"'

Western rationalist theology has managed somehow to distil love, to extract a heady essence from it, as the power of choice. Love is a choice to connect, we are told sometimes. That extraction is quite an achievement, true as far as it goes, but perhaps limited by fear, by the fear that love's many emotions make it a potentially explosive mixture. Using reason to control destructive passion has, as I explained before, in my view spilt over into preaching a blanket pronouncement that emotions are in themselves un-spiritual and soulish features of the fallen nature. Our experience of emotion in the South Highlands extended Christian family, however, is that it is a God-given feature of humanity *in relationship*, of humanity created in the image and likeness of the tri-une *Personal God*. Because of the dangers of the passions, people worry that their emotion will separate them from God. The opposite is true. Emotion connects, and thus enables people to be full of grace.

Jesus went on to speak words of life to the dead Lazarus out of love and in the presence of onlookers. He took a risk. Was that risk emotional? Were his emotional inner movements and preparations transformed to some extent by knowing that he was not separated from his Father? Perhaps in Jesus' earthly walk his emotions did not move in individualistic separation and worry, as ours might, but we can learn to be like Jesus in his relationship with Father, his Source and ours too. Like Jesus, in Christ, we can maintain two sets of emotive relationships simultaneously, with the fallen world and with our Father. There, where his spiritual and physical natures met, he wept.

Mostly Jesus' emotional intelligence is subtly there in scripture, under the surface of his teaching, like multi-coloured stones causing ripples on the surface of a stream that runs down from those hills above. When we look carefully through the surface of the waters, they add depth and explanation to the Truth being spoken as words.

God is Love, we are told repeatedly by the apostle John. He was the disciple who had leaned back and rested his head on Jesus' chest at the last supper and had asked Jesus who it was that was going to betray him. John, now called St. John, had at that time probably felt Jesus' heart-beat through the rough material of his garment, and perhaps even heard the heart of a man who knew that he was soon to be sent to torture and death. What sort of aroma was in the room after the meal, and was it added to by the sudden emotional tension? Was Jesus' heart racing, or pounding, as any other human being's would, as he dipped some bread in the wine and gave it to the one who would betray him. Picture it. Put yourself there. Was it emotional? Was Jesus' choice of action emotionally intelligent?

The betrayer had received communion at Jesus' own hand, and by his will. What emotions might that knowledge evoke now in the person who had chosen to turn his or her back on God, and who then met him, eye-to-eye, through the emotionally intelligent actions *of one of us*? Emotion at such a moment would not be a sign of disconnection from God. Surely, God's heart and ours would be beating in unison.

What sort of God would a penitent person see through us; a vision of a personal loving God, or one obscured by reason? If emotion is purely physical, soulish and feminine, and if emotion merely interferes with pure reason as a way to see God's truth about life, then why is the Old Testament packed full of references to God's emotions?

In Jonah, God is compassionate and concerned enough for the Ninevites (the residents of the Assyrians' capital city, who so violently oppressed other nations) to deliver a prophet to them in a most uncompromising manner, because they did not know their right hand from their left. (God, by the way, is also concerned about how they looked after their cattle.) In Exodus 20 God describes God's own nature as jealous, sufficient to say this is God's name —Jealous. Throughout the Pentateuch God's anger burns against those who stand against God's People. In Deuteronomy God has made a covenant of love with God's People, and throughout the Prophets God tries time and again to call his wayward beloved back to the covenant relationship. Are these mere words? How can we understand this feature of Godly nature without attaching our human standards to it?

I believe we shall discover that emotion in Godly nature is all about intelligently sensitive action and choice, while humans may get caught up with the feelings, and forget the intelligent action. But we humans can learn and grow...

In the Western Church for centuries, Christians who commonly worry that their emotions separate them from God have hoped instead that their beliefs connect them. Many consequently try to get rid of their anger, and hide their guilty feelings as if they meant they had done something wrong and unforgivable, and they fear that shock and doubt and anxiety make them weaker witnesses of an all-powerful God in whom, *good* Christians tell themselves, 'all things are possible'. Christians commonly feel they should not be depressed when they have such a glorious salvation to celebrate, and although they secretly know that they cannot pull themselves out of 'it' by their own efforts, they nevertheless cannot ask God's help when they believe that God will look on them as pathetic failures and not worth the effort; and fearing to take risks is another failure for this courageous army; and sadness is wrong and if that keeps breaking into my bubble I must have an illness called depression, and I shall need to see a doctor. All of these misunderstandings about emotion are self-fulfilling curses that Christians speak on themselves, which I aim to lift for God to abolish in a way that only God can.

In fact, as I hope to show, emotion is the level at which people connect with each other and with God through grace at the very ground of their existence. In spirited life, e-motion = personal energy in motion. Only a small proportion of this grace-laden movement enters consciousness as our feelings. If God and human beings in their different natures are both e-motional in their moving connections, they do not need to look on each other strangely, as if something is amiss. The movement sparks awareness… "There is a person here, if not Three, and I am among them."

Love's grief: seven Stepping Stones back to joy

Joy and grief are equally important features of love in the life we are called to live as Family with God. Both contribute to the movement of Family life. Grief is fulfilled and dispersed in joy restored. Family honour, in the eyes of onlookers, grows where people grieve truly and constructively.

Talk that acknowledges unpleasant grief emotions does not have to be morbid, as if grief refers only to endings or failures. These unpleasant emotions are all God-given to move you in unusual ways towards restoring right relationship, when changing circumstances have pushed you out of a comfort zone. The emotional energy turns to personal growth as the motivators for re-gathering. In so doing they can *restore* Godly life, and in doing that increase the possibility of re-discovering joy in love. The problem is that these grief emotions *feel* unpleasant, and that distracts us from their useful purposes to guide intelligent choices and action.

In the midst of any change, human nature mostly seeks low risk solutions; but what if Father God is asking us to engage with risk, releasing Holy Spirit to guide and empower the movement? A sense of riskiness will accompany *any* choice for intelligent action that includes an assessment of the meaning of unpleasant emotions. Just trying to get rid of them instead may seem easier and safer; but such an attitude may underlie the problem that Marian and I had encountered between local church communities. Criticising others unemotionally may seem tough and powerful for a season, but its heavy weight loosens a plank in the high viewing platform of grace. Unresponsiveness to God, and hard-heartedness to each other, may open a chasm beneath. On saying farewell to a true friend, don't say, "Take care"; say, "Take risks lightly!"

In Jesus' life, even when filled to overflowing with Holy Spirit, unpleasant grief emotions still arose. They are there in Scripture, as we shall see below. We have our own experience of shock, anxiety, irritability, anger, self-questioning, apprehension, depressive emptiness, sadness, and so on. Jesus, in his human nature, experienced these also. Can you risk imagining for a moment that Jesus' loving Father in heaven experienced an equivalent also, as humankind dished out its treatment on his Son? If there is movement within God through grace, then we can be sure that Our Father did.

By that grace of God, we are forgiven, welcomed and adopted into the Family, healed, restored and strengthened to reach out now to others, empowered to do so by lived connection through Holy Spirit into Christ where we abide with our Father. The emotional attachments of this mean that we are moved potentially by God's purposes as much as by our own. From our Father's deep grief for his Son's treatment, the grace of God is poured out from the Father, and this is the Source of life for the healing of humankind and the world.

Being familiar with grief, like the suffering servant of Isaiah 53, does not mean being 'all emotional' in situations. It means that you and I need to have a mental framework that makes sense of unpleasant emotions within a loving God's creation of ever-renewed life. Through South Highlands and our medical work, such a framework has emerged and has proved effective to help people adjust constructively to change. It goes by the unusual name 'Emotional Logic', which is another name for intelligent kindness.

The Logic is the process of adjusting. It is a logical process. A person can reason and decide where he or she wants to be in it. Emotion is that person's energy organising and preparing in different ways to put those adjustments into effect. Reasoning and emotion thus work together in partnership when understood as parts of a process of adjusting to change with others.

Your Emotional Logic is your inbuilt capacity for one emotion to evolve constructively into another *as you prepare in different ways to adjust to change.* Jesus in his earthly walk and ministry lived Emotional Logic. His emotions evolved appropriately from one to another in situations. He didn't get stuck, ruminating on the feelings. Seven categories of emotional preparation for action or withdrawal are described in Emotional Logic, all identifiable in Jesus' life. We call them 'emotional Stepping Stones', because each is a firm state of inner organisation and social messaging, on which a person balances while preparing to adjust with a further leap on to cross the river or swamp of the situation. Each emotional Stepping Stone is associated with a range of feelings, uniquely for different individuals. First we land on an emotional Stepping Stone; then we balance as we think and feel about what is going on and where we need to go next; and then we do it.

An emotional Stepping Stone is more than just the preparation to react, however. It includes giving feelings a meaning because they have a place within that process of adjusting. This opens out our observation of the world to include new possibilities, and so knowing the useful purposes of our emotions can even guide choices. Some of the seven core preparation states organise a mind frame that directs personal energy and movement *outwards*—as an urge to go out and change the world out there in order to adjust to the situation. Others organise a different sort of mind frame that directs personal energy and movement *inwards*—as an urge to reflect and to change the person I am inside in order to adjust to the situation. All of this is included in the notion of an emotional Stepping Stone. Therefore, the names we give to these preparation states have capital letters (a proper noun, such as Shock), to differentiate them from the fleeting feelings of emotion (such as shock).

The Stepping Stones are, in fact, *categories* of adjustment types in-built into our survival mechanisms, which Jesus in his humanity would have shared with us. Jesus can be seen in scripture to have prepared for change going 'out' into the world with Denial, Anger and Bargaining; and for change going 'in' for reflective review of his situation with Shock, Guilt and Depression. Do you get a sense of outrage or doubt that your Saviour could be so human? He also came to a point of Acceptance, you may recall, in Gethsemane. We cannot know how our Saviour felt at those times, any more than we can guess how any other human being feels while preparing emotionally for change. But we can be thankful that whatever he felt, he felt it openly with his Father. Perhaps honestly so can we.

Shock

Could it honestly be that the Son of the living God ever felt shocked? Jesus in his Godly nature, in continuous communication with his Father, had access to all knowledge. So, surely, how could he have been surprised or shocked by anything? Jesus also shared our human nature, however. I would like to suggest to you that the emotional intelligence of grace in Jesus' Godly nature enabled him to respond to humanly shocking situations *in the most constructive way*. The point is that Jesus could 'go to' his emotional Stepping Stones, but not get stuck there ruminating on the unpleasant feelings, instead turning them straight away to their God-given useful purposes. We see this in Matthew 14:10-13.

> ... *(Herod) had John (the Baptist) beheaded in the prison. His head was brought in on a platter and given to the girl, who carried it to her mother. John's disciples came and took his body and buried it. Then they went and told Jesus. When Jesus heard what had happened, he withdrew by boat privately to a solitary place.*

Jesus, on receiving the shocking news that his cousin, John the Baptist, had been beheaded in such outrageous circumstances, withdrew to a quiet 'safe place'. We can surmise from other scriptures that he probably went to pray to his Father.

In Emotional Logic terms, Shock's various unpleasant feelings *alert a person* that something valued may be lost in a changing situation. The feelings arise from a pulse of hormone messages 'from your guts', from your adrenal glands in fact, which via your blood stream within seconds shifts every cell of your body out of maintenance mode chemistry and into survival mode. At a whole person level the shock feelings mean that temporarily you are doubting your resources to handle this new situation *until you can make an assessment of it*. Clearly, training can accelerate people through this stage, for example in the emergency services or armed forces, but many trained people will experience the shock later, and then call it post-traumatic stress. This sudden change of preparation state does not feel good for most people, but it has a useful purpose towards which the energy of the shock reaction can be turned when it is recognised. Shock's useful purpose primes a person to, "Stop what you are doing! Find a safe place where you can review your resources to manage this unexpected change".

However, we usually tell ourselves off for having the shock feelings such as anxiety, fear, numbness, paralysis, trembling, sweating, and so on, seeing them as signs of weakness that we need to push on through. Jesus' most reliable and effective resource, however, was his ongoing relationship with his Father. If he heard Father's words, then he would act on them; and so he chose to take himself away and listen.

We all need safe places to reflect. For many people a safe place is like a bomb shelter that you go into when there is danger, and emerge from unscathed when the danger is past. But in Emotional Logic terms a safe place is more like your War Office, or your planning department, and so it was for Jesus. It is not a place where you just 'switch off'. Jesus would have been actively asking Father, I am sure.

There are three sorts of safe places for we followers of Christ: a physical place, such as a walk by the river, or a favourite armchair, or a sanctuary; *a frame of mind,* such as re-focusing by looking to a horizon, or counting to ten to calm down and think, or reasoning about known motives, or taking a piece of paper and jotting some notes quietly; and a *relationship,* contacting someone trusted, perhaps by phone, text or prayer. When Jesus withdrew, he probably activated all three safe places at once, to face the turbulent emotions of his human nature and to calm them into his ability to make constructive choices, with the energy now released to move on.

Therefore, in future, when you get feelings such as anxiety, panic, stunning, numbness, and so on, you can now value and respect them as 'my Shock Stepping Stone', which is appearing out of the mists to equip me to 'Stop what I am doing!' for now, and find a safe place to identify, assess and adjust to some significant new change. Then, recovering balance there, we can congratulate ourselves for taking note of these important messages, before taking the next risky leap on with Holy Spirit.

Denial

Matthew's account of John the Baptist's murder leads within the same verse 13 and on into verse 14, straight into one of the most remarkable events recorded in the Gospels.

> *... Hearing of this (that Jesus had withdrawn), the crowds followed him on foot from the towns. When Jesus landed and saw a large crowd, he had compassion on them and healed their sick.*

This re-adjustment continues directly into the miraculous feeding of the five thousand, the disciple John's account of which (and the subsequent teaching) I mentioned in Chapter 1. This miracle thus took place while Jesus was grieving for his murdered cousin.

Denial has a bad press among some counsellors, and perhaps among the general public, who may consider it to be a sign of failure to face reality. *Nothing could be further from the truth!* Every one of us is using Denial every day simply to organise our day's activities. It is the process of mentally shelving something for the sake of getting on with something else for now that is important. Jesus did this about John the Baptist's murder for the sake of having compassion on the crowd. That is emotional resilience, and strength. Denial only becomes a problem if, when a safe opportunity arises to reflect on the difficult or painful issue, you refuse to look at it to consider your adjustments. After a time the storage shelf can become a bit crowded, and energy is required to avoid looking at things. People become prickly and irritable if someone gets too close. Some issues are so painful, particularly involving abuse, that people effectively put the memories into a deep freeze. When eventually a safe set of relationships develops, perhaps many years later, the memories may emerge, but as emotionally raw as when they first were put there. That's when counsellors are helpful, who understand how safe places are so important. That is what a good friend is also, and hopefully a true life partner.

So, safe places are vital to both the emotionally intelligent handling of shock feelings, and to the emergence of painful memories from the Denial Stepping Stone. Many people think that shock only arises when they first experience a difficult situation. However, people repeatedly re-shock themselves whenever they remember certain situations, when they 'pop out' from Denial. Shock hormones course through the arteries around the body when memories influence the mind, and they are released even when dreams are disturbing, so that people can wake up feeling shocked. Repeated re-shocking can present as generalised anxiety and panics, but choosing to call it 'my Shock Stepping Stone appearing to stand on' opens the logical next step after emergence from healthy Denial: find a safe place and get inside the situation to name some hidden losses, and then to plan the relationship developments needed to address one.

Simply choosing this strategy, as an alternative to 'worrying about my anxiety', could liberate many people from the traps that prevent lives from being fulfilled in Christ. Much that people call depression is, in fact, the disabling effect of recurrent re-shocking, but unrecognised as such. Anti-depressant medication, so effective in the short or medium term for true clinical depression, does not work against shock feelings. *And* God cannot simply remove them, in response to a misguided plea for 'healing' or cure, because they are God-given in the first place for a useful purpose, as part of God's plan to restore the joy of love. "Stop what you are doing! It is leading you into trouble. Take note of that feeling." Learning Emotional Logic, however, can prepare people to be released from these misunderstandings, setting captives free from their traps.

Jesus went on, even while grieving, in the power of his love for his Father to feed five thousand men and many families miraculously. In this he showed the useful purpose of Denial, shelving his hurt to show compassionate and intelligent kindness that renewed and restored life for others. Take note carefully, however, we should never doubt the importance of our quiet times with our Father, with our Source. Here we can find that our safe place is in Christ, in the centre of God's will in a place full of grace and truth, where we can be at peace even alongside others from whom we differ. They are, nevertheless, our brothers and sisters, some of whom will unexpectedly have exactly the right answers to help us, when we feel safe enough to allow it.

Anger

In Mark 11:15-18, Jesus' zeal for His Father's house led him to take firm action to clear the temple courts of traders and money changers.

> *On reaching Jerusalem, Jesus entered the temple area and began driving out those who were buying and selling there. He overturned the tables of the money changers and the benches of those selling doves, and would not allow anyone to carry merchandise through the temple courts. And as he taught them, he said, "Is it not written: 'My house will be called a house of prayer for all nations?' But you have made it 'a den of robbers'."*

The 'house of prayer for all nations' is vitally important to remember here. It comes from Isaiah 56:7, in a section from verses 1-8 that is often overlooked when attention turns to Chapter 58 on true fasting, or 61 on declaring the year of the Lord's Favour. Chapter 56 is on 'Salvation for Others'. In this scripture the Sovereign Lord declares that eunuchs and foreigners (Gentiles) who keep the Sabbath rests, and who love the Lord and hold firmly to his covenant will be acceptable in the temple alongside the chosen people Israel, who are to be re-gathered from exile.

It is a most astounding prophetic declaration. It was made even before the Jewish Nation went into exile! The Church of Jesus Christ potentially fulfils this prophecy, as 'eunuchs and Gentiles', if we others, Christian Gentiles, are capable of being moved with the same measure of emotional intelligence (and perhaps zeal) that Jesus showed in Mark 11 to prevent the destruction of his house of prayer for all nations.

If any reader doubts the central importance of this to Jesus' mission on earth, then read again Acts 10, where St Paul agrees to visit the house of Cornelius, the devout Roman Centurion, and the whole Gentile household is filled with the Holy Spirit. That moment was a tipping point into the new world order, and the fulfilment of Jesus' anger towards the Jewish traders who had been corrupting his Father's home, his house of prayer for all nations.

Throughout the world many cultures teach that people should get rid of their anger, because it is a dangerous, uncivilised, contra-spiritual emotion. However, anger is God-given, built-in as part of the grieving half of love. This true Anger is not the dangerous, hostile, destructive *aggression* that people mistake it for. The Anger of grieving is more like a passionate drive releasing personal energy to move people with an ability to *engage with others despite danger* to prevent the loss of something valuable that is at risk. It is more like a passion for some higher purpose. Jesus had a passion not to lose the salvation that God had purposed for Gentiles and eunuchs and all the outcasts from poor, proud, stiff-necked, lost Israel who were keeping the Glory all to themselves (and the priests especially) instead of being a light to the world. That purpose was worth engaging with some pesky robbers and profiteers, and showing them the door. Would you and I do that? We certainly need some Godly Anger to have the courage and the voice to stand up against injustice. Every one of us needs some Anger just to hold life together in a creative order, and to provide safety and a nurturing environment for the next generation.

The major point that must not be lost is this: Jesus also *taught* in his Anger. He explained, probably loudly, why he was taking this action. People would have no doubt in their minds which loss Jesus was preventing so vigorously—a House of Prayer for all nations—and that makes all the difference. Anger means that someone is trying to prevent the loss of something valuable, and its useful purpose is that it enables others to take note of what that loss is, so that they then have a choice about their own response. Their choice, whether to co-operate or compete with that purpose, determines their futures.

There are other occasions when Jesus showed this Anger with his disciples, when they were going seriously wrong in their thinking or faith. In Matthew 16:21-23, Peter tries to rebuke Jesus, when Jesus has predicted his own death:

> *From that time on Jesus began to explain to his disciples that he must go to Jerusalem and suffer many things at the hands of the elders, the chief priests and the teachers of the law, and that he must be killed and on the third day be raised to life.*
>
> *Peter took him aside and began to rebuke him. 'Never, Lord!' he said. 'This shall never happen to you!'*
>
> *Jesus turned and said to Peter, 'Get behind me, Satan! You are a stumbling-block to me; you do not have in mind the concerns of God, but merely human concerns.'*

Was that an emotional moment for Jesus? If we are to be emotionally intelligent, as Jesus was, we shall need to know ourselves and our values well enough to declare what we are worried we might lose. That is like seeing the multi-coloured stones that create the ripples on the surface of our moving lives. Naming our own hidden potential losses is not morbid or a sign of our weakness. It is Godly honesty about the valuable material of our lives that God can mould into a vessel, or a temple, for Holy Spirit to move among. Naming our potential losses is, in fact, naming our values, but we only know what we value when we feel that we might lose it. That familiarity with our own grief is part of an emotionally intelligent Christian conversation with Father, in Christ. Emerging from that conversation we can then teach others God's values, perhaps even sometimes with a passionate re-connection in Godly Anger, if that is wise and intelligent. Jesus did not want to lose Peter!

In Mark 9:14-21, Jesus shows his Anger at the whole 'unbelieving generation' of the Jewish Nation and the spiritual realm, which included teachers of the law, the local population, and the disciples who had insufficient faith and knowledge to deliver a boy from a troublesome demon.

> *When they came to the other disciples, they saw a large crowd around them and the teachers of the law arguing with them. As soon as all the people saw Jesus, they were overwhelmed with wonder and ran to greet him.*
>
> *'What are you arguing with them about?' Jesus asked.*
>
> *A man in the crowd answered, 'Teacher, I brought you my son, who is possessed by a spirit that has robbed him of speech. Whenever it seizes him, it throws him to the ground. He foams at the mouth, gnashes his teeth and becomes rigid. I asked your disciples to drive out the spirit, but they could not.'*
>
> *'You unbelieving generation!' Jesus replied. 'How long shall I stay with you? How long shall I put up with you? Bring the boy to me.'* (This sounds to me like Godly Anger.)
>
> *So they brought him. When the spirit saw Jesus, it immediately threw the boy into a convulsion. He fell to the ground and rolled around, foaming at the mouth.*
>
> *Jesus asked the boy's father, 'How long has he been like this?'*
>
> *'From childhood,' he answered. 'It has often thrown him*

into fire or water to kill him. But if you can do anything, take pity on us and help us.'

'"If you can"?' said Jesus. 'Everything is possible for one who believes.'

Immediately the boy's father exclaimed, 'I do believe; help me overcome my unbelief!'

When Jesus saw that a crowd was running to the scene, he rebuked the impure spirit. 'You deaf and mute spirit,' he said, 'I command you, come out of him and never enter him again.'

The spirit shrieked, convulsed him violently and came out. The boy looked so much like a corpse that many said, 'He's dead.' But Jesus took him by the hand and lifted him to his feet, and he stood up.

After Jesus had gone indoors, his disciples asked him privately, 'Why couldn't we drive it out?'

He replied, 'This kind can come out only by prayer and fasting.'

Matthew 17:21 adds into the teaching:

Jesus replied, 'Because you have so little faith. Truly I tell you, if you have faith as small as a mustard seed, you can say to this mountain, "Move from here to there," and it will move. Nothing will be impossible for you.'

Is prayer and fasting emotional? Jesus' firm and resilient Anger enabled him to engage with the deaf and mute spirit, and once again to teach the Jews, in that crowd alongside the boy's father, about the *hidden loss of belief in God's power* that prevented them (and us now, perhaps) from living a kingdom life. That loss of kingdom living is worth a bit of Godly Anger to prevent.

To overcome the widespread cultural restraint to 'niceness', Ephesians 4:26-27 is relevant.

'In your anger do not sin': do not let the sun go down while you are still angry, and do not give the devil a foothold.

The first part quotes Psalm 4:4, so it is written into the history of the Jews. Anger, therefore, is not in itself sin. However, *Anger misunderstood and misused* may give the devil a foothold in our lives. I shall have more to say about that in the chapter 'Deliver us from evil'. That foothold can be created when we fail to use our Anger for its God-given purpose to creatively restore loving connection around important values 'before the sun goes down'. Ruminating on our feelings of anger instead, or on injustices or hardships, will create the foothold. In Job 36:21 the young but wise Elihu speaks for God when he says to the good but ailing Job who has turned angry at God:

Beware of turning to evil, which you seem to prefer to affliction.

Remaining angry while ruminating on our own affliction is not the way to turn Godly loss emotion to its useful purpose. If there is nothing that he or she can prevent, the emotionally intelligent Christian will know how to move that personal energy of their anger on to other emotional Stepping Stones by assertively managing one or two named losses that are more appropriate, without turning to evil or allowing evil in.

So, there is more to emotional intelligence, and to Emotional Logic, than first meets the eye! Where else can that energy of inner re-organisation go? I shall describe the four remaining emotional Stepping Stones, and along the way explain the overview that can help you to make appropriate choices that allow your emotions to evolve constructively.

Guilt

A nano-second is a very short period of time, yes; but have you heard of an ohno-second? An ohno-second is that *gap* in time as you realise you've just made a bad mistake!

Many emotions can be rolled into an ohno-second, and Emotional Logic uses 'Stepping Stones cards' to help people map the emotional chaos that can reign over their lives for that moment. Figure 1 shows three such patterns, demonstrating how unique every individual is in the way he or she adjusts to potential loss.

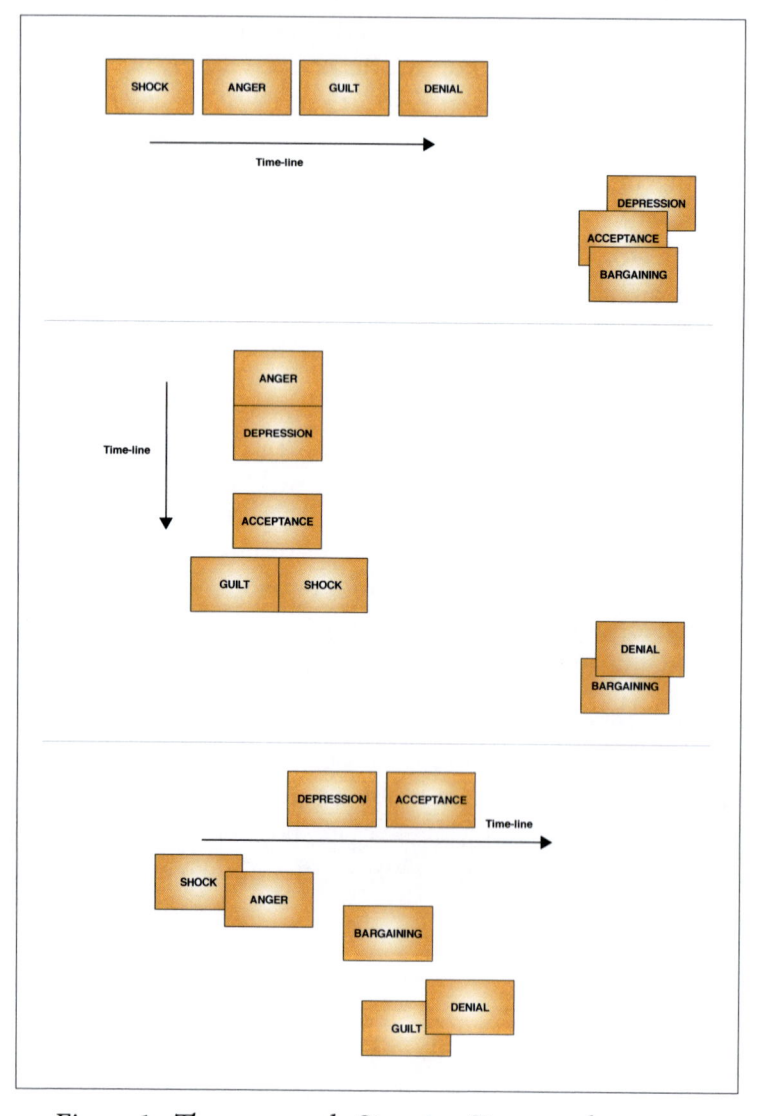

Figure 1. Three example Stepping Stone card patterns

Even though there are only seven emotional Stepping Stones to make adjustments, there is an infinite range of potential patterns with which people experience them. These unique patterns can become the starting place for 'creative conversations', which are like re-arranging big pebbles in your river bed to make them into Stepping Stones to get yourself moving. In a creative conversation both people learn more about how to recognise and turn all that emotional energy to its constructively useful purposes.

In the midst of all that emotional chaos may be the horrible feeling of guilt. I imagine Adam and Eve having a recurring ohno-second whenever they look metaphorically into each others' eyes, and one or the other remembers losing Eden. We all inherit some of that tendency for our feelings to knock-on to others. At such times it is too simplistic to say that one or the other feels only 'guilt', or 'guilty'. Stepping Stone card patterns show how emotions all pile in together as implications knock-on to activate reactions for other associated losses, all happening now at the same time. The situation becomes horrible, or feels terrible. Words become insufficient; and that is why we use cards. "Don't tell me how you feel; show me, using these!"

Guilt is useful, in among all the others, because it is the emotional Stepping Stone where we get organised to ask ourselves a few awkward questions. Should I, could I, take some responsibility for what has happened? Was there something I did that brought it about? Could I learn to do things differently to prevent it happening again? The drive to self-question leads to undertaking a life review, and to then building an action plan upon it. *It is the drive to learn.*

However, the *feeling* as we organise ourselves to conduct such a life review is the weak spot in our human nature's grieving system. That drive to self-questioning feels like, 'I must have done something wrong!' This feeling of guilt and its accompanying self-belief of error can dominate people's ability to think. This saps the potential energy for that Stepping Stone's preparation to fulfil its

God-given useful purpose, which is to move people to adjust their own lives in ways that eventually will enable them to re-connect with others.

The feeling of that drive to conduct a self-review makes people want to hide away; and there many people remain, hiding. That is why it is truly possible to say that Jesus, in his human nature, was not a sinner, because Jesus was able to ask awkward questions of himself in public, conducting his life review in Gethsemane in the presence also of his loving Father, confident that the Father's guidance towards renewed life will follow. He then went on from his self-questioning Stepping Stone, which may have felt like guilt for him—we cannot know, but it was intense—to constructively use his self-review to life-giving purpose for others. We know from John 14:30-31 that he must have conducted a self-review, because he knows that the prince of this world has no hold on Him (See Chapter 11).

> *I will not say much more to you, for the prince of this world is coming. He has no hold over me, but he comes so that the world may learn that I love the Father and do exactly what my Father has commanded me.*

How could Jesus have known that the prince of this world has no hold over him? It was not by remaining a mindless child under protection by his Father from harm, as we may be tempted to remain! Jesus knew that his Father was asking him to suffer affliction and face oblivion for us. This was a mature relationship between a Father and his adult Son. The Son makes choices in such a relationship. This is the garden of Gethsemane, not a dream of lost Eden. The choices were hard, enough to make him sweat blood. Jesus needed every ounce of emotional intelligence to choose to say, 'Yes', while despairing of his friends who fell asleep while he was facing such a difficult decision. Had it all been worth it? Could he trust them to carry on when he had gone? These are emotional decisions of the sort that we have to face sometimes. If Jesus had chosen to say, 'No', it would have been equivalent to saying that he believed his Father did not love him. That was, and is, the lesson. In this, Jesus' honour grew, because honour grows where people grieve constructively.

Jesus knew that the prince of this world had no hold over him not because he believed in his Father's protection. He knew because he believed in his Father's love, and that is emotional intelligence.

Jesus knew, because of this life review, that he could overcome any accusation that an evil-minded person might throw at him, as they later did when he was dragged before the ruling worldly authorities. It is not belief in theology that gives such an assurance, but belief in the love of the Father, knowing that grief marks the path to restore joy in re-gathering.

We frail humans often believe instead the *feeling* of guilt, rather than see it as a preparation drive within to review and learn. We believe the feeling that in some way we are 'wrong', and lose the belief that the Father's love includes this grief for a good and useful saving purpose. The genders have different ways of showing this weak spot in the human love system of grief-and-joy. Women tend to stay too long on their Guilt Stepping Stone, ruminating on the questions; men tend to prefer anything other than going there, usually leaping towards anger or aggression and not wanting to take some responsibility for the way things are. It's nothing that a bit of learning and toughening love cannot sort out.

Guilty feelings are simply the price we pay for loving. The doubting St Thomas went on from his lesson, via a self-review, to found the Church in the Far East. The persecuting Saul spent three years in the Syrian Desert going through his self-review, before opening the Kingdom of God to the Gentiles. You have your calling…

Bargaining-Depression-Acceptance

The examples of Stepping Stone card patterns show the reality of how grieving feels. Curled up inside those patterns is an interesting feature of God-given grieving. Shock, which is commonly one of the first emotions experienced, means that I am doubting my resources to handle this unexpected change. Bargaining and Acceptance, on the other hand, are two Stepping Stones on which people prepare to explore new ways to manage difficult situations. They are outward rather than inward looking aspects of grieving, standing on which we develop and hone new resources. They are our 'growth points' within the grieving process.

Bargaining means I must try doing something to get back what has gone that I value. Acceptance however, is not just letting go of something valued, but also the start of an exploration of something totally new in life despite sadness. The God-given loss reaction thus moves from doubt about personal resources, which may include finance, knowledge, skills, physical abilities, and so on, to developing new resources—a process of personal growth, being able to make use of opportunities rather than let them slip by. People thus can come out stronger from grieving.

In Matthew 26:36-46 you can read the account of Jesus' inner struggle in Gethsemane, before the arrival of his betrayer. Jesus was *'overwhelmed with sorrow to the point of death'*. Three times he appealed to his heavenly Father to take the cup of suffering away. He was trying to recover the things he humanly valued, things that he knew he had lost already as events closed in around him. If you were facing the inevitability of imprisonment, or torture, as many Christians world-wide do, what would you be most worried that you would lose? Can you name those things? Perhaps mobility if you were crippled, or sexual function if you were assaulted, or comfort if you had residual scarring that was painful, or sleep if you had nightmares. Then, or course, there is the shame that victims of torture may feel as they lose self-respect, and the sense of alienation from people who do not seem to appreciate what life can do as they lose connection. That's six 'hidden losses' we have now named, and there will be many more. We could, for example 'get inside' those feelings of shame and alienation to name some more practical things that have actually been lost. It is upon these practical aspects that an action plan might be built, enabling this person to work towards recovery and restoration. In empathy take some time to hear someone (be merciful and connect), by asking, "Yes, this is terrible, but tell me, what you have actually lost?" "As a result of feeling so alienated, what can you no longer do that you used to be able to do?" "Can I help you to recover the ability to do that?" Learning to think in this way is the path to becoming an emotionally strong and resilient Church.

NAMED LOSSES	SHOCK	DENIAL	ANGER	GUILT	BARG'N	DEPR'N	ACCEPT
Painless movement	✓		✓		✓		
pride	✓			✓		✓	
meeting friends			✓				
relaxation			✓			✓	
reason to get up	✓			✓		✓	
sleep						✓	
belief in myself	✓		✓			✓	
intimacy	✓		✓	✓	✓	✓	
independence	✓		✓			✓	
interest in life			✓			✓	
direction			✓			✓	
being understood	✓		✓	✓		✓	
self-respect	✓	✓	✓	✓		✓	

Figure 2. An example Loss Reaction Worksheet

Figure 2 shows how this sort of life review might look on the Emotional Logic 'Loss Reaction Worksheet'. On the left we gradually build up a list of hidden losses, which is really a list of previously un-named values, and at some point we ask people to map their emotions across onto that list, going down the list one by one and asking, "Even though this might have happened some time ago, what do I feel *right now* about this one?" The resulting tick pattern shows the pre-tensioning of someone's inner heart in the present moment. It is like an X-ray or a reconnaissance photograph of the soul. It is out of that entire pattern, showing inner tensioned preparations for action or withdrawal, that a person's 'knee-jerk reaction' emerges when confronted with a difficult situation. Emotional Logic tutors learn how to interpret the patterns, and give constructive feedback and teaching about the useful purposes of those unpleasant emotions. Then people can use this map to untangle the chaos, and turn all that emotional energy to constructive action to grow through the situation, and emerge stronger and more resilient, more able to build substantial relationships with their new-found emotional intelligence and grace.

Bargaining, in Emotional Logic terms, is what people *do* to try to get back the people and things that they have already lost. If a person believes that a loss can be prevented, this belief will drive a person to try to control situations, for which anger and guilt are the relevant emotional preparations. Believing you can *control life* is a trap that sets people up for failure and more grief. It creates a foothold for revenge to take root in the heart. Bargaining, by contrast, is all about letting go of control, and instead gaining in *influence*. Influencing involves risk, because the attempts to recover named losses by Bargaining with unpredictable others may fail, which could add even more grief. Many never take that risk as a way to avoid further grief. They prefer to accept feeling powerless but safe, rather than engage and confront to re-build life around other important values. However, effective Bargaining for a single named loss is, in most life situations, as realistic a growth point to aim for as Acceptance of that loss.

In Gethsemane, each time Jesus Bargains, he was able to turn that inner cry of want and yearning around into a genuinely forward-looking Acceptance of his situation, *"Yet not my will, but your will be done."* But the distress is so intense that he cannot remain in Acceptance. Twice more he goes around that cycle of Depressive emptiness and powerlessness, then Bargaining to gain influence, in the attempt to recover those things and people he values. Then again he is back to Acceptance that, if he is going to take back to his Father in heaven the keys of death that trap all humanity in fear, then he is going to have to let go of life on earth in pain, and explore instead the dark unknown alone.

In the Emotional Logic Centre we call this process of going round and round Bargaining-Depression-Acceptance the 'Growth Cycle'. Unpleasant though the emotions are, people thus find and explore their personal growth points while on the emotional 'Stepping Stones' of Bargaining and Acceptance. It is here that people develop new resources to adjust to situations. Jesus, however, did not need to discover those sorts of growth points in his life, as we do. He was on a different process, a process of self-emptying, of kenosis. Jesus wanted us to be free to explore a path to that high viewing platform, where we could recover eternally renewed life together, sharing in God's loving grace without fear. Jesus was Bargaining there to recover you and me.

The Serenity Prayer

The 'Serenity Prayer' is famous as the foundation upon which Alcoholics Anonymous helps people to re-build their lives. It is now known widely in all walks of life as a guide to facing difficult change. The Growth Cycle described above fits as an exact parallel to the Serenity Prayer.

"God (or 'Higher Power', or the 'Big System' in which I belong), grant me serenity to accept the things I cannot change, courage to change the things I can, and the wisdom to know the difference."

Serenity is a feature of the Acceptance emotional Stepping Stone, and courage is a feature of the Bargaining Stepping Stone, the willingness to face risk and to experiment with some new ways of relating. That leaves Depression. Could this be the emotional place, the preparation state, where I grow in wisdom?! We say that the Depression Stepping Stone is the place of decision. When I begin to recognise that I have limits, but cannot accept them, I am left with the question, "Do I go back to Bargaining, and explore some new way to try to recover a loss that I value and yearn to have back to fill the gap; or do I go on to Acceptance, and explore some way to live without that aspect of life I have so valued, some new way to live, even beyond death?"

That decision may need to be applied separately to each significant loss named in a situation. The Growth Cycle does not apply to whole situations. That is the mistake that many people make when they feel stuck in their feelings of depressive emptiness. To turn a feeling into a firm Stepping Stone of useful Depression, where I can grow in wisdom to adjust by making difficult decisions, there is a creative approach. It is to break big situations into small manageable bits that are each a named loss that was previously hidden un-named in the situation. Each named loss requires a different response. Choosing just one to focus an action plan around requires wisdom. That sort of process can happen even if the overall situation cannot change, or continues even to deteriorate. That is the development of personal strength and resilience. That is the planning that needs to go on in one's safe place.

So, even Jesus was forced by circumstances to his Depression emotional Stepping Stone. His loud cry of dereliction from the cross, *"My God, My God, why have you forsaken me?"* is reported in Matthew 27:46 and Mark 15:34. Did his emptiness and powerlessness overcome him there...? As with Jesus' baptism, which he submitted to for our sakes, I find myself asking if he declares that feeling of forsakenness *to affirm his humanity for us*. I question this, because in Luke 23:38-46 we read that in his Godly nature he was able, even when facing death, to turn that terrible condition into one of hope for others!

> *There was a written notice above him, which read: THIS IS THE KING OF THE JEWS.*
>
> *One of the criminals who hung there hurled insults at him: "Aren't you the Christ? Save yourself and us!"*
>
> *But the other criminal rebuked him. "Don't you fear God," he said, "since you are under the same sentence? We are punished justly, for we are getting what our deeds deserve. But this man has done nothing wrong."*
>
> *Then he said, "Jesus, remember me when you come into your kingdom."*
>
> *Jesus answered him, "I tell you the truth, today you will be with me in paradise."*
>
> *It was now about the sixth hour, and darkness came over the whole land until the ninth hour, for the sun stopped shining. And the curtain of the temple was torn in two. Jesus called out with a loud voice, "Father, into your hands I commit my spirit." When he had said this, he breathed his last.*

In the Emotional Logic Centre we say that in true Acceptance people are not diminished by loss. Certainly there is sadness in Acceptance, when valued aspects of life are gone, and that sadness can be intense and deep and recurring. However, in Acceptance people do not need to 'live in' the sadness. In true Acceptance all the personal energies of the other grief emotions are released into the potential to explore something completely new in life, which restores joy after grieving. That does not dishonour the lost, or devalue what has been let go of. It is life renewed. Life can be ever-renewed if we are able to see, and choose to move on, into new opportunities in Christ alongside others in God's Family. That is how Acceptance differs from Depression, and how the courage of Bargaining mixes with this, all to allow new life to grow and personal development to flourish, perhaps unpredictably. This was certainly the situation for Jesus, whose free-will choice to Accept the path before him opened a new way for people to follow, if they choose, deeper into Him to fulfil all God's purposes.

Constructive and destructive grieving

The basis of an effective and emotionally intelligent Church, in and for the world that God so loves, is a Christian's capacity to name hidden losses for oneself and for others who are different from you, and to respond with a Growth Cycle and Serenity Prayer appropriately. This capacity results in oneself and others developing new resources, often unexpected ones, to recover some losses and to let go of others, while wisdom grows quietly in the background within to weigh which is the better choice. That sort of resilience and strength opens the door to true celebration, to joy on re-gathering, even when circumstances look bad. In Psalm 23, the Lord prepares a table before me in the presence of my enemies, which sounds to me like a bad set of circumstances. Who are my enemies? Only those whose stories I have not yet heard. Asking about our enemy's hidden losses is a great response to find alternative solutions than aggression when conflict arises. A story properly heard shows true spiritual love. That is constructive grieving, as an alternative to revenge. That is where honour grows.

Learning this Emotional Logic framework will not make grief emotions or their feelings disappear or feel more pleasant. That flattening of relatedness into a bland tranquillity is not ever-renewed life. Learning the Emotional Logic framework will, however, make it far less likely that a person, whether enemy or friend, will get stuck with their unpleasant feelings. When feeling stuck with accumulating unpleasant emotions, people can act out and display their inner tension by behaving destructively or withdrawing and feeling overwhelmed. Destructive passions can arise when two God-given loss emotions get drawn into whirlpools, in which neither of the emotional preparations can fulfil its useful purpose. Their potentially constructive energy gets sucked down instead into the depths of the heart to disturb relatedness and personal identity. This is destructive grieving. It can impact others, turning potential friends into enemies.

A few examples of whirlpools might help. I interviewed many people with chronic fatigue. The same pattern of ticks appeared on their Loss Reaction Worksheets—lots of ticks in the Shock and the Depression columns, and none in Anger. Is fatigue a Shock-Depression whirlpool? The hormones involved in Shock (adrenaline and cortisol) affect the immune system. They initially alert it, switching it from 'healing and repair mode' into 'defend against attack mode'. But if the stress continues without a break for too long, these same hormones then exhaust the immune system, but tell the brain "Go to bed and rest. Your immune system is busy down here and needs the energy." The lack of passionate, constructive Anger can seal the illness as a withdrawal from the world. Getting gently passionate about something, paradoxically while continuing to rest, is part of the healing process.

Similarly, on interviewing people in the medical practice, Anger and Guilt are repeatedly revealed where there is obsessional or compulsive or impulsive behaviour, such as self-harming behaviour, bulimia, obsessional cleanliness, and so on. I can confidently say that these behaviours are not signs of *mental* illness, but of *normal grieving* that has been pushed to an unhelpful extreme in whirlpools. Learning the useful purposes of the emotional Stepping Stones involved is part of the healing process of re-connecting the underlying loss emotions with the challenged values that set them moving in the first place, before they became entangled and obscured.

Two others are vital to know in relation to the classical

passionate vices. When Shock and Anger get entangled people cannot think clearly, and they may feel odd and 'out of it'. It easily becomes a spiralling trap of increasing anxiety and panic directed out into disturbed thoughts and behaviour. Finally, and perhaps most importantly, when Anger and Depression get tied together into a whirlpool of emotion, the resulting inner tension feels as if it can only be resolved by smashing something up. Why? Anger is the drive to go out into the world and prevent the loss of something valued. Depression directs the person inwards instead, feeling empty and powerless. Imagine how it feels when someone who is feeling powerless also *gets angry about having that feeling*. A behavioural drive can get moving to *do something out there*, anything, just to prevent that horrible feeling within of emptiness. Irrational action results, destructive or confrontational to try to fill the void. If the drive becomes turned against oneself, unfortunately, irrational suicidal thoughts can result. All of this is normal, healthy grieving but pushed to an extreme, dissociated from the values that have started the emotions moving. The whirlpool develops a disruptive life of its own. The person, not knowing from where all these disturbing thoughts arise, starts telling lies to himself or herself about their identity, such as "I'm weak; bad; mad; ill; dangerous."

NO! This is the grieving you! If you understood your grieving better you would not be like this. You only grieve if you have loved, so that makes you more of a human being, not less. Join the human race. We see people's sense of identity flourish when they can understand how their unpleasant emotions do not mean there is something wrong.

An emotion will evaporate when its preparation state has fulfilled its useful purpose, which is usually about connecting with others in an appropriate way for purpose. To simply acknowledge and name the emotion, ideally with someone else, is halfway towards releasing its tensioning physical preparation state. The other half is to jointly guess which hidden losses have set all this in motion, and then to pick one for which to explore a bit of Growth Cycle.

Sozo: healing-salvation-deliverance

So, bringing this to a conclusion now, love is deeper than joy and grief. Love's relatedness brings feelings of joy on gathering together, and grief's many emotions when there is separation, brokenness or misunderstanding. We can now start to turn our fleeting feelings into the firmer preparation states for action or withdrawal of Shock, Denial, Anger, Guilt, Bargaining, Depression and Acceptance. These move us to re-connect with others in unexpected ways, there to re-discover the joy of love. In doing this, we learn to live each unpleasant feeling with grace.

Tears and weeping do not indicate any *one* of these emotions. People can cry when on any of grief's Stepping Stones. Think about it! Some people cry with their anger, for example, or in guilty self-questioning, or in shock, or when feeling depressed. Weeping is a sign of engaging with the whole grief half of love… and in fact, if you think further about it, people can weep for joy as well, on even thinking about re-connection, or reconciliation! Jesus wept for the wholeness of love he felt for Lazarus. Perhaps Jesus wept thus for us all. John 11:40-44 records the teaching that Jesus gave along with the miracle of resurrection to life:

> *Then Jesus said (to the onlookers at Lazarus' grave), 'Did I not tell you that if you believe, you will see the glory of God?'*
>
> *So they took away the stone. Then Jesus looked up and said, 'Father, I thank you that you have heard me. I knew that you always hear me, but I said this for the benefit of the people standing here, that they may believe that you sent me.'*
>
> *When he had said this, Jesus called in a loud voice, 'Lazarus, come out!' The dead man came out, his hands and feet wrapped with strips of linen, and a cloth round his face.*
>
> *Jesus said to them, 'Take off the grave clothes and let him go.'*

'Take off the grave clothes and let him go.' This is the most profound, brief statement of salvation that I have come across in the Bible. We too can learn to speak words of life to others, in Christ's loving grace. This simple theology of salvation connects with the picture of Christian healing with which I ended Chapter 1. In fact, I would like to end this Chapter by filling out your picture of salvation and wholeness.

When the woman who had been bleeding for many years touched the hem of Jesus garment in the crowd, and he knew that power had gone out from him, Jesus said, "Daughter, your faith has healed you. Go in peace and be freed from your suffering." (Mark 5:25-34) The Greek word used for 'healed' there is *sozo*. The same Greek word is translated a hundred times elsewhere as 'saved'. It means 'to make whole'.

When the possessed maniac in the region of the Gerasenes is delivered of 'Legion', of many demons (Mark 5:1-20), Jesus said to him, 'Go home to your family and tell them how much the Lord has done for you, and how he has had mercy on you.' He was set free into his right mind, made whole by merciful connection, and saved, a picture of *sozo*. But please note, he was saved *into* family reconciliation.

When the four men lowered their paralysed friend on a reed mat through a hole in the roof to where Jesus was healing people in Capernaum, Jesus asked the doubting teachers of the Law (Mark 2:2-12),

> "Which is easier: to say to the paralytic, 'Your sins are forgiven,' or to say, 'Get up, take your mat and walk'?' But that you may know that the Son of Man has authority on earth to forgive sins..." He said to the paralytic, "I tell you, get up, take your mat and go home."

And he did. In so doing he showed that forgiveness of sins and healing are features of one process of movement, of *sozo*, healing, deliverance and saving as movement into wholeness of living. And why did Jesus once again emphasise home?

Our spiritual home is in Christ by grace sharing life with Father and Holy Spirit, the ultimate wholeness of life together with others who are different from us. There, as Family on that high platform of grace with God, we all can look deep into the hearts and movements of humanity, and know that's also where we belong. That's our earthly home, where heaven and earth meet in grace.

Chapter 4
Stepping into a hologram of the Bible

Meanwhile, back at South Highlands where our understanding about *sozo* was emerging out of chaos, our 'therapeutic environment' was turning into a home where we daily invited God to move among us. We shared our differences, and we learnt from each other's unpredictability that people can be surprisingly good.

It was the 1980's. The population of Ivybridge on the southern tip of Dartmoor had grown rapidly from three to twelve thousand. European grants had made the nearby city of Plymouth attractive to high-tech industry planners, and the married military needed homes among local communities. The secondary school erected a dozen 'temporary' classrooms to cope with the expansion.

Tucked away near the town's centre, in large grounds hidden behind trees, was our extended Christian household. In former centuries the town had been a coaching station on the London to Plymouth road. Nine inns had served the formerly small population, and three mills had provided employment. The original hump-backed ivy-clad bridge is still in use. It spans a tumbling, boulder-strewn river, turbulent and moody as it filters off Dartmoor down through a steep-sided, winding valley, arched with trees covered in moss and ferns across the river's course. Each tree is a micro-environment shared with neighbours, unique and beautiful when bathed all in mist or sunshine. At Ivybridge the river used to fan out into a swampy, silted plain that has now been drained, and the river's course clarified. Builders occasionally find a rusty old cannonball when working on house foundations, lost since the English Civil

War when Cromwell's New Model Army had accidentally tipped an ammunition cart over the bridge on their way to besiege the Royalist garrison at Plymouth Barbican. Conflict in religion is not new, and it tends to be mingled with power politics.

The General Medical Practice in Ivybridge needed to expand to match the most rapidly expanding town in Europe. I had become a fourth partner, but differences in approach to medicine had appeared over the first three years, made worse on the arrival of a fifth. We had a parting of the ways. I set up a new practice in the town, which gave me the freedom to be innovative and daring. They took in a more traditional replacement.

My new medical practice opened on Ist April 1986, after a remarkable series of events. The initiating one of these I shall describe for you, to explain why it is that Marian and I talk about 'God-incidences'. Following the incident I am about to re-tell, we bought and converted 'Highlands Health Centre' in such a limited time-frame that, on our opening day, the senior partner of my former practice took a photograph while passing by that he pinned on their notice board with a scrawled caption saying, "Easter miracle?"

So what was this initiating event, this mini Big Bang? Highlands Health Centre sits 20 metres back from the main street of Ivybridge, and its rear boundary abuts South Highlands' paddock, the land rising steadily to the hill on which South Highlands stands half way up. From our home we have views across the rooftops of the town centre, to the valley plain and the hills beyond, and access to the town was convenient for residents along a private drive beside the detached house that was about to become Highlands Health Centre. A nurse, widowed for twenty years, had lived there quietly alone, regularly out to do her work, but her life at home otherwise hidden from the town by a twelve metre high hedge of Leylandii trees. I knew that many business people had asked to buy her home. The location was so ideal for clients. She had consistently refused them, because of the convenience of the site for her own way of life.

As I looked for suitable premises for my new General Practice, I had not even approached her out of respect for her desire for privacy. I was investigating two other sites instead, and was content to do so. However, one evening I was sitting in South Highlands lounge when, completely unprompted, into my mind popped a voice-like feeling, as if someone emphatically said, "Phone her now!" I knew instantly that 'her' was the lady in the detached house. Motivated in this strange way, I picked up a telephone directory, was surprised to find her number there, and rang. She answered hesitantly. I explained who I was, and my purpose in calling. She replied, "That's amazing. My daughter just happens to have dropped in this evening, and we are *right now* talking about the fact that I am getting near to retirement, and that perhaps the time has come to consider selling! I would like to think my home might become a General Practice. Do you want to come down now and talk about it?"

I did; and with the security of her daughter's presence to strengthen her, we agreed the sale there and then!

That prompt at the right time is what I mean by a God-incidence. The builder who did the conversion also became unwittingly the route by which my former senior partner described the following events as an Easter miracle. He motivated several tradesmen with different skills all to work at the same time on site to complete within deadlines—a feat that is normally impossible, I am told.

Intuitive prompts. Constructive responses from people contrary to their normal ways. This is not the stuff that naturalistic science would normally investigate. It is all too unique, unrepeatable, uncontrollable, and unpredictable for that sort of study. These unscientific types of events are, however, life-giving. Does that mean they are unreal?

Healing, cure and change

A brief aside question will set the scene for the next part of this story.

Are you clear about the way I differentiate healing and cure? Healing creates a context in which people grow to feel they belong, and can integrate within and beyond to become whole; cure has a focus on a localised point of attention at which some specific change is hoped for. 'Healing, cure and change' make a triad that matches the healing-deliverance-forgiveness of *sozo*, all of which are parts of taking off the grave clothes and letting people go.

We, as Christians, can learn to let people go, rather than trap them as jewels in our crowns! People whom we have helped to set free will then start to explore the unpredictable development of their personal lives. Our role transforms into one of prayerful trust in God's guidance, of them and us *simultaneously*. That is true relationship. Then the glory of God, rather than the glory of Trevor Griffiths, shines. We shall look at that true glory more closely later.

Following on from that question, which is so fundamental and important—about the way healing, cure and change are related, as context of, and focus in, a transfiguring life—I would like to make this comment about 'change'. The changes that we see in life may be predictable, and they may be unpredictable. Most people need the comfort of some predictability, and they also need to go out and 'get a life' by seeking a bit of unpredictability as well. Each individual differs in their preferred balance of these.

Now, what do you think of this idea? If you constantly narrow the way you look on life, to give it a clear focus in which things happen predictably, then change that results when the whole wider context moves, which is 'out of focus', can appear as if from nowhere. It may appear as something like a God-incidence. This is simply the nature of interactive 'systems', as they adapt, however. The unpredictable happening locally arises from widespread shifts of organisation dispersed throughout an inter-connected system. It is a principle that can be scaled up from the local family, for example, to God's whole Creation. The surprise and even disbelief that people express sometimes about the God-incidence at the very heart of Highlands Health Centre is partly an effect of three hundred years of narrowing attention, which is associated with *believing* in the old-fashioned type of science. This 'Old Science', now taught in schools from an early age, teaches people to focus on the processing of matter *first*, and to focus on this with a very linear sense of time-sequence. In this view a material cause has effects, which may be called 'life'.

However, the Bible is full of references to the living God of eternity. What if 'life' precedes matter, even causes what we consider to be energy-matter? What if the Big Bang of Creation arose out of the life of one Creator God, with linear time as only one optional feature of that Creation? The New Science offers a way to understand how God is synonymous with creative life everywhere now. It is important for Christians not to disdain this way of refreshing the ancient Creeds of the Church, not contradicting them but allowing their wisdom to flourish again. I intend to set people free, who are captives to that Old Science's way of thinking. I intend to untie its 'first focus' on material causes, and replace its effect with the New Science way of focusing *first* on the wider pattern of relationships as an inter-connected 'system' that moves many situations locally. That's life. Those relationships may be purely physical, such as snooker balls bouncing around—if that is where you are focusing your attention—or may be 'patterns of activity', for example among networks of brain cells as thoughts are active (as seen on real-time brain scanners), or may be among a social gathering of people all self-motivated to communicate with each other; or may be between one person and their Big Picture of the greatest whole they can imagine life to be, in which they live their spirituality. In all of these settings, there are patterns of relationships that 'tension' a local situation. There are also strange effects by relationship that can bring an unexpected peace and orderliness beyond focused understanding.

We shall be looking at how to attain that state, described so beautifully in The Message's free transliteration of the Bible.

Matthew 11:28-30 reads:

> *"Are you tired? Worn out? Burned out on religion? Come to me. Get away with me and you'll recover your life. I'll show you how to take a real rest. Walk with me and work with me—watch how I do it. Learn the unforced rhythms of grace. I won't lay anything heavy or ill-fitting on you. Keep company with me and you'll learn to live freely and lightly."*

In such a state of being, I hope to encourage Christians and others to welcome the New Science first focus on *context*. It will renew minds, and in such a way that allows God-incidences to be a natural part of the life that God created. It is a view that does not play down the importance of purely local material interactions (They are special cases of a more general triune principle of organisation.), however, it raises to equal priority the *personal choices* that make life happen unpredictably through the quality of our relationships. *That* sort of healing of the mind, after three centuries of cultured disbelief, can set deliverance and Christ-like forgiveness simultaneously on the move as parts of ongoing salvation.

Here is the plan. Through the Highlands story, I aim to show how emotion, properly understood, is information about the context in which people self-motivate and choose their movements. Emotions are signs of people's connectedness in the whole. They are our radar into the interactions of and with others—our sonar echoing from distant forms that interact to make life the way it is at *this* place and time we call the present. Interpreting these signs of the distant times brings reason and emotion into a partnership. It is a partnership that will be most creative when made in the presence also of echoes from God.

I'll say a little more about the New Science of order emerging unpredictably out of chaos, but only after taking you deeper into the real human story behind Highlands.

A meeting of cultures

Four months from that evening of the intuitive prompt, Marian and I were in a unique and unpredictable position. We owned a property from which we could freely develop a whole person approach to medicine. (No, we did not proselytise.) An NHS General Medical Practice had come into existence *sharing a boundary* with the home where we were developing a whole person approach to healing through prayerful hospitality in the presence of God. The personal prompt *pre-ceded* the physical existence of the Health Centre (upon which people tend first to focus, and then look for material causes). Co-incidence? God-incidence? Changing context and focus at the heart of shared life?

I employed a receptionist at our new practice and her husband as our part-time book-keeper. They were fascinated to discover the way we lived at South Highlands. They were dedicated Christians, and their daughter was also. She, it turned out, worked as a Personal Assistant to a Russian Orthodox priest who was based ten miles up the road in Totnes. Father Benedict Ramsden had an unusual parish in the UK—the whole of Cornwall, even though he lives in Devon. He is a truly English gentleman, who converted to Eastern Orthodoxy from the Western Church while studying at Oxford. The Russian Orthodox Church has a Centre there in the UK. Although traditionally highly geographical in their boundaries, the intensity of persecution of the Orthodox Church by the Communists had forced a Diaspora to take root outside Russia. Initially they had settled in Paris in exile, and later moved to Oxford. It has been through this Diaspora that the Western world has begun to learn the treasures of Eastern Orthodox thinking (thanks to the Communists).

My receptionist, called Traudel and her husband Angus, told me in outline that Father Benedict and his wife Lilah had also developed a ministry of hospitality, after needy people started knocking on their door. Not only were this brave couple growing a family that expanded to eight children, but also they had started to take in far more disturbed people than those with whom Marian and I shared our home life. The whole ministry had expanded into a community of helpers and residents in eight homes dispersed through Totnes and its surroundings. I had to find out more!

I was introduced through Angus and Traudel's daughter, and met Fr. Ben, as he asked to be called, at the Old Priory in Totnes, their original family home and now the centre for their 'Community of St Anthony and St Elias' (COMAE). I was delighted to discover he has a cultured and relaxed tone and manner as he strokes his grey beard (an essential part of the Orthodox priestly condition, but his more trimmed than some I have seen since). A continuous smile in his eyes and a quick, perceptive humour lighten his conversation as he contemplates briefly his responses, and advances his challenges as we get to know each other. We talked on and on. Every aspect, it seemed, was identical in the ways we created environments in which people could explore new ways to live and relate; except that Fr Ben was far more organised and focused than I, with a large staff and severely troubled residents, and his spirituality included a rhythm of prayer that was entirely liturgical—smells, bells, vestments and sung liturgy unchanged over 1500 years or thereabouts, candles and icons—the exact opposite to everything I had felt gave me the freedom to explore—and yet, here was Fr Ben and his family having explored far more bravely than I.

Each home had three *forensically mentally ill* people, and at least two live-in helpers staying as a single shift for three days and nights, many of whom were trainee psychologists. Social Services funded his residents' stay and support, because the Social Workers recognised and valued the stability and social integration that most of the residents managed to achieve outside the locked, secure units in which they had previously been held.

Fr Ben described his aim in this way: that by home-like hospitality, challenge and supportive feedback in guided community these people might discover their potential for living. For both of us, adventure and unpredictability within a supportively structured and responsive social system were important parts of the challenge. They led to personal development, and to self-respect for both residents and staff *alike*.

I was more intrigued than ever. I was about to learn that the charismatic freedom I moved in at my church could equally be lived in other ways, neither more 'right' than the other. I later visited the small public Orthodox chapel at Fr Ben's home, richly decorated and beautiful. Fr Benedict explained, as he showed me the icons and the screen illuminated by small oil lamps, that this is mysteriously the focal point of family and community. The Life celebrated regularly at this chapel is a heart-beat present in the background of his life, telling repeatedly a higher order story that may turn the minds of inquisitive individuals into a shoulder-to-shoulder body of people, a community, even a family. The common theme of that celebration, that all can hear if they listen, is that each human being is a respected person; no, much more than respected—a revered person—and that together they are a people, in which each belongs.

Exploring Russian Orthodoxy

I had to learn more about this angle on Christianity. Everybody reads a story differently. Each person identifies differently with it, or finds their juxtaposition to it. That's the diamond-like beauty of a story or a parable. The Gospels were written in a story-telling culture, and the Orthodox liturgy developed thus also, repeatedly re-telling the story. I wanted to turn this diamond in my hand, and see the light of God shining through it for myself. My Protestant friends were mostly dismissive about ways of worship other than their own, and they were wary of theology that did not precisely match theirs in detail, and they quickly could step away from those ideas before even trying to understand from whom they were thus disengaging. But I am an innovator by nature, an explorer and adventurer, an activist as a learner, comparative and inquisitive, so that makes me dangerous and a risk-taker to find the Truth. That visit was the start of my ten year exploration of the Russian Orthodox Church. It changed my views of history, and of Church history, particularly of the argument between Rome and the Protestants, of theology and anthropology, and of the nature of religious and personal conflict; and it has strengthened me, not weakened me.

The same might be true for those of you who open your minds to this new and balancing perspective. But be warned, it opens a colourful and four-dimensional space to dwell in eternally. The Orthodox are Biblically-based (more than sixty percent of the Bible is read aloud every year through the liturgies and vigils), and every feature of a chapel points to some aspect of the Biblical account of prophecy fulfilled in the life and resurrection of Christ. The chapel itself is like a hologram of the Bible, with an added dimension of time eternal into which we participants in the liturgy step and stand alongside all the believers of old, and those still to come. Each feature of the chapel and liturgy does not point one's focus just to an idea, for a mind to reason about. Each feature points one's mind through the physical to the living person or people beyond, in the Kingdom of Heaven beyond time in which we share with them even now. That is how stepping into an Orthodox chapel is like stepping into a hologram of the Bible. The people come alive and present in 4-D. The charism of Holy Spirit is shared among all. I liken the array of icons to a family photograph album. When you recognise how far back your family goes, and how impressive some of your relatives are, you sometimes cannot help but be moved emotionally to be counted among them. I belong in *this* Family! And you may then want to touch the source of that memory, re-discovered, even to kiss this loved one's photograph as the memory brings the person beyond in this moment close once again, ever-present.

It *adds* to rational Protestant grey-stone Puritanism, and to Roman hierarchies of authorised truth and grace; and it does not diminish the value of either of those different expressions of spirituality. I have found it highlights their unique qualities—more of which later. I have concluded that *all three need each other to be different*.

One Sunday in four, with the blessing of my Protestant Pastor, I started to attend the Orthodox morning liturgy, and the monthly night vigils in which the heart of Orthodoxy is revealed. These times were mostly accompanied by long conversations and feasting afterwards with the other attendees, with Fr Ben and his wife Lilah, and perhaps some of their children (of all ages). I learnt about the way of life and the meaning of all that I was experiencing. The other Sundays I worshipped with the Protestant charismatic free-church as before, playing bass guitar in the music group, worshipping in the Spirit, singing in tongues and extemporising and reflecting mood musically during free praise times, and I took part in its mid-week church house-groups, where the fellowship of believers is built up and character is strengthened. I also developed links socially with the Roman Catholic priests in our area, talking philosophy and theology over a brandy (The Orthodox seemed to prefer whisky at their feasts).

As a local GP I worked with the Roman and Protestant church leaders in our locality to successfully develop a truly ecumenical neighbourhood befriending scheme. 'Open Door' made pastoral visitors from all the churches available, under priestly supervision, to help others in the wider community who were isolated by illness or unfamiliarity. It was a non-religious, non-proselytising act of service from all the churches in the local community—helping to turn the town's individuals into a community.

So an integrating core had begun to emerge in all this exploration. Father Benedict was playing a significant role in broadening my horizons. Seeing how the Community of St Anthony and St Elias worked was a valuable comparison to the calling Marian and I were following. There, Christianity was more of a background grace, held in peoples' hearts, unspoken but 'at hand', made real in the way the staff were inspired to *reverence* the residents, which is more than respecting their human rights. Some subtle difference in attitude was making all the difference.

Healing into a paradoxical wholeness

I would like to share with you three insights that I gained through the vigils, breaking through some Protestant boundaries to make further connections in the Person who is Truth. I am not saying the Eastern Orthodox Church has a better way! It is a route by which I broke out of limited thinking to grasp the fully *triune depth of diversity* that moves continuously in grace within the appearances of things. And more than that, I grasped how this movement through grace may appear meaningfully in the fabric of each person's life as *emotion*. All this exploration started from trying to identify the roots of conflict and division in the Church.

The Oxford Dictionary definition of paradox is: a person or thing conflicting with preconceived notions of what is reasonable or possible with a seemingly absurd though perhaps actually well-founded statement.

In a four-hour vigil, Truth can be presented as multi-faceted—presented as a human-divine paradox. Vigils are extended Bible studies that are sung as a biblio-drama, all set in a hologram of the Bible into which the participant steps by choice. They reveal the grace and truth hidden behind what we take to be reality. They present these scriptures in a way that the Holy Person who is Truth can seem startlingly different from the positions different people take to view and understand Him. Comparing personal perspectives, or stories, after the vigil generates new ways to respond to life's events.

For example, one paradox that I find particularly moving is the story of the old man Simeon in Luke 2:21-40.

> *Now there was a man in Jerusalem called Simeon, who was righteous and devout. He was waiting for the consolation*

of Israel, and the Holy Spirit was on him. It had been revealed to him by the Holy Spirit that he would not die before he had seen the Lord's Messiah. Moved by the Spirit, he went into the temple courts.

He must have felt an 'intuitive nudge' when moved by the Holy Spirit (then as now!) to enter the temple courts just when Mary and Joseph had arrived to present their baby Jesus to the Lord on the eighth day, in accordance with the Law. Simeon (v28), having taken Jesus in his arms, announced that he can now die (be 'dismissed') in peace because

'with my own eyes I have seen the Lord's salvation, a light to the Gentiles and the glory of Israel'.

The liturgy of the vigil brings out the paradox. Simeon is holding in his arms the One through whom the whole universe is created, and in whom now all things hold together. So, who is holding whom? And into whose peace is Simeon now released?

It is this inside-outside paradox that the Orthodox are so good at maintaining, and at living out daily in their walk with God. It keeps celebrants mentally 'on their toes', unable to settle into one extreme of inside-outside belief, because the opposite is so clearly also true.

Try this paradox also: it is one that could hold in creative tension opposing ideas that have separated Christians in different Churches from sharing the sacrament of Communion. The bread and wine, in an Orthodox liturgy, having been prepared and acknowledged behind the screen (iconically 'in heaven'), are carried in solemn procession out of one door in the screen, and returned through another door (in a biblio-drama representing Christ's birth/arrival into the world and death/departure from it), before being brought out again through the central door for distribution to the faithful within the worldly arena of the chapel. This represents the resurrection and renewal of Christ's eternal life given for us. But, as Father Benedict explained to me, God is everywhere, and so during the procession, although the priest has solemnly acknowledged that Christ is *in* this bread and wine, as the sacraments are processed through the church, Christ does not move. The procession moves through Christ.

Are you beginning to get a feel for the 'earthed' yet deeply spiritual nature of Orthodox belief? It has vitality, offering a place to belong and to participate fully in the life freely given and shared among the Family of God in and for the world. We each walk through God, breathe and speak in God, and in time we may know that God, being totally other than us, delights in our walk together.

One final example of paradox. It is another important way in which the inside-outside distinction is made permeable and not a barrier to living as Family in the presence of God.

Orthodox priests are absolutely clear that the liturgy is a play—nothing more—except that it is a play in which the *real presence* of God is celebrated. The play repeatedly enacts the Biblical story, making visible in that chapel the dynamics of ever-renewed life that are on-going *everywhere now*, but which are easily hidden from our minds in the normal busy walk we make daily through the world.

Those dynamics are on-going even in your kitchen at home, for example, or in your place of work, or where you mix socially with others. You can remind yourself anywhere and anytime of the rich sensory experience of that candlelit chapel filled with sung liturgy and incense, and recall how every iconic picture and action is a doorway to heaven through which you have the choice to look or step, even now, into eternity. This is the eternal now.

You have a choice to recall that hologram of the Bible at any time as a framework of mental categories, a mind frame, against which you can compare (or within which you can place) your ongoing, daily, present-moment sensory and motor-action experience. That act of comparison will affect your emotions, and so influence the way memories are laid down to rest in Peace in your brain. Your life will thus be moved and transformed by the renewing of your mind into more of the likeness of Christ. In that physical transformation of your brain and relationships, you become 'a little Christ', a Christian.

So where is the paradox? When you step into an Orthodox chapel, and in so doing relationally interact with the hologram of the liturgy, are you stepping out of worldly existence to create a mere mental image to think about, or are you stepping into a higher relational reality that you in some mysterious way *co-create*?

And when you step out of the chapel, are you stepping into a fully human reality, or are you stepping out of fully relational humanity into a world that lives in a dream of its own self-existence?

When the leaders of an organisation have a 'dreamtime' as part of their long-term planning, the personal honesty involved in sharing such hopes may be uncomfortable for others to hear, but more stable agreements for the future can result. The personal truth needs to be shared and received with grace if the honest diversity is to be brought into a creative unity within the organisation. The outcomes may be unpredictable, but they may be unexpectedly good.

Perhaps people could learn how to turn the discomforts of truth before God to a constructive purpose, if they knew how to apply their Emotional Logic moment by moment. We may even thus become risk-takers, able to let go of the facts that have made sense in our limited contexts at one particular time, and to grasp hold firmly instead of the freedom that we belong in Christ, there with the Family on a high viewing platform of grace. From there, in Christ's inner heart, we may adapt over time to be available for the healing of the world that God so loves, and respond to the call to participate.

Bridging across social and physical limitations

Let me give you a practical example of how the spiritual inspiration of 'resting in God with paradox' can turn around an old science mind set. It is about revising our picture of health.

To be 'healthy', such things as physical disabilities, traumatic damage, or illness, may seem to set limits. But physical health and being a healthy person are not the same. Health comes from the same linguistic root as whole, and a person can be whole even with physical limitations or illness. That is because personal wholeness includes the notion of movement into connection with others. Ultimately this is the nature of the kingdom of God. A whole person is incomplete alone.

So, personal wholeness includes the potential pace at which a person can change, or develop, or grow wilfully from a place of disability, damage or illness into their complementarities with others. Residents and carers at South Highlands mingled as equals, each with their different starting places and paces for change and development. The same attitude prevailed at COMAE, which was a valuable affirmation of this personal development principle.

Individuals have undeniably different limits in the physical perspective on their lives. Both Fr Ben and I had seen how these limits can seem to change over time, however, given the right social setting. The opposite is also seen, however. Old habits and physical limitations can re-emerge in certain settings when they had disappeared in others. So, behaviour varies in context, and can recur in context, including bringing a recurrence of brokenness, separation or misunderstanding. Perhaps the New Science, which is all about communication patterns, can bring some light to bear on what is happening here.

First, a reminder: cure of a condition may be limited by peoples' genetics; healing of a person may be limited by contextual conditions.

Health includes an ability to explore our limits socially, otherwise people would be like prisoners who remain in the cell by habit even when the door has been unlocked and left ajar. There are mental habits, and emotional habits, and physical habits. So, are genetic limits just *chemical habits,* which might also shift as people explore different environments? Well, the New Science does in fact offer a very different picture of how genetic chromosomes work over *extended time-frames* to the old science 'snapshot' view of genetics with its linear view of 'cause and effect' (from one snapshot to the next). The old view was that the genetic material (DNA) is like a blueprint for a ship, for example. The linear cause-effect relationship was that the blueprint causes the ship's final shape, because it directs the activity of the workers who make it. But this is simply no longer a true picture of *life*! The New Science of adaptive systems has shown that the biochemical activity around chromosomes is far more affected by feedback from the environment than previously thought. Different areas of the chromosomes open up and close down in response to body and environmental changes. It is not a linear cause-effect process, but a microcosm of systemic activity that opens up ranges of potential responses to changing circumstances. Pregnancy, aging, climate changes and so on open up different areas of the human genome.

In 2010, the ability to clone genetic offspring led to a remarkable finding. Everyone expected that clones would be identical physical replicas of the original mother. Horror stories were rumoured that cloning had the potential for new 'new model armies' of cloned soldiers invading across the world. But clones are found to be non-identical physical replicas! A telling photograph appeared in The Times of the first cloned pig's litter, all nine piglets suckling at the same time. All nine bottoms clearly had a *uniquely different shape*. The development of physical body form does have more varied influences than purely genetics. It startled and shocked people out of that 'inevitability' frame of mind about genetics. The way piglets crowd each other in the mother's womb, the differences in placental feeding, the assertiveness of one piglet for the nipple more than another, and so on, all make each individual pig unique in its history and potential, activating different parts of the individual's stored genetic material along the way. This is true equally for human beings, whose personal environment for development includes choice-based freedom in relationships. A person's Big Picture of where they belong in the universe may affect this feedback as well, opening or closing the way for the living, responding, communicating, ever-present God to speak words of life by relationship also.

These environmental influences are now called 'epi-genetic factors'. These influences in a child's early years can shape connections in the brain long-term, affecting the body's chemistry via hormone feedback loops. In the midst of this transforming dynamic of life, chromosomal DNA opens and closes its stored historical record of feedback loops to activate those that have worked sufficiently well in the past for the organism's former family to survive in *their* changing environments.

The New Science view of genetics is that each human being inherits a unique *range of responsiveness* through their genes, which can open up in different settings. Genetic material codes a memory of chemical responses that develop into a living, transforming collection of dust that is a living body—not a blueprint for a shape.

Thus, environmental influences 'speak' to us at a deeper level than previously imagined. They can influence epi-genetically the way our physical forms emerge and perform in different settings. Our choices feed back in the midst of this process also. It does not just happen automatically as if pre-programmed. Parenting is far, far more than just begetting—it is environment-making, and memory-making.

Now, I want to shift this idea to a different level, heading along the path up to that high viewing platform of grace. This section gets a bit 'heady', so hold on to something and go slowly.

Along life's way, without clearly thinking about it, every day we are Bargaining to try to recover something valued that has been lost, or that we worry might have been lost by making certain choices. Bargaining involves personal choice, and goal-directed behaviour, with feedback about how well we are doing. In South Highlands, and in COMAE, we had been led to create environments in which people could explore new potentials with a managed amount of risk, so minimising loss and maximising recovery. What if God— No, surely this concept is too outrageous—What if God could Bargain to recover us by creating and influencing our environment, called Creation (or the cosmos, or the living universe)?

Creation emerged, I believe, from the unity among three sub-states before the Big Bang of Creation. It emerged, and is continuously emerging, from the unity of 'God'. If so, then maintaining unity is inherently part of the image of God in Creation, and it is there to be found *in and through us human beings* (and perhaps all other living organisms). If so—and this is a big step up towards that high viewing platform—could you imagine that *the choice for unity* is grace; and that making this choice continuously is the 'fabric' that runs substantially through all Creation?

Picture grace as the waters of Genesis 1:1-3.

In the beginning God created the heavens and the earth. Now the earth was formless and empty, darkness was over the surface of the deep, and the Spirit of God was hovering over the waters. And God said, "Let there be light," and there was light.

I am told that in Hebrew it reads 'In beginning...'. This is an active, continuous verb; not a static noun. This verb actively could be at the source of every present moment in time everywhere now —as God.

I am suggesting to you, for you to consider, that 'the waters' were *not* some pre-existent material or force other than God. I believe that 'the waters' are the 'chosen unity among God's personal sub-states', over which hovers the Holy Spirit, hovers until the Source we call the Holy Father speaks change; upon which the Holy Spirit becomes the utter connectedness (or relatedness) of grace so that the spoken change spreads into the wholeness by grace. Across these waters of chosen unity the Father spoke waves that are the

Word we know as Christ, the wholeness of grace in movement, the only begotten true Son. These waves of grace within the Son heap up and interact with each other and criss-cross to make interference patterns that give parts of Creation an appearance of self-existence—but of course these parts are emerging from movement within and simultaneously beyond themselves. All things hold together in Christ, we are told in Colossians 1:15-17; all things are in movement in Holy Spirit; all things now and forever owe their existence to the uttered Source of change we call Holy Father.

If this is grace, the chosen unity of God's three personal sub-states, then could that Source of all environments somehow also modulate local contexts that 'Bargain' with us, by opening our minds, from limiting belief in our self-existence, to peace discovered by resting in wholeness? If that can be imagined as an image of the living creator God, then Fr Ben and Lilah, and Marian and I, had been led or called independently by God to co-create with God smaller local environments that Bargain to restore wholeness in Christ for those who live in them. People chose to step into them, just as other people may choose to step into a chapel hologram of the Gospel. Is this an image and likeness of one living God in humankind? Could each one human being have some inner capacity to do that creatively for others?

Furthermore, the influence of those co-created local environments can alter the physical potential of the persons who dwell there. The environments could feedback into the activity of their genetic material even. Beyond the limits of old science beliefs, we can become sources of renewed life, 'new creations'.

> *Therefore, if anyone is in Christ, the new creation has come: The old has gone, the new is here! (2 Corinthians 5:17, NIV)*

> *Therefore if any man be in Christ, he is a new creature: old things are passed away; behold, all things are become new. (King James Authorised Version)*

Substantial grace

So, by *substantial grace* I mean that the substance of One God mentioned in the Nicene Creed (the essence, or Gk. *ousia*) is the chosen *unity* of God. We experience this chosen unity, as God chooses us, like healing waters when we know God's grace. But think again about an old translation that may be *unhelpful* in English. In English the word essence means 'the indispensable quality that makes a thing what it is', from the French 'to be'. The Greek ousia (for essence) was translated into English as 'substance' from the Latin sub (under) sto (stand) via the ancient French substantia, meaning 'that which stands under something else', its existence—a rather Platonic concept. However, there is another more direct translation of sub-sto that makes more sense in everyday English. It is to *under-stand*. The grace of God becomes the *mutual understanding* of the three Holy Persons of God. Out of this chosen unity is birthed a Creation that has both material essence and conscious mind in its creatures. The essence and the mind of God come together in this concept. Where wilful choice is part of a creature's life, in humanity, then image and likeness of this indispensable quality of God is to be found in human being also.

This direct translation of *substantial grace* that I am presenting to you, the mutual understanding between persons in God and in the life of Creation, gives equal place to emotion alongside reason in God's kingdom living. E-motion is the evidence in us of our engagement in the movements of God's grace. It is where our spiritual and our physical natures meet.

Chapter 5
Unearthing the roots of conflict

How is Creation built upon the substantial grace of God? It is built upon the mutual understanding that endures through all changes that are spoken by Father; and by the mutual understanding of grace Holy Spirit moves through connection to diversify those changes into each and every part that responds from its unique place of belonging in the whole; and all those diversified changes are held in unity by grace as the only begotten firstborn Son despite affliction and tension, in whom eternally all things hold together. It is an emotional process, diversifying and holding in unity, especially when human will gets involved as well. In these final two chapters of the first Part, I shall present the opposite to this image of God in human being—a 'model of mutual misunderstanding'.

This model is designed to help you notice other peoples' curious ways, but specifically then to help reconciliation to flourish. Make every effort to keep in unity of Spirit with others while being moved by the Father's words. Where the Family of God dwell in unity, God commands a blessing to flow out.

Trying, and failing, to 'bottle the secret'

Some people in health and social care planning wanted to 'bottle the secret' of what made Fr. Benedict's Community so effective for their seriously ill people. Some people have 'It', they decided. Perhaps, if they could identify what 'It' is, they could replicate the success of the Community by training 'It' into people.

A focus group I ran as part of planning local mental healthcare services set about trying to define what a trainable 'It' might be. Unfortunately the wider context for this focus group underwent a change, which affected our work. Including residential communities within National Health Service provision became a highly controversial idea against an emerging background trend that focused on behaviour, towards which protocol-driven cure strategies could be written. We never succeeded in our task. However, our conversations did alert me to an interesting observation. I noticed that as soon as the focus of attention goes to behaviour, the *spirit* of belonging in a network of moving interactions is lost to sight. There is a profound and surprising consequence to this. The importance of personal choice and responsibility 'in context' evaporates; in its vacant space appears a target to aim one's behaviour towards. Who sets up and moves the target is the boss.

Where is belonging now? Who belongs to whom when targets are being moved? The personal freedom that accompanies spiritual 'belonging-in' is replaced by the linear focus of captured 'attention-upon' the one *outside* you who seems to know enough to rule your life by moving that target.

This distinction, I have come to realise, is vital also in the story about brokenness in the Church that I am telling. The 'It' we had hoped to bottle about the Community is, I personally believe, the ability of the family-type healing community to maintain an inside-outside paradox *about the development of personhood*. The Western Church pulled away from this 'honest freedom for personal development' a thousand years ago. It pulled away from maintaining a *paradoxical* place of personal development through worship, and made instead the life of Jesus a model target to be aimed at behaviourally, enabled through receiving sacraments materially as the cure of souls. This is a valuable perspective on God's life, but 'It', personal development through living paradox, cannot be thus bottled.

Healing, cure and personal growth; forgiveness, deliverance, and salvation; context, focus and change… We are stepping onwards now, balancing carefully, up towards that high viewing platform with God.

Just as context and focus are needed for life to grow, so East and West need each other's different views on life for the Church to be a living source of healing for the world. Each has their values built into their perspectives on God's kingdom. When diversity becomes stark difference, however, these values may cause offence, and raise a defence against the risk of loss. That is a spiritually emotional process, which can develop its own sorts of complications that Emotional Logic can untangle. The values will be important to recognise and name. For example, the psychologist who suggested that we try to 'bottle the secret' of the Orthodox community was a Roman Catholic, for whom the notion of collecting a dispensable sacrament in a bottle or wafer was something valued as normal. The model of misunderstanding I shall be presenting can give a non-judgmental account of this, one which intrinsically points the way to mutual respect, reconciliation, and blessing.

Eastern Orthodox theology maintains that we humans should not try to name or describe the invisible God. God is beyond even the dispersed whole life context at source everywhere and continuously. Words divide and reduce. Eastern Orthodox Christianity takes an 'agnostic' stance to this invisible spiritual system of interactions, but is willing to show the story as a biblio-drama. It is akin to the Jewish tradition of respectful humility, leaving God un-named. For the Eastern Orthodox, the still, quiet voice of God emerges from a place of paradoxical mystery, deeper within and simultaneously further beyond than human minds. If God, as the source of life's universal energies, is beyond all humanly constructed categories of existence, what then can be said of God?

For example, this approach to keeping a living and respectful relationship with God is called 'apophatic theology'. In the English language this approach should make us wary of that little word 'is'. In an apophatic mindset, saying 'God is love' is risky. Perhaps the love that God is, is not love as we know it. Human minds so easily take that extra dividing step to say, God is love and I have got it. Perhaps God loves my enemies as much as God loves me, and wants me to love them in God's way too, so that the spiritual work of reconciliation can begin. The problem of the little word 'is' could be avoided simply by worshipfully knowing in your quiet heart-source 'God who loves me and you'. I shall return to this towards the end of the book.

Apophatic 'unknowing' does not prevent Christians from honouring God as the mysterious heartbeat at the source of a community or a family. A community or family is continuously co-created by the feedback among its individuals. An attitude of respectful 'unknowing' about the presence of God simply protects the individual members of that community or family from being manoeuvred by others' words into a *restricted* view of God. Restricting someone else's view creates the conditions in which they may be psychologically manipulated. With apophatic 'unknowing', however, the infinite is moving deeply within each human's experience, leading individuals quietly into the liberty to develop all their relationships, including theirs with God. But it may be an uncomfortable place to be, made potentially joyful when people know how to handle their grief constructively together. The 'leadership' of any church or community or family may make recommendations about how best to relate to God, but it is the Body of the Church as a whole that has the ultimate authority of love to relate by God's personal inspiration as best they can.

In the Western Churches many people have a mind set, however, in which they find 'unknowing' to be an unsatisfactory way to honour God. God *does* have attributes that can be named. The Bible gives us many pictures of God's attributes or names, for example Wonderful, Counsellor, Light, the Rock, Almighty, everywhere-present, all-seeing. These are valuable for reflection and contemplation. Used pictorially they can inspire faith, hope and love that rational minds need to live out God's call upon their individual life. This approach to building a living relationship with God is called 'cataphatic theology'.

If a Christian needs named attributes to *know* God's nature as *different from* human nature, then philosophically-speaking he or she is adopting a 'positivist attitude' to God. This focus of mental attention is favoured by Western Christian thinkers, and it explains why attempts in that Western-minded focus group to 'bottle' the mystery at the heart of Fr. Benedict's Community failed. There is no positivist element in wine when 'It' is consecrated. Western minds may need to emphasise instead how great and wide and deep is the unending love of God, as substantial grace moving continuously through the wine.

The apophatic way of knowing God, the Eastern and as we shall see Celtic way also, is not 'negativist' by contrast with the cataphatic 'positivist' way! It simply gives attention instead to context, somewhat unfocused. It emphasises a human person's subjective experience of *living dynamically with* God—in God's love for your and my personal development together. It is an approach that philosophers call 'phenomenology'. In this mind set, the phenomena of daily living are all clues to the presence of God interacting across the divisions that are being spoken into existence by humans. It is the mind set that opens into eternity the doorway of a human being's 'eternal present' moment; it is the route of mystical spirituality walked by Eastern Orthodox Christians, Celtic Christianity, and all in the West who are true worshippers in spirit.

These two mind sets, apophatic and cataphatic, emphasise how people's relationship with God has multiple aspects. To assert that one is more orthodox (in the sense of doctrinally right) than the other will lead almost certainly to misunderstanding, separation, brokenness and conflict. To recognise instead the different values they point to may bring closer the humane possibility that constructive grieving could restore joy in reconciliation to unity. This is only possible as the Church cultivates emotional intelligence.

Back to the beginning, to the source

Marian and I have been moved now for many years by a mystical call to find the source of conflict between Christians, and to contribute to its healing. A 'cognitive' issue, for example the apophatic/cataphatic diversity, primes people for misunderstanding. Then separation, brokenness, false pride and conflict are not far away. It is like the old story of the three blind men who grab hold of different parts of an elephant, the trunk, the ear, the belly, and claim the description they each give, like a snake, like a huge leaf, like a boulder, describes the whole elephant. Cognitive mismatching is not confined to the major mind set differences of East-West. Context mismatches happen every day, even along the main shopping street of Ivybridge.

I needed to lay bare the roots at this depth of misunderstanding between people. If its cause could be *visually* present, then people could step over the problems without stumbling in their spiritual walk. Those roots are not problems in themselves, as we shall soon see. They are the very source of life, running deeper into grace than any parts of the mustard tree of the kingdom of God we can focus our minds upon. We just need to learn to walk carefully over them. Divisions of roots and branches have their source and also their fulfilment in unity.

Figure 3. *The triquetra—an image of dynamics*

I realised that the Celtic Christian symbol for Holy Trinity, the triquetra in Figure 3, could show also how a human being might be made in the image of a living God. The name comes from the

Latin *tri* (three) *quetrum* (corner). A triquetra (single, not plural) is a three cornered shape that is not a triangle.

The triquetra is an image of dynamics. Run a finger along the lines, and you will get a better impression of the utter interrelatedness of changes angling at nodal points, from where some new direction takes flight. The Ancient Celts may have used this image to display the eternal change of *life* that underlies our impression that the world is constant. It is the visual partner of the French proverb, *Plus ça change, plus c'est la meme chose.* (The more a thing changes, the more it is the same thing.) In the next chapter you will see how this dynamic can be interrupted, however, to show brokenness and conflict appearing within its unifying dynamic. Those diagrams are where the roots of the tree of life have come to the surface and may trip up the unwary.

Figure 4 Networks of triquetra

The Celts made geometric patterns out of these triquetra, as shown in Figure 4. I realised I could use this diagrammatic feature to demonstrate networks of people interacting with each other, as communion, and as a falling away from that perfection into restricted group mentalities and identities that, once again, can end up in conflict with each other.

These networks might exist at numerous different levels of life, for example a community of people, or perhaps even the material processes of life. Imagine that this network of triquetra is light; imagine each triquetra is a photon, a small package of energy streaming across the universe, each one of which can activate a human retina's light sensitive cells (rods and cones). Each photon is a squiggle of changing relatedness, which can entangle with others to make and illuminate forms. Light is the first level of God's Creation, out of which all else is made. Here in a single triquetra you have a picture of a quantum of energy (a light photon), squiggling into entanglements with others to make atoms, each atom a network of triquetra. How different a picture of an atom is that to the old 'solar system' picture! The electrons (quanta of energy) no longer need to be pictured as circling around a nucleus like miniature lumps of rock, but instead they leap at the speed of light to entangle wherever the change takes them next.

The same image of dynamics gets scaled up through different levels of organised *life*. Atoms entangle into molecules that transform continuously in the biochemistry of living bodies, which gather into inter-active families of people who develop their diversity with others in neighbourhoods, and aggregate into warring tribes or nations struggling to secure more resources from each other. Or perhaps people might connect more constructively with each other by co-operating in a more extending network rather than competing.

In-and-out of this entire material struggle of entanglements is the Trinity of Holy Persons of God. The holy *tri-unity of sub-states separately conjoined* of one living God is the source of all quanta of energy. Out of the grace to conjoin (and not to separate) emerges the spoken movement of created energy. That created energy is nothing in itself other than 'changing integrated patterns of relatedness' moving through grace.

Chapter 5 **Unearthing the roots of conflict**

The triquetra displays *triune principles of organisation*. Its dynamic is the verb 'create' with a lower case c. Its cyclical standing waves become the noun 'Creation' with a capital 'C'. All are contingent on God's grace.

It is this dynamic of creation that shows how the God who called Abraham is a living God. Only a living God can call to human beings. Figure 5 shows how these triune principles of dynamic organisation affirm that one creator God can have Personal *sub-states in unity*. Not being separated, they are not three gods, but one mutual understanding with diversity that integrates the Source of all life.

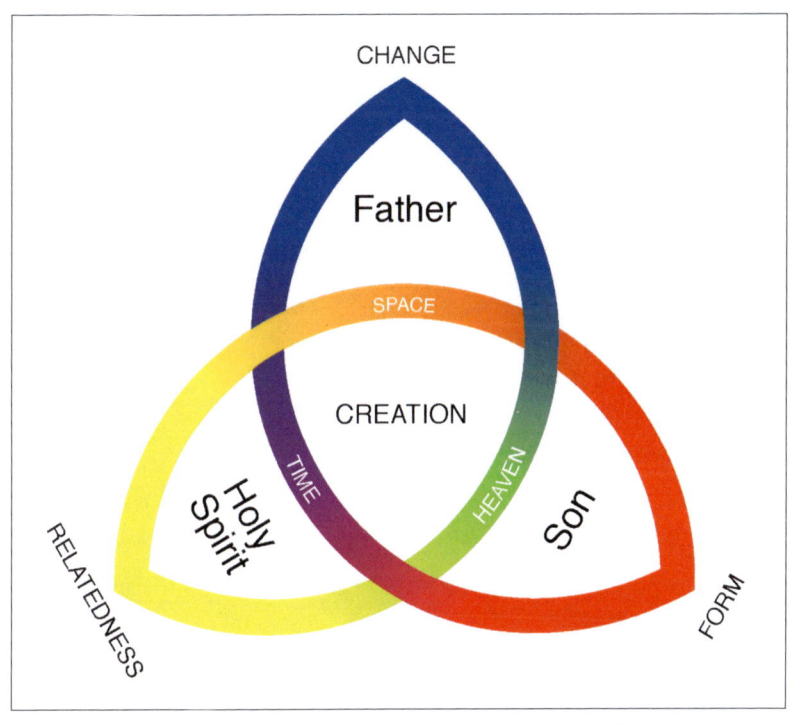

Figure 5. One living God as a Holy Trinity of Persons

Basically, the Father by divine nature sources change that courses through space; the Holy Spirit by divine nature interrelates all change across time for eternity; the Son by divine nature contains all changing forms in Creation in a loving embrace as the living presence of heaven. This is kingdom living.

Godly kingdom life resounds like a call through that central space of grace, emerging as Creation in standing waves of grace. Several eras of prior organisation have been spoken as 'Days' before we humans appear on the scene. We arrived into a thriving context of continuous creation, whether by a single act or by its evolution—it really is not worth falling out about when this model so clearly shows the living Word sustaining and allowing it all to transform. Death had no sting in the continuous creation shown by networks of triquetra, because the dissolution of a creature's bodily form back into continuous creation is not an end of connected relatedness with God. Bodily dissolution did not mean spiritual or personal separation. A call from one who loves you can set up new standing waves of grace in ever-renewed life. It is from here, in the centre of God's creative will, in the centre of the triquetra of Creation, that each one of us thinking creatures looks 'out', through the phenomena of our existence in this shared world, towards God as our dispersed source.

In the next Chapter we shall see how humankind can break that created unity into bits, and separate out grief from love in the process. That separation makes people fear bodily death, introducing a sting that can emotionally trap people in a separated and broken state. The triquetra in the next chapter will demonstrate how. In such narrowed views on life and death, people lose sight of the spiritual life of eternity, like the night sky being hidden behind a passing dark cloud.

This is scriptural, not mere philosophy, poetry or physics! These *triune principles* were revealed at Jesus' baptism, where all three of the Family of the living God were present simultaneously: the creative voice of the Father heard to say, "This is My Son, in whom I am well pleased. Listen to Him!" The connectedness of Holy Spirit (hovering like a dove of light) personally associated with the Father saying, "Listen to Him!" We choose whether or not we let the Holy Spirit in (or out *from* within) as we listen, and are thus transformed. In this is my spiritual connection with an utterly other but living God, and yours.

Imagine that the three semi-circular lines of the triquetra represent three paired relationships of mutual adjustment between the sub-states of Father, Son and Holy Spirit. Now imagine this… that the third sub-state is able to 'look on' that dynamic relationship of any pair and 'understand it' by making its own responsive change to remain in unity. In this way, each of the three sub-states might gain what we call a 'Personal Identity', contributing as a part of the one God, whole and living and communicating or 'calling'. Thus the mind of one God is made, by three different personal perspectives on love choosing unity through mutual understanding.

Human beings have that potential, as an image within, as we shall see, but so seldom can we humans reach mutual understanding between these perspectives within our own minds, let alone with other people's differing thoughts and beliefs. But we shall see how Emotional Logic can restore love after separation, and brokenness, and misunderstanding.

The 'dance of love' within God from a distance may look like an explosive change, one that flings out stars and galaxies, and grief also! That's love. Like gravity in the processing of energy-matter, love re-connects people through grace.

Humankind as the image and likeness of God

Through my contacts as a Protestant with deeply committed Christians whose spiritual homes are in the Russian Orthodox and the post-Vatican II Roman Catholic Churches (more of which in the next Chapter), I was forced to the conclusion that God has a loving purpose behind why all three of these major historic branches of the One Christian Church *need to be different from each other*. My conclusion is that by this diversity we more fully reflect for the world the range of qualities of ever-renewed Life that are within God, and are being continuously seeded by God in the world that God so loves. The problem is that Church-orientated people have not handled well the grief that accompanies diversification within God's Family. They have separated out grief from love, tried to control it or get rid of it, and lost the likeness of God as a consequence, because grief is the movement to re-connect when change has moved someone out of a comfort zone. Yes, God's love is as much the presence of grief as eternal joy, but God does not get stuck in the grief as we may do. God turns it to redemption.

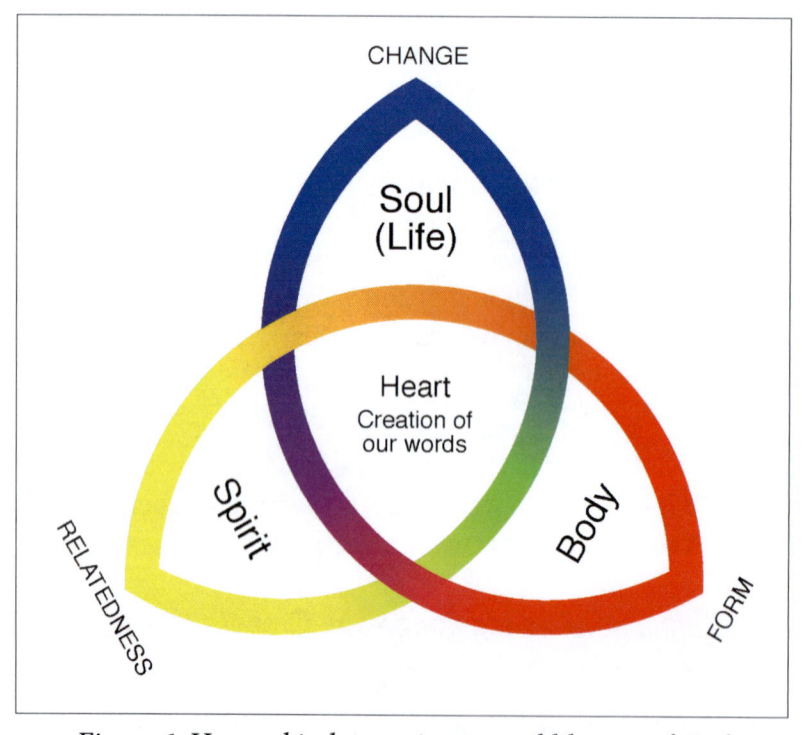

Figure 6. Humankind as an image and likeness of God

Triune principles of organisation *require* grief to re-integrate after change, as we shall see in Chapter 6. For now, let us move further along the path to that high viewing platform of grace by looking at Figure 6, Humankind as an image and likeness of God. This Figure shows how the human brain can use the same *triune principles of organisation* that energy-matter uses to construct physical bodies. Instead of organising molecules into cells and bodies, and so on, the brain constructs out of the 'elements' of temporary brain states an organised, consistent *picture of life*. Brains and bodies are thus putting together something *similar*, but at different system levels, both using exactly parallel triune processes that therefore can achieve 'a fair match'. Now this is important… The matching process between the way the body is self-organising in the world, and the way the brain is self-organising sensory inputs and memories, is kept 'fair to middling' by continuous feedback between the two systems. Inside and outside more-or-less match most of the time when sensory input from the body is allowed to mingle with the memorised temporary brain states; and so I become a self in the world. Stop the feedback between them, however, and the physical world and peoples' mental worlds rapidly diverge. Wake up, day-dreamer, wake up! Look ahead to Figure 8 to see this process of feedback between people.

When the brain is connected by feedback with the peopled world environment, the thinking person can look either 'out', or paradoxically 'in', and see the same triune principles of organisation at work. Because of the image within, of *chosen unity by grace*, mutual understanding between Creator God and created human being is possible.

In practice, Figure 6 shows how a person converts chaotic signals that are flying around the dust of the brain's neuron networks into an organised set of 'accords', just as the mind of God is made. The triune model presented here selects three fundamental elements (form, change and relatedness) from the wider range of elements that the brain 'extracts' (for example, colour, sound pitch, etc) because these are essential to becoming orientated as a person in the world. The other elements fill out that picture. Each semi-circular loop represents pairings of these fundamental elements, ongoing in the brain's three 'association areas'. Together these three fundamental accords or pairings can generate the impression of being an orientated person, conscious in space, time, and real presence (reality).

Space is constructed from forms relating.

Time is constructed from forms changing.

Presence is constructed from relatedness changing.

These accords, shown in Figure 8, are built into the brain's structure. They can all be disrupted by drugs, anxiety, brain injury, epilepsy and dementias. Mental orientation is a construct, continuously made using the same triune principles of organisation that can describe the creation and processing of energy-matter.

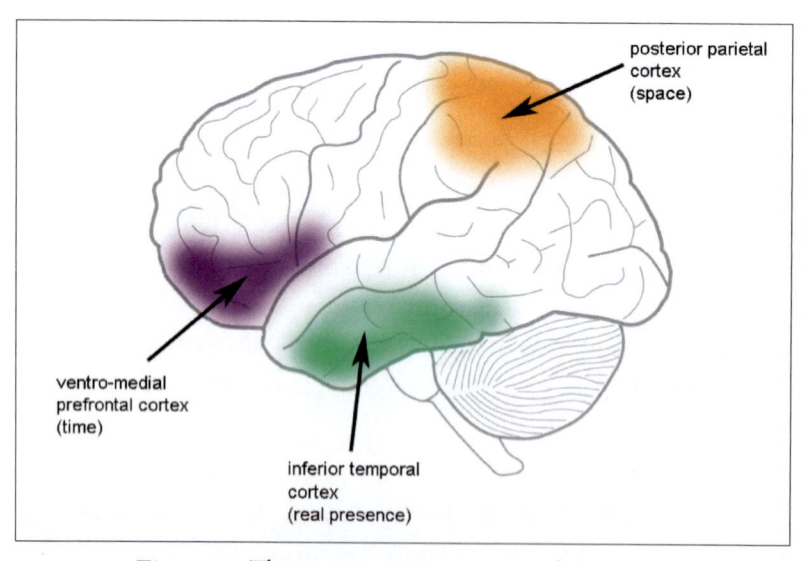

Figure 7. Three association areas of the brain

Figure 7 shows how neuroscientists have found three 'association areas' of the human brain that construct precisely these three features of conscious orientation as a person. (More detail is provided in the Appendix for those who are interested, which would be better read after finishing this and the next Chapters.) Whether evolved or created, the human brain is built to identify the same fundamental features of shared life to those revealed to be at the heart of a triune creator, God. We can lose the likeness of God when the human brain does not keep all this integration in *full accord*.

Thus we humans have the capacity to focus our minds with a context of time and so to understand the phenomena of relatedness in that context (See Figure 8). We can also choose to focus our minds differently, and then understand the phenomena of change *in a context of space*. We can focus our minds differently again, and understand the phenomena of forms *in a context of presence*, which we know as the realities of matter (objects), energy (power), or people (personal presence as an organising or disorganising influence). We can bring all these together, creating an interpersonal context for conversations, and for silent accords, with another person who is integrating mentally in a similar way.

The human being is not a creator in the same way that God creates energy-matter out of God's own loving grace. However, by understanding life using the same triune principles as God, we humans can choose to become *co-creators of life* with God. Through our conversations and silent accords our choices can generate a spread of grace, with unpredictably creative effects. We have the choice also to turn our backs on God, and to go our own way. However, the chances are that our grief locked into making that choice for 'independence' will lead us to speak words of deathliness to others, despite our best efforts sometimes. If we remain disconnected from the Big Picture (from Father God, and our older firstborn brother Jesus Christ, and our mysterious spiritual relative, all sitting together at that iconic communion meal table on the high viewing platform), we shall always be somewhat lost, turning life into an enormous, uncontrolled social experiment.

Of course, within Creation we are *not* alone. The French Existentialists wrote about 'existential aloneness', but their message is a sad lie from the misery and poverty of those who were lost. A whole person is *incomplete alone*. We only have to ask, and the offer is already there to connect. The wise criminal on the cross beside Jesus asked him for that hope, acknowledging his own error. Christ gave him an assurance of eternal connection, even there in the pain and shame they shared. So also can you and I *ask*. It is our call, to God.

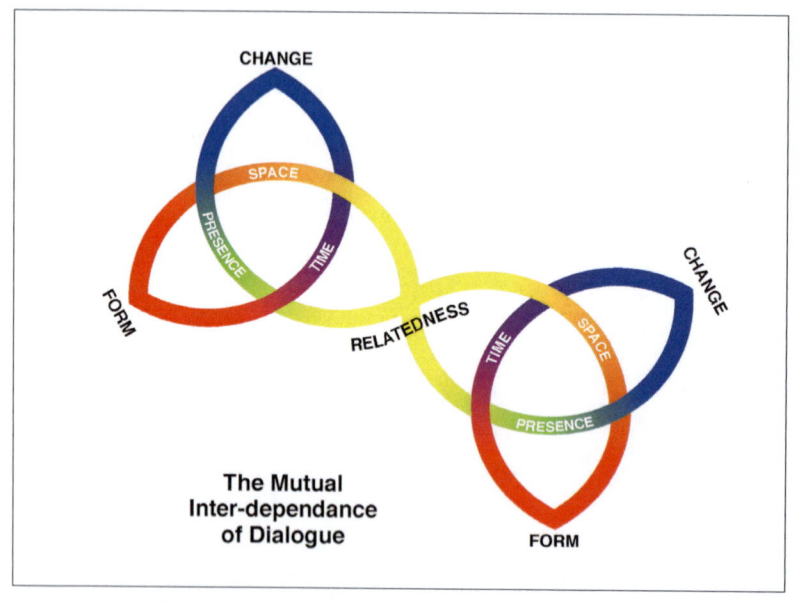

Figure 8. Dialogue—The conversational orientation of personhood

Figure 8. This is the *core diagram* of 'the 3+1 model of personal development', the origin and development of which I shall explain in the next Chapter. Dialogue in conversation or in silent accord is mutual transformation. It is mercy—listening and being heard, and modifying one's response accordingly. It is the business of Church to promote this saving dialogue. Given the right chosen unity within the Church, this dialogue could spread like a wave in grace through God's Creation.

This diagram, Figure 8, shows the 'conversational orientation' that results when the human brain is working in complete accord internally and in relationships with another (or others). The focus of attention is on another person, or on life processes altogether, engaging actively with them as a whole person with your other. This is a view of humanity that I call 'speaking life'. It is a 'Christian anthropology', a model of the human person made physically in the pattern (or image) of God. The two connecting triquetra may represent two human beings in conversation, or a person relating to their physical environment, or a person relating to God and in so doing being transformed, liberated and transfigured into salvation. Relatedness is essential to personal wholeness.

Run a finger along the lines of Figure 8, and you will get a better feel for the mutual transformations that are this life-giving dialogue. Emotional Logic has been developed to foster the emotional intelligence needed to overcome the grief and discomfort of misunderstandings that can lead to brokenness while this type of exploratory life diversifies people. Disagreements about words, power and material possessions can break the dialogue, lead to conflict, and to dismissive rejection of others who think differently.

Meanwhile God loves creatively, guiding people to turn the feelings of love's grief into the strength needed to overcome disconnection. Our capacity as human beings is to listen, to hear, and to transform words into material form or the energy for change, so that God makes the world new every moment through us. These are the triune principles by which human beings are made in the image, and by which we together can transfigure beyond time more into the likeness of God.

Chapter 6

The grace to reconcile

My introduction to Eastern Orthodoxy had followed a path emblazoned with unexpected experiences. So too was a path that criss-crossed with it, along which I occasionally meandered inquisitively, while Marian got on with the business of physically living out Truth in our extended Christian family.

I found myself involved with Polish Roman Catholicism while the Polish Pope, John Paul II, was spreading Light from the Vatican. Remember, all of this exploration followed from the drive Marian and I felt, to question why and where the roots of conflict and division between Christians writhed across the surface of God's world. Marian's practical footsteps criss-crossed with mine daily as I wandered 'head in the clouds and feet on the ground'. She would repeatedly remind me to check that the high-flown ideas that I talked of so enthusiastically were relevant *now* to the personal development of the people around us. "Come and do the drying up while you talk!" Together we edged towards that high viewing platform where, with others, we could view life alongside our Holy Trinity. My meandering took me eventually to meet the Pope, at a General Audience in St Peter's Square in Rome.

How did that happen? And what happened?

Well, it started like this. During those early exploratory years in the 1980's and 90's, Marian and I had become centrally involved in 'Christians in Caring Professions' (CiCP), a charismatic Protestant national healthcare movement. It was the continuation of the 'doctor-clergy seminars' that had brought Dr Peter Quinton to

Plymouth at the start of our exploration. Gathering from every branch of healthcare and counselling, people were discussing and comparing stories of how to include sensitivity to the intuitive prompting of the Holy Spirit safely among the high standards of their professional work. There were some unexpected carers and counsellors among the flock, including a barber who reminded us that men talked while he snipped, and he needed Holy Spirit inspiration to know how to respond constructively to their tales of woe.

A number of CiCP's leaders built connections with a parallel charismatic Protestant organisation in Germany, the IGNIS Academy for Christian Psychology, which had opened in 1986. The IGNIS folk had a well-established counsellor training course based at their teaching centre in Kitzingen near Würzburg. They trained counsellors to use methods that helped people achieve their goals in ways that were consistent with a Christian view of the person. They seemed more organised than we Brits, with an impressive journal, and qualifications. We in the UK had a range of dis-connected counselling courses, with quality assured through on-going supervision by more experienced counsellors or clinical psychologists. However, the pressure was on politically in the UK, with a widening presence of counselling in the NHS, to start regulating the training standards. IGNIS had a model we were interested to learn about.

I had noticed during this time that the counselling I had pioneered in General Medical Practice in the UK was being pressured away from my original intentions. I had joined General Medical Practice at a time when it was still known as Family Medicine. Physical health for individuals is, to my mind, inseparable from that person's relational development. To fulfil a role in a relationship requires physical development and character development, whether that role is competitive or co-operative. Those roles transform throughout life, and the most significant ones for the long-term stability of society are learnt in families. Within General Medical Practice I saw counselling as a way to help people break the cycle that passes on bad emotional habits from one generation to the next, both within families and organisations. I saw counselling as a means for whole person and family development.

This goal was shared by an NHS senior clinical psychologist, Ron Wood, with whom I had worked closely for many years to develop a safe counselling system. Ron initially supervised our counsellors in General Practice, before political-financial pressures forced him out of the NHS. (Clinical psychologists are expensive for managers, especially when they approach retirement age). The problem with our approach was that the social benefits of emotional re-learning would mostly be seen many years later, in the next generation's way of relating. Giving a firmer hope for the future was, within the old-fashioned, person-centred style of Family Medicine, a reasonable goal to work towards. However, the political climate had changed. General Practice had been re-branded 'Primary Healthcare', and this was supposed to emphasise that its role was closely integrated with hospitals, where 'secondary healthcare' is practised. Families were 'out' as the focus of our attention as personal doctors; disease management was 'in'.

A new wave of central control swept GPs and hospital-based specialists into a different way of thinking. It was cost-cutting and de-humanising. It wanted protocol-driven interventions with *measurable outcomes* within a politically short time-frame (from one General Election to the next), not the enhancement of human values that could be noticed in the general 'feel' of society over subsequent decades. This new wave saw only a limited place for counselling, as a crisis intervention short-term service to minimise sickness absence from work, and as behavioural training to improve 'coping skills' that might reduce medication prescribing and the number of referrals to secondary care, all measurable you see.

And, more shockingly, its ideal outcome was 'independent living'; not mature, *mutually inter-dependent* personal development.

It saw people now as numbered individuals, clocking into work to perform designated, pre-defined tasks. I saw problems coming.

Through our CiCP visits to the IGNIS Academy in the charming old riverside town of Kitzingen we discovered that we, in the UK, were not alone in feeling that a robust statement was needed of a more person-centred outcome to therapy than efficient, symptom-free, task-centred functioning. IGNIS had become a focal point for Christian counsellors and psychologists from several European countries, all of whom were facing the same issues! Where was this financially-driven revision of healthcare values coming from, I wondered? What role did the World Bank have to finance healthcare, and perhaps to set financial targets for governments rather than personal ones?

In 1992, in response to these international political shifts, the Association for Christian Counsellors (ACC) was founded in the UK. Its aim was to get one step ahead of the proposed professionalising of training and outcome standards for counsellors by introducing a voluntary standard-setting validation of courses and qualifications. ACC's approach was ground-breaking, and it has subsequently been reproduced for Christian Counsellors in many nations.

Christian personal development

Through this mix of working minds worshipfully seeking guidance, I came to see how central the idea of *personal development* is to Christian living, as it is in any human life setting. But in Christian settings, of course, it carries an extra depth of meaning, because the term person was first coined by the Early Church Fathers.

In the secular world the word personal has become twisted from its original meaning of a 'sub-state of a greater whole', to mean instead 'private', concerning an individual's inner values that you have no right to infringe, or even to enquire about. In a secularised frame of mind, personal development commonly means choosing a self-willed 'direction' to life, or perhaps the opposite, abandoning self-willed direction and letting go into conformity with a group that seems to know better.

The status of 'person', in truth however, is intrinsically and utterly relational, akin to father, sister, cousin, citizen, friend, employee, and so on, but more generalised. If I am to be to be a person, there must be an 'other'– an employee has an employer, for example; a citizen has a state. A person is an individual of a people; a whole person is incomplete alone.

The Christian concept of personal development, or personal growth, is rooted firmly in a balanced triune picture of personhood that allows exploration, mistakes, self-correcting, self-forgiveness, forgiveness of others and so on, all taking place within a social and spiritual context where maintaining unity by grace among developing diversity is the primary purpose to sustainable life. Christian personal development is to explore how to participate in the divine nature by Holy Spirit filling us to unite us in movement *in* the Personal wholeness of Jesus, in and for the world God so loves.

That sounds outrageous—human beings having a divine nature with their human nature—and it is outrageous! It shows how brave the Early Church Fathers were in confronting centuries of Greek philosophy, Roman paganism and Jewish Kabbalah. The notion that two natures, divine-human, can be in dialogue in one person (as in Figure 8) often makes people angry. What are they worried they might lose if it is true, I ask? They may want little Christs (Christians) to fall, and even persecute them to see if they do fall, as a way to hide their values defensively from a conversational God.

This is where Emotional Logic may enable grace to re-shape personal development. For Christians to become strong and resilient together in and for the world God so loves, their roles and identity need to develop around recovering and preserving Godly values in their own hearts. Understanding the grief that triune principles include to re-make joy is a vital part of letting go of the old to join the new. That sort of *personal development* leads to the strength and resilience to stand in Christ, in every situation, and, having done all, then to stand in the world to give testimony to the glory of God –doing so alongside others.

Standing alongside others

But I rush ahead of the story. It was at the IGNIS Akademie that therapists, healthcare professionals and theologians from across Europe gathered to look afresh at how to describe this view of personal development in a way that would be of practical use. We wanted a benchmark against which to judge the outcomes of healing and curative interventions, Christian and otherwise. It had to give Christian counsellors the ground to stand and justify working towards politically-incorrect outcomes, not independence in the post-modern sense of about 'me creating my own world'. We wanted outcomes that were systemically relational, about 'me standing where I belong with others'. Such an outcome could seed 'ever-renewed life' back into a society that had become corrupted through self-advancement. This model of personal development needed also to fulfil the Christian criterion of 'humanity made in the image and growing more into the likeness of God'. Integrative therapy in a Christian mindset could follow in line with this anthropology.

So in 1997, arising out of this gathering of friends, the first Symposium of the 'European Movement for Christian Anthropology, Psychology and Psychotherapy' (EMCAPP) met in Kitzingen. [Actually, I am shortening history here; it was originally EMCPA, but nobody could say that!]

From the outset my contribution was two-fold, [a] to keep the psychology grounded *physically* in medical science and neuroscience, and [b] to assert that a description of balanced personal development would need input from all three major branches of the One Church—Eastern Orthodox, Roman Catholic, and Protestant.

Europe's unique history, it seemed to me looking back on it, had been largely shaped over the previous 1500 years around the conflict and reconciliation (or lack of it) between different dominant mindsets within vast populations. These are evidenced in the way people in the Church had separated away from each other, attracting political and military support around their beliefs to make spiritual strongholds at war with each other. Each faction could claim they were 'right', and had God's support to justify their atrocities. I had noticed that all the attendees at this Symposium were Protestant. All, that is, apart from Anna Ostaszewska. She was the visiting Lead of the 'Association of Christian Psychologists' (ACP) in Poland. She also led the Polish branch of ACC, through which her eye focused on standard-setting. Anna was Roman Catholic. After making enquiries I discovered that nobody other than I had any connections with priests from Eastern Orthodox churches, whether from our Greek, Serbian or Russian neighbours in Europe. I had previously asked Fr Benedict if he would attend this Symposium, but he could not add any more commitments to his already busy schedule. Perhaps I was to be the bridge across which the Eastern Orthodox 'earthed' way of seeing spiritual life might walk into the midst of our two Western mind-sets, and speak to them both.

All participants at this first Symposium gave an introduction to the work and organisations they were involved with. We Protestants thus discovered, to our surprise, that ACP in Poland had a highly developed three year training programme for Christian Psychologists. It had input from university level teachers, theologians and clinicians, but was struggling to get its course validated or promoted by a university. The capacity to build such a course had opened after the fall of communism during the 1980's. These Poles had clearly taken firm hold of the opportunity.

Around the Symposium we discovered that no specifically

Christian course had university validation, even though the evidence base for therapy practice by Christians was the same as that by secularists. We clearly needed to define where a boundary existed (if any did) between evidence-based and faith-based interventions–not such an easy task, given that secular interventions are based also on faith—faith in the primacy of matter to determine human life, rather than inter-personal grace.

Good personal connections were made at this first Symposium, with Anna gaining an increasingly central place. We decided that it should continue in the future to be a gathering of interested individuals from diverse backgrounds, not a meeting for representatives of organisations, but rather friends exchanging views as whole people. Nobody should feel they needed to go back and check something out with a committee, but each should consider what was said from different viewpoints with respect and curiosity, so that a balanced sense of unity could emerge from our diversity, and so influence our writings.

And so it was that we Protestants began to mix with Roman Catholic psychologists, and later with theologians, around shared values. The second Symposium was held two years later in Poland, in Płosk, in a Seminary thirty kilometres from Warsaw. To explain what happened there and following on from it, I need to mention briefly how the 3+1 model of personal development shaped up during those two years. It was a busy time.

Three sources

Three exploratory bore-holes all released new waters that irrigated the land where kingdom roots were edging out.

Firstly, having seen the limitations imposed on counselling based in NHS primary healthcare, I succeeded in getting funding to pilot basing a systemic family therapist at Highlands Health Centre for comparison with individualistic counselling. The pilot aimed to discover if an approach that worked directly with the 'communication context' of a distressed person (the habits of communicating in family, workplace and/or community), could help adults who had life problems that had not been helped by the counselling or medication that was already available. The systemic approach develops the feedback within patches of relational networks in innovative ways to help an individual thrive better within the relational system. It thus works directly with the mutual inter-dependence that is humanity.

We were fortunate to employ Ros Draper, a leading light nationally in standard-setting for training systemic family therapists. Ros lived locally, and had developed ways to extend the systemic approach from appointments with a whole family, to working with a single distressed adult. Through her, our pilot influenced the lifelong consequences of emotional habits learned in childhood or teenage years to survive difficult relationships. This went straight for the heart of personal development.

The pilot successfully showed that adults can gain in self-respect and capacity to build relationships through re-learning how to interpret emotional feedback from others. The Plymouth and South Devon family therapy course changed as a consequence, so that the first semester module could be studied by any care professional as an introduction to how systemic principles affect their own specialist areas of work. We thus *generalised* the teaching of systemic principles of family communications. I then further generalised this for Christian psychologists and theologians at the Płosk Symposium. The Early Church Fathers were the original systemic thinkers. Tri-une principles are systemic.

The second bore-hole started to water the land as I began to talk with my patients more about the *loss reactions* that I was becoming increasingly primed to see running through the stories my patients told me. These were not the major upheavals of bereavement, but rather multiple, small setbacks and disappointments that affected valued aspects of life day on day. The associated loss emotions accumulate, to the tipping point where they are overwhelming and confusing. Doctors then diagnose common mental illnesses such as anxiety and depression, but I was shaping a picture of emotional overload, emotional chaos, causing distress and tension that showed in disturbed behaviour or communication.

In the medical model, in principle, a diagnosis describes a set of symptoms that follow from a single cause, all of which would improve if that single cause could be removed. It has proved startlingly effective for physical disease, but it does not work well for mental illness or socially disruptive behaviour. The other model that could guide a doctor's or nurse's actions for these is the 'bio-psycho-social model', previously mentioned, which is another term for systemic. It emphasises the inter-connectedness of physical healing with belief factors and with social communication. Consistent with this model I developed a new lifelong learning approach, to help my patients *understand* what was happening to them in changing life circumstances. Understanding how loss reaction emotions feed back physically into health and social well-being then empowers the person to make different choices, and so the bio-psycho-social model comes alive.

Emotional Logic was thus born. I introduced Emotional Logic's core ideas into conversations in our extended family home at South Highlands, just up the hill from the Health Centre. I discovered there that improved courage to experiment with new ways of living and relating could follow when one or two small insights from the overall structure of Emotional Logic were tipped into these informal conversations. I was seeing 'systemic family therapy', but *not conducted as therapy*. I was sharing 'given wisdom' about love's dynamics (wisdom given to me and everyone through the Gospel of love) in small doses. Learned thus conversationally in a home setting, *this* type of delivery of the power of love brought maturity to developing life. It did not bring conflict within the family.

I had found a teachable overview of how reasoning and emotions work in partnership to father and nurture personal development. This teaching could spread through any setting where people gather when conversations are influenced by someone who understands emotions within this overview. There are no negative emotions, we can truthfully say in love, only unpleasant ones that have useful purposes to turn distressing situations around into a dynamic for growth.

In 1999 Paternoster Press published my self-help book, making this approach more widely available, *Lost and Then Found: Turning Life's Disappointments into Hidden Treasure*. There were two reprintings. Its influence birthed a charitable trust to teach counsellors and care workers how to use the method in their professional work. Initially the project was called 'Realisation: Training in resources for personal growth'. It is now 'The Emotional Logic Centre'.

The third bore-hole that watered the land between the EMCAPP symposia was further work on the triquetra diagrams to show what happened in peoples' hearts to divide the Church.

The core diagram of the 3+1 model of personal development is the paired triquetra displaying 'conversational orientation' (Figure 8). This diagram represents how, while in a conversational mindset, the three association areas of the brain shown in Figure 7 might work in balanced, integrated harmony. The human being has evolved or developed as a social creature, and we have a socially-shaped brain to match that. However, by subtly shifting the electrical connections between these three brain areas, totally different and even incompatible concepts of what is inside and outside 'the person' can be generated! During these two years I developed the diagrams to demonstrate how this can happen. These perspectives on life, or mindsets, I had realised map onto the mindsets that predominate in the theology and practices of the Eastern Orthodox, Roman Catholic and Reformed Protestant movements of God's one Church.

These mindsets generate the inside-outside paradox that is

revealed in the Orthodox vigils. I call these mindsets 'analytical perspectives on life', to contrast them with conversational orientation where two people share together in life. There are three patterns by which any one of us can (and do most of the time) fall away from conversational orientation into these *primary analytical perspectives*. The thinking (re-connecting) brain enables that person to look at life from different angles, then mix and match the way life looks from these different viewpoints in any combination, like a colour chart mixing ideas and perspectives, to make an infinite variety of dimensional worldviews, all of which are *secondary analytical perspectives* on life. Conversations among a group of people, who seek security and affirmation in their agreement with each other, can drift over time into a group preference for just one or two of these primary analytical perspectives set over against the third. A 'restricted group mentality' can thus emerge, in which people feel they belong only by rejecting and criticising others who do not see life the same way.

I have already outlined in Chapter 5 the mental backdrops to each of these primary analytical perspectives. One uses a concept of 'space' in which to analyse changing life processes. One uses a concept of 'real presence' in which to analyse forms and structures. One uses a concept of 'time and eternity' in which to analyse the utter relatedness of life. Whichever preference a person has, that relevant association area of his or her brain is preferentially connecting forward to the motor planning areas of the frontal lobes of their brain, priming them for action and reaction. This 'cognitive priming' gathers with it simultaneously the potentially intense *emotional preparation*, for example when a value such as group identity or belonging is imagined to be under threat. Grief can thus lock thought into these patterns, and drive people further into the restricted mentality. Understanding grief and finding ways to turn it to growth can release both new thought and release trapped energy to explore ways of living that seem totally new.

I checked out the mental consequences of being in these

analytical frames of mind with some friends from a wide range of religious and spiritual backgrounds, so I am confident that the picture I shall present to you is balanced and acceptable. It is an important part of the human story behind these ideas to mention this group, who met repeatedly for discussion, and who presented the model at two teaching conferences with me.

Trisha Horgan, a senior psychiatric nurse from North Devon, has a Degree in Trinitarian Theology having studied under Colin Gunton. For several years she, Ron Wood (the western Buddhist psychologist) and I had an extended conversation as we developed the counselling services and systemic family therapy pilot. Trisha's charismatic Protestant background gave her a powerful grasp on how forgiveness and healing are connected with advancing the kingdom of God, preparing the way for reconciliation when that extra step is wise.

George Giarchi joined us when, as Professor of Social Science and Social Work at the University of Plymouth, he wanted to reflect on this new 'speaking life' anthropology, as I later called it. He was a devoutly liberal, post-modern Roman Catholic. George and I knew each other socially from combined charismatic church events that he and his wife Claire would contribute to in Plymouth. He invited me to teach the 3+1 model of personal development on his 'MSc in Pastoral Care' course in Plymouth. The particular aspect that he valued was the way it showed how different perspectives on life could each truly claim to see the whole truth, while equally each was only one angle, or 'take', or colour, on that whole Truth. The '+1' part of the model was the missing ingredient that was needed to bring them all into balance, and this was the ingredient he felt his pastoral workers would need in good measure.

Fr Benedict Ramsden agreed to join, bringing the Russian Orthodox critique alongside the Protestant (Trisha) and Roman Catholic (George) perspectives. Ros Draper, our family therapist, also joined enthusiastically. She was a convert to Protestant

Christianity, a Messianic Jew who had developed her faith with Francis Schaeffer while living at his L'Abri community in Switzerland. Ros brought a lively sense of connection to Old Testament ways of seeing God. Both the Jewish and the L'Abri backgrounds are strong on community as living human systems. She was intuitively systemic as a therapist for families and individuals, and strong on how living faith within a community differs from, and yet fulfils, the Law of Life that was once written in stone.

Everyone's contributions refined the model by feedback. We were all activists in our own ways, so talking was not enough. Words took shape in actions. We turned the subject into a two-day workshop, and ran it twice, once at South Highlands, inviting a wide range of care professionals and churchmen, and once at a Christians in Caring Professions weekend conference in The Midlands of the UK. Sadly, the time commitment was too great for us to continue the series. The experience gained, however, refined and strengthened the 3+1 model of personal development. My thanks goes to them all.

The reason this ecumenical team was so strong in its teaching, was that we could all support each other constructively and enthusiastically when explaining the diverse views among the major world-wide branches of the Church. It was not emotionally charged to say that the Roman Catholic Church prefers to look on Godly life as 'structures in real presence', while the Eastern Orthodox Church prefers to look on Godly life as 'relatedness in time and eternity', and the Reformed Protestants prefer to look on Godly life as 'changing life processes in relevant spaces', and while the Messianic Jews look to the first Century church communities to model life without wanting to name G-d. We were one team.

A history of divisions overcome

Before explaining in more Technicolor detail how Church life has fallen out into conflicted brokenness around these patterns, I would like to introduce you to Anna Ostaszewska. Anna was for many years the head or lead of the organisation in Poland that is equivalent to the IGNIS Akademie for Christian Psychology in Germany. Tall, lanky, a broad forehead with dark perceptive eyes under dark curly hair, her expression was at once thoughtfully serious and quickly breaking into infectious laughter. Respectful curiosity about others guided her movements among people, introducing one to another and revelling in the conversations that followed. She knew everyone, and moved easily among them as a natural leader, widely respected.

I made a big mistake on our first evening at the Symposium, but by grace not a fatal mistake. Having been introduced at a meal table as one of the UK visitors, there was much good humoured joking and laughter among us all. I heard briefly about the backgrounds of the various psychiatrists, theologians and psychologists there. They were a high-powered bunch, heads of this Seminary and of that Department of Theology or Psychology at this or that University, psychiatrists and psychotherapists. Someone was explaining to me that Anna had been involved in the Solidarity Movement that had led to the downfall of communist rule in Poland during the 1980's. She had later, in recognition of her leading role in helping to dismantle the communist machinery of state, become the first woman to be elected vice-President of Caritas in Poland, the Roman Catholic social care organisation. Anna was then telling me her personal story, that she had felt a calling from God and a revelation of her salvation while working for the government. Despite the communist hatred of the Church, she had pursued her call, and made those connections in the Roman Catholic Church that had led to her involvement in the social and spiritual revolution of Solidarity. Just in passing, by way of light conversation as one might in England, I asked her out of curiosity what work she was doing in the government…

The atmosphere in the room suddenly froze. All eyes were on me, staring, fixed in suspicion, inscrutable. After some seconds, the friendly psychiatrist I had been talking with earlier said quietly,

"There are some questions we do not ask."

I apologised sincerely. I said that I had never lived under oppression, and I had not realised how deeply the memories must run.

People relaxed. My apology was accepted. To my relief, the conversation did not drift back to superficial niceties. Instead, it opened out into a very personal sharing of the experience of Solidarity's revolution. There was no doubt in my mind of the conviction these brave people expressed that it was their Christian faith that had given them the strength to resist the Communists. Why else would they have met in forests to pray?

I was humbled. On a later occasion, as we walked into Warsaw for a dinner, the conversation returned to the same theme. They pointed out the streets where the Soviet tanks had appeared when Solidarity was outlawed and martial law imposed. What sort of a dream world do I live in, in England, where we equate oppression of Christians with someone disparaging our ideas? Here, in Warsaw, my values were being shaken down to the ground I stood on.

The next day, sight-seeing in the afternoon, I saw the last remaining wall of the Jewish ghetto, where an estimated 100,000 Jews died of starvation and disease, and 300,000 were sent to death camps. In the final destruction of the ghetto after the uprising in 1943 more than 50,000 died as it was levelled block by block.

We walked the streets and squares of the re-built city centre, a festival spirit around us as preparations were in progress for a public holiday celebration. There was a palpable pride in the new life springing up. A combined restaurant and antique shop offered excellent food in surroundings filled with the memorabilia of the previous decades, with early spy cameras that had watched peoples' movements mixed among art and lacework, stuffed animals and lamps, all for sale. It was the dawn of free trade and hope.

But if life had been hard for the Poles under German

occupation, they kept a special hatred in reserve for the Russians. I had marvelled at the spirit of reconciliation I had seen between the Polish and German psychologists, remembering their earlier history. But as we walked below the walls of the old city, at a breach in one place, a statue of a child commemorates the Polish youth and intelligentsia who had resisted the Germans and fought and died in the streets of Warsaw. This young resistance movement had attacked the occupying German forces when they knew that the Russian army had arrived on the far bank of the river. They had expected to help the Russian liberators to advance by weakening the Germans from within. Instead, for three weeks the Russian army waited on the banks, waited so that the Germans would kill off the intelligentsia and strong, so that the Russian Communists could in their turn occupy and dominate.

I saw the scale of task that I felt was set before me to achieve. Here was the Protestant part of Germany and England meeting with Roman Catholic Poland in a spirit of reconciliation and mutual curiosity, and over the previous two days of the symposium I had been repeatedly saying that we needed to have the Russian Orthodox input if we were to formulate an all-round model of human personhood...

I recognised more clearly than before the depths from which a long history of human conflict emerges, crawls out of the rubble even, to influence peoples' choices now. How small the issues that had divided the two churches in Ivybridge seemed now; but I was sure that the deep source of rejection, division, conflict and oppression was the same.

And, now I reasoned, grace must run deeper or life would cease. Healing must be possible when people hear the higher call. Renewed life can grow where the soil of the land is drained and fertilised, and when the hard stone of a human heart is softened into living, active flesh.

Let us look a little deeper now, as Anna and her brave colleagues did, into that source of defensive division, rejection and oppression. Three years later the Russian Orthodox priesthood and Russian psychologists were equal members of EMCAPP, and I had presented a copy of the model of misunderstanding to the brave Polish Pope.

A preference for structure

The Roman Catholic hierarchy is based historically in a view that there is an unbroken succession of 'laying on of hands' to transfer the Holy Spirit from St Peter through to the present day Pope and bishops. Physical contact is necessary. Acceptance of this hierarchy is a requirement to join the communion of the Church Family. At Mass, the emblems of bread and wine are mystically 'transsubstantiated' into the physical body and blood of Jesus Christ. A bell is rung at the point in the time-sequence when that happens. There is a preference here for material to structure and form the shape of the Church in the world. Such shaping of the mind also requires submission to priesthood by the body of believers, priests mediating the Holy Spirit by grace *through sacraments*, physically or in formal ritual. Such is, was, the only way theologically that grace was shared in and through the Roman Church. Was, until Vatican II, which has changed the Roman Catholic Church in the modern world in ways that others *do* need to note with care, and with their own courage consider the call to change as the Romans have done.

The Second Vatican Council started in 1962 under Pope John XXIII and released sixteen statements over the next three years, of which 'Church in the Modern World', commonly known as Vatican II, is perhaps the most remarkable. It gave the church laity increased roles to support the priesthood in the ministration of grace into the community by their actions and lives. In practice, the priests now can release a blessing directly into the body of the Church upon those who take action in faith to make real the living Word in modern life. It has enabled diversification of ministries and communities within the Roman Catholic Church in the world, kept in unity within that body by that priestly blessing. That changes everything. The old academic theological statements remain, framed centuries ago to address issues that were relevant then by asserting structured hierarchy. Now the same preference for structure has moved beyond academic statements that once attempted to capture eternal truths about *life*. Life is structured movement in the eternally relational present, and the priestly blessing maintains structured relationship while allowing life to move more freely under direct Holy Spirit inspiration of church members. That is the post-Vatican II Roman Catholic Church. Those whose attitudes towards her have been framed by academic theology since Martin Luther's protest may find it easier, post-Vatican II, to let go of their purely theological response, a response generated from a *different association area* of an academic's brain (as we shall go on to see). Instead we might stand in awe conversationally alongside those who choose to minister blessing in Christian faith into a community, even while they have a preference perhaps for a more structured Family of God than 'ours'.

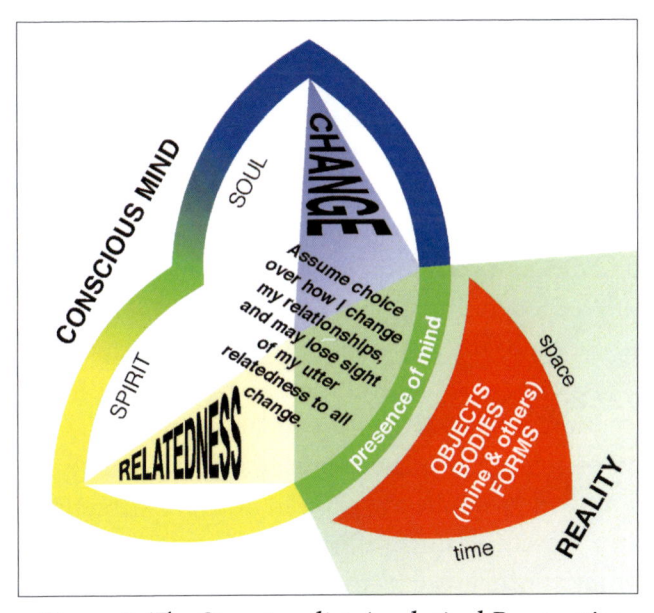

Figure 9. The Structuralist Analytical Perspective

Figure 9 shows how a 'structuralist observer of life' is preferring to connect their inferior temporal association area (generating an impression of 'real presence'—in the diagrams coloured green by blending blue-change and yellow-relatedness) with action planning in the frontal areas of their brains. When thus 'connected', a viewpoint on life is generated in which the structured forms of life take on a real presence as matter, observed by an equally real presence of mind. The other two association areas do not become inactive, however. They continue to sort the fundamentals in accords that generate the impressions of time, and of space. These become subordinated in this focus of attention, however, to 'objects'. Space and time become mentally projected 'out' of the person, as the environmental *context* in which the real presence of matter 'makes sense'. Real life looks then like objects in space-time, all bouncing around with each other. Does that sound familiar? Life seems now to be about mind and matter, no longer about persons conversing. Reason, structured logic and cognition become the 'stuff' of pure, observing mind, not the so-called touchy-feely distractions of personal inter-connection. However, please remember, all this is only one of three *equally valid* ways to understand life.

In this structuralist view, the focus of attention on objects (that must 'exist') finds a line of connection between a cause and its effect. That causal line, through time and space, makes movement seem to transfer from one object to another (momentum), which happens through a series of 'present moments'. This may be imagined as a string of picture snapshots, which disappears off into the distant future, and back into the distant past, all connected by causes. Time, in this perspective on structure, is a linear 'arrow of time' moving in one direction, and so time thus means 'time-sequence'. In this perspective on life, eternity therefore looks like an endless sequence of present moments—quite a scary and not very attractive prospect if life in the present is uncomfortable or boring! Christ, or God, then becomes another 'cause' to transform that hope. But God is more than a prime cause, or just the far end of an invisible line. God is, apophatically, not only alpha and omega. All in between and beyond moves and breathes in God. There is something missing in this analytical, structural view of God and Creation. The malaise of Western society may be evidence of it.

Perhaps the two other primary analytical views on life can fill out this concept of eternal salvation, when mixed all together, to make it more attractive and alive and free to develop.

A preference for change

A Western Christian delegate, at about 1,000 CE excommunicated the whole Eastern Church over a number of disagreements in a defensive outburst that was energised by grief aggressively protecting his western structuralist mind-set. It was a remarkable and disturbing end to the golden age of Church diversity-in-unity. Another 500 years was to pass before printed bibles became available, and a scattering of free-thinkers across Western Europe realised, each uniquely, that there was more to spiritual life than the way it had been presented by the Roman priesthood of that day. They became the Reformers, Luther, Calvin, Zwingli, Knox and Cranmer. Each brought out different aspects of the potential for new life when lived directly by faith *in* God, rather than by restricting grace through structures mediated materially *from* God. The new focus of attention was on inner transformation. Salvation followed the individual's choice within to repent, to re-think.

These free-thinkers conversed with each other, and with potential converts, in a totally different mind-set from the established western Roman priesthood. Living by faith is an ongoing free choice. The individual person can become a co-creator of life with God, by choosing to remain in fellowship with the self-revealing God, made possible only by God's free-will given grace of forgiveness.

Figure 10 shows how this view can be generated when the posterior parietal association area (orange in the diagrams) preferentially connects with the frontal action planning areas.

Life seems then primarily to be about souls transfiguring and developing as personalities and communities. It is all about change and turmoil getting organised as we speak into chaos. Preaching brings to the fore our likeness to Christ, whose character we might aspire to when changed within by indwelling Holy Spirit. Grace becomes the 'unmerited favour of God', God's personal choice for distribution. No longer is grace the ground of all being by chosen unity that sustains the whole of Creation.

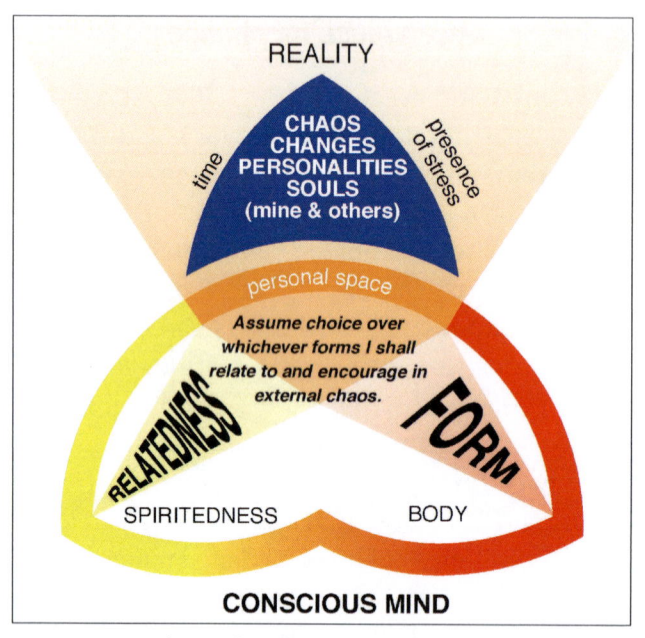

Figure 10. The Individualist Analytical Perspective

In this view, space, time and eternity can seem very different from the linear time-sequence that a structuralist observes. The notion of space becomes an internal 'personal space'. It becomes 'my bubble' in which I create my choices as if assembling thoughts on a workbench. I retain choice over who I allow into my bubble, and I relate to the world beyond it by exchanging information, which seems in this worldview to be the 'stuff of life'. To construct this individualist mind-set, the focus on change in life is made real by projecting 'out' a context that makes sense of change. This context is constructed mentally by mixing the impressions of time and real presence, which are being generated in the two other association areas. When mingled, these create an impression that a time-frame has real presence. Time-frames, even chosen ones, become sufficiently robust to structure life's choices within them. Time-frames become pressure cookers, in which the individual must generate a certain number of changes as information to feel fully alive. It can become a highly stressed way to live, always facing time deadlines. Relativism of time-frames becomes acceptable also, so norms of structure and cultural rituals that can bond people together disappear. Life is what you make it. Nobody has a right to tell me what I should do in my bubble. Salvation has to be a choice made before the last physical breath of my time on earth. Purgatory will not do for a Reformed Protestant Christian. Eternity is just another time-frame. Or for some secularists it might even be a number of parallel time-frames, but personally I think that is going too far for one created universe...

In this mind-set freedoms are gained, but the potential for unity becomes complicated and obscured. When it comes to one Family of God, something is missing. Are all families that chaotic? What has happened to choosing to co-ordinate time-frames at shared mealtimes? Does completely independent living lead to truly personal development?

Perhaps some of these gaps can be filled by mixing this view with the other two mind-sets. But that will mean staying connected with others who see life differently to me. It leads to the sad situation of marital instability, how long must I remain connected before I can gain my freedom again?

A preference for relatedness

Until the severe communist oppression of all religion, the Eastern Orthodox Church quietly, consistently displayed in her liturgy the eternally present grace of God poured out on all humanity. In this liturgy, I am inclined to agree with the Eastern Orthodox, is the most balanced triune expression of God's relationship with humankind, one that sustains mystery and awe at the heart of Godly love, and in a peace that surpasses all understanding.

I must ask the Orthodox to be patient, therefore, while I explain that nevertheless there is a weak spot in a tendency of the Eastern mind. Remember that 'the most balanced triune expression of God's relationship with humankind' requires you and I to step into the hologram of the liturgy and share *in* the life that is being displayed. It is balanced because it establishes that 'conversational orientation' shown in Figure 8. However, as soon as anyone takes a step back from that balance, to mentally analyse what is going on, that conversational orientation is lost in which personal development and healing might otherwise have happened. If anyone is tempted, and this includes myself, to explain or justify the Orthodox teaching or praxis, then it is no longer 'beyond human understanding'!

The Eastern cultured mind, when analysing, tends to take a mental step back in a way that focuses on how the relatedness of life generates knowledge. Consequently, differing qualities of *knowledge* can arise from differing qualities of relatedness. Another name (Greek) for knowledge is 'gnosis', and the weak spot in the Eastern cultured mindset is that reflective analysis can seem to set the quality of knowledge of some restricted groups above others in value. Even while the Eastern Orthodox liturgy declares that all are equal, communicants can be thinking that they have a 'special knowledge' that sets them apart from other groups. This tendency to exclusivity among groups of people is quickly detected by Western minds, which are sensitised by their focus instead on mutual change, or on uniting structure. I am not saying that one is more right than the other. Humility is required all around to sustain balance!

I would like to emphasize again that the Orthodox liturgy is not exclusive or Gnostic. Orthodox communion, if it is analytically interpreted as a ministration of grace (which for the truly Orthodox it is not, even though Romans might think it is!), may *seem* to be so because of its exclusion of the non-Orthodox (a problem for Protestants). But, on the contrary, Orthodox communion properly and mutually understood is a confession in humility of being part of something greater. It is a statement declared publicly of mutual submission to participate in community, in Godly Family.

Such a simple thing, then, as a geographical boundary, or a tribal dialect, can set a collective, exclusivist tendency on the move spiritually. By comparing 'our group' with neighbours, with 'them', (rather than loving our neighbours as if they were our own family, and grieving with them until we celebrate in joy together with them), the message that is lived in the Eastern Orthodox liturgy, of mutual inter-dependence with 'others', can become corrupted. That small hint of exclusivity can start a mental roll towards the Gnostic view of spirit as a *thing in itself* that can be distributed unequally between people or groups (which is not the Orthodox balanced view!).

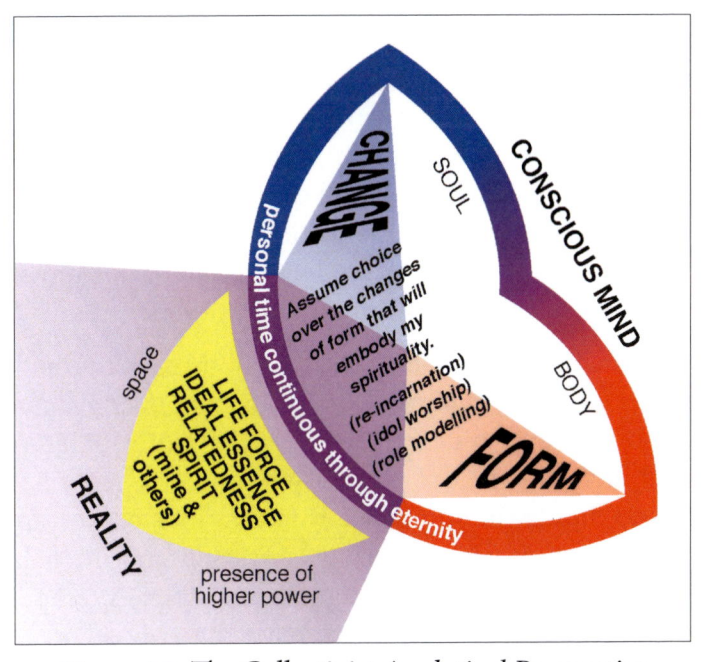

Figure 11. The Collectivist Analytical Perspective

Figure 11 shows how taking an analytical focus on relatedness can shift conversational orientation in life into a perspective in which life itself is objectified into a vitalist *life force*, such as Tao, or Hegelian spirit, or New Age energy, or Platonic Ideals, that somehow course through the universe 'out there' and *through* me. It happens when the time-generating sensory association area (above your eyeballs—coloured purple in the diagrams) is preferentially connected to the upper parts of the frontal lobes for motor planning. The other two association areas then create the *external* context (space and real presence) in which this *objectified* dynamic becomes the focus of attention. Relatedness becomes some objective *thing* or force coursing *through space as a real presence,* to which I must choose to submit my life, because it has the power to determine the life quality of individuals in different collectives or groups. Believing you have special knowledge of this life force through the quality of relatedness that 'it' brings to people (or by a feeling of inner energy derived from 'it') is Gnosticism.

Christianity is not Gnostic. Knowing our one living God as three inter-relating Persons protects Christians from seeing Holy Spirit as a life force entering us from outside. Holy Spirit is the mutuality of changing forms—the dynamic movement of the whole network of God's Family at the source and in Creation—by which the Family moves also the world in Godly ways. These are the unforced rhythms of grace, Spirit-connected, not moving by special knowledge, but by prayerful love for others.

Have you noticed how, on generating all three of the analytical perspectives on life, a different sort of inside-outside element is introduced into each mindset? The presentation of paradox in a worshipful liturgy is the only safe way I know to overcome these mental strongholds that limit our thinking into one or another perspective, and thus prevent a truly conversational and balanced and living relationship with God and each other. Attempting to compare this relational perspective with the two other equally valid perspectives could generate a sense of mystery and awe, in which it is reasonable simply to celebrate the eternal renewal of life in God.

Taken alone and out of balance, this collectivist analytical perspective, which objectifies relatedness as a life force, has also an intriguing consequence in belief about souls and salvation. In this focus on life, eternity and time become fundamentally wrapped up with the person. To understand this twist, look again at Figure 11.

In this collectivist perspective, a participant in life has a conscious thinking mind that looks 'out' at the imagined reality of a life force coursing through the spatial environments people share, and also looks 'inwards' at itself. There the nature of the self seems to be not an observer of life, and not a creator of life, but a soul and a body combined—a soul-body. This soul-body needs to be activated by 'the life force' to come fully alive. The soul-body needs, in the imaginations of its mind, to submit to the real external 'it' for health to flow through the space presently occupied by this soul-body. This soul-body has its own personal time, however, in which to learn to submit. Failure to do so can mean that this soul-body continues its own existence in eternity, from where it can return to the world *in a changed form* to continue the learning process. In this perspective on life, re-incarnation is a logical deduction!

Of course, re-incarnation is not a Christian doctrine. However, in a fully triune Christian balance this analytical perspective on life does *contribute* to the wholeness of salvation. It appears there as an assurance of *resurrection* into eternally renewed life in Christ. This resurrection will be in a bodily form as different from our earthly one as a seed of wheat is to a whole sheaf gathered from it. Unless a seed falls into the earth and dies, it remains only a seed (John 12:20-28). In this resurrection body we gain a *knowable form* with and in Christ, and become participators somehow alongside knowable others in worship of God by Holy Spirit-filled relatedness from within as our Source through grace.

A preference for Family

So here is a much fuller picture of salvation into eternally renewed life. The two 'Western' perspectives, on uniting structure and on mutual change, both *protect against* an over-balanced fall into a Gnostic perspective, which would evaporate the *Christ-like person* of a human being's divine nature, by *objectifying* the soul, and also the spirit.

How can each one of us gracefully turn from our fascinations with the way life looks in each of our favoured perspectives, and explore instead how all three perspectives might work in together, softening their conclusions and hard little 'facts' like triune clay being moulding to the movements of Godly life? Is each view like a different field on God's hillside? Do the fences that mark out the fields separate them, or are they where the fields meet? Could the awareness of these fundamentally different worldviews start now to stimulate conversations that turn mental barriers into personal meeting places?

An *infinite* range of possible 'world views' can be generated in peoples' thoughts by mixing these three primary perspectives, like a colour chart. Because each primary is constructed by an equivalent shift of assumption base from fully conversational orientation, no-one can claim a greater *logical* justification for one over the other. Some features of the various world views are incompatible. For example, although re-incarnation makes sense in a collectivist view, it is incomprehensible in pure materialism. People may try to reconcile these by proposing two worlds, one physical and one spiritual, or in the post-modern age an infinite number of parallel universes—which of course is nonsense, because the uni- part of universe means 'one turning around on itself', and any 'one' created with God's triune principles has the potential for *all* diversity to flourish within it.

At one level it is possible to reconcile these ideas. Each has a different view of 'the stuff of life'. Materialism sees it as matter (or energy-matter); individualism sees it as information carried on matter; relational collectivism sees it as energy moving *behind* matter. In a fully person-focused view of life, however, we need to shift our primary focus off matter and instead stand on substantial grace, as if on that high viewing platform together with others. Substantial grace, the chosen unity of mutual understanding in the one living God, endures between human people also by wilful connection that endures through change. This is the resilience and strength of an emotionally intelligent Church. Substantial grace may be understood also by us as the ground of eternally renewed life, and also as the source of the dust that makes the Promised *Land*, out of which our bodies and minds form, and through which we meet and interact. This land, this earth, this mind-blowing dust collecting as our bodies, can be analytically understood without contradiction *from all three primary perspectives simultaneously*. Grace is the inner essence of matter, enabling personal information to be carried on matter, and holding all movements of Spirit together behind matter in Christ. God's grace is multi-dimensional. It is at the source and fulfilment of all life, and as such grace is between the alpha and the omega of Christ.

This view of grace, and matter emerging from grace, relies on seeing human persons as mutually inter-dependent sub-states of Creation, as Family first. All the material of land is God's. Its sacred dust is gathering into our living bodies, so that we people relate through the land, as living clouds of self-organising dust communicating. As triune creatures with mutual understanding, we also know that we misunderstand each other sometimes, and can be curious to know why. Life shapes up materially around personal interactions by sub-states calling to each other across the mysteries of time and eternity. From the smallest particle to the Biggest Picture of Creation, all life is in the overall context of God's grace.

Misunderstanding between people is rife, though. Mismatches of inside-outside beliefs are often accompanied by outbursts of grief, which leads to confusion, doubt, fear, and protective separation.

Family and society become broken. Others can manipulate that grief, and force even greater divides, thus to gain power over others to oppress and control and abuse them. Such is our fall. God cannot simply take away grief, however, because that set of unpleasant emotions is all part of love, moving us if we only understood the feelings to find new ways to re-connect, and thus to re-discover the joy of love in our diversity.

To live in the movement of Holy Family, watched over by the presence of a loving Father as we diversify, is an awesome experience that sadly many have been denied in the fall of humanity. To equip the Church with the emotional intelligence needed for disciples together to become that presence for others is achievable. It is a reasonable and relevant goal in the next two decades. One Church can restore compassionate care for the world God so loves as this third Millennium opens out. Our older brother and teacher walks among us even now, saying to this day, "The kingdom of God is at hand."

Communion, and restricted group mentalities

I would like to round off (visually, as well as conceptually) this introduction to you of the 'cognitive level' at which similar sorts of misunderstanding may have led to back-biting in Ivybridge, and to slaughter across Europe's history. I have been repeatedly emphasising the family and community nature of conversations among groups of people, in which the living Word can be active to restore and reconcile. I have been showing how the humanly unpleasant emotions of grief are God-given to put in the energy for change that can reconcile these networks of human relationships. All that is needed is for people to understand the importance of making choices that maintain grace.

Figure 12 portrays diversity-in-unity. It is a picture of true communion, a conversational state showing the different types of connection that can be made between people as they explore

Chapter 6 The grace to reconcile

the ways they differ from each other. This type of communion is personal fellowship deeper than sacraments, rituals and beliefs. It shows the personal level of Church, where St Paul in his first letter to the Corinthians (11:29-29, in the context of 17-34) said that before taking the bread and wine people should examine themselves, and wait for each other. In true communion people could meet not only to celebrate the living experience of their relatedness, but on any occasion also to compare notes about the structures they see that shape life, and the activities they might or might not share an interest in. There is, however, a very interesting and perhaps unexpected feature revealed by this portrayal of true communion among diversity. Look at the ligands that extend out from the group. What do you see?

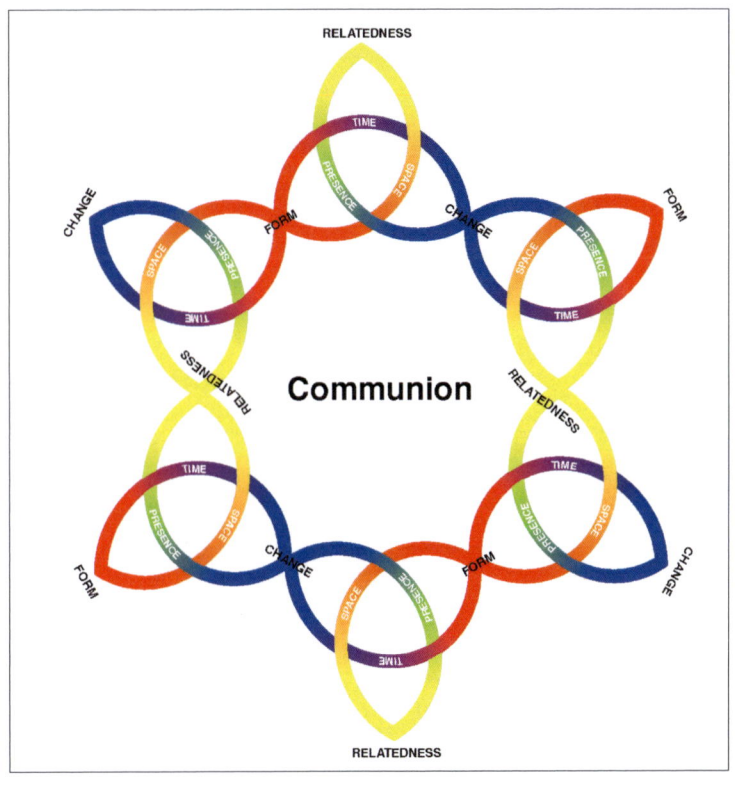

Figure 12. Communion

If you imagine that these ligands are hands extended to welcome others into the fellowship of communion, then offers are being made that welcome all diversity to join. If self-examination and waiting for others is truly part of the activity structured into the fellowship of Godly Family, then this type of Church will truly be 'in and for the world that God so loves', welcoming all.

Contrast now what happens when people gather as a group around a restricted, analytical, cognitive way to understand life. They connect through their shared cognition, not conversationally through their shared grace.

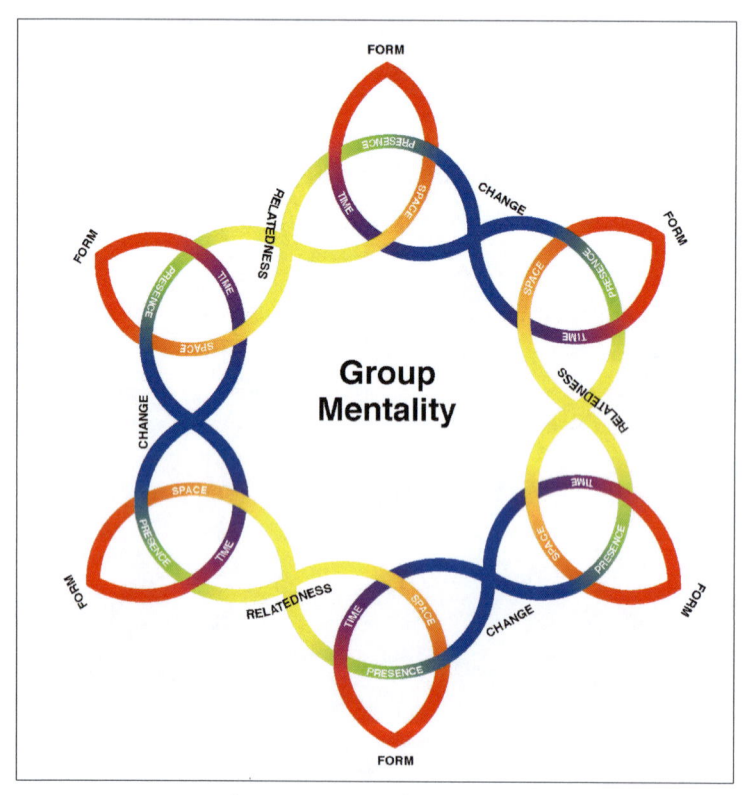

Figure 13. Restricted group mentality—a preference for structure

To understand Figure 13, look again at Figure 9. A preference to see life in terms of forms, structures and order creates a cognitive mind-frame in which the person becomes an 'Observer of Life', a presence of mind, where pure reason reigns and emotion gets in the way. When people connect around the ideas that are logical when deduced from this twist of the triune assumption base, the group becomes exclusive. The ligands that extend out from it have conditions attached to the welcome offered to others. They can join if they conform to our ideas and structures. But grace...

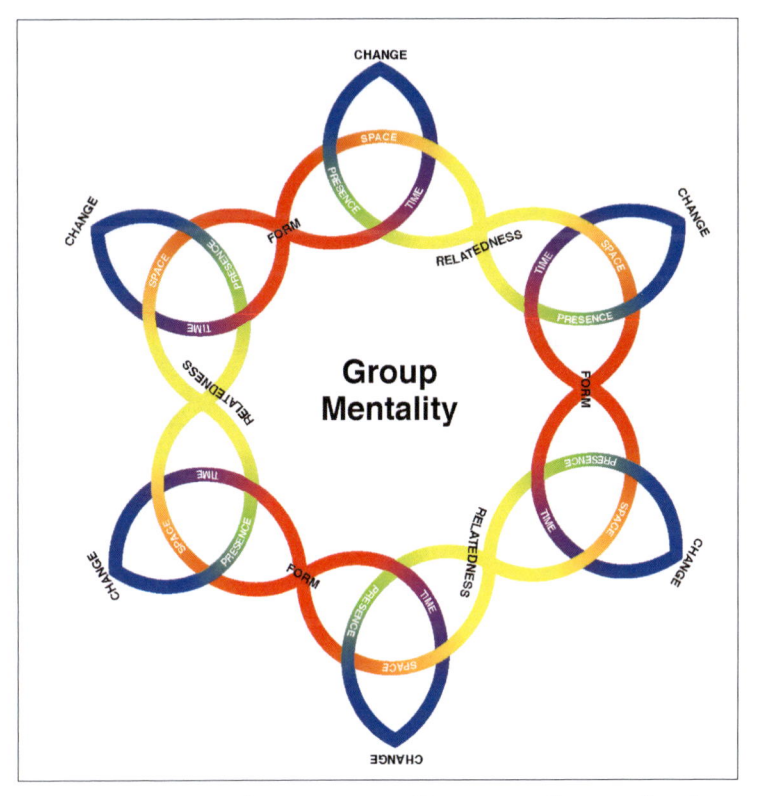

Figure 14. Restricted group mentality—a preference for change

Figure 14, on the other hand, shows a different sort of restricted group mentality. This pattern of connections arises when people gather whose preference is to see life as the changes that are ongoing in different time-frames, shown in Figure 10. The thinking person develops an identity, then, as a 'Creator of Life', an individualist inputting their information to a system (putting their formations in to a system) to bring about change in a relevant time-frame. Figure 14 shows how people can team up temporarily in a project to achieve an agreed target, and then disperse once the goal has been met feeling they have achieved something useful. Others are welcome to join on the condition that they work towards the same goals, and don't try to shift the goal (which would hijack the group). If they lose their usefulness towards this mission, then perhaps it would be best if they leave the group, and thus don't become a waste of personal space. But grace...

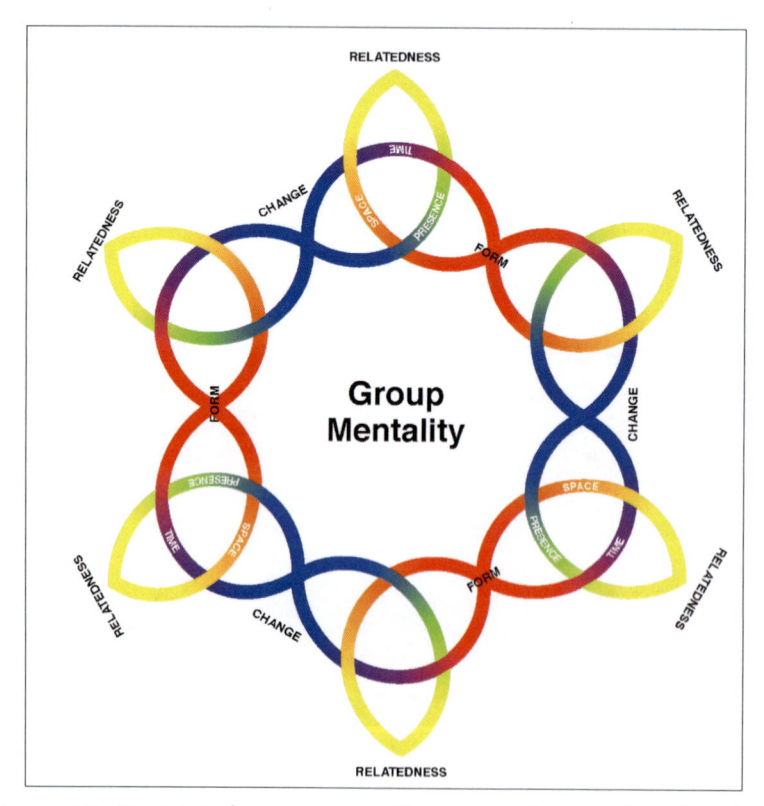

Figure 15. Restricted group mentality—a preference for relatedness

Figure 15 portrays a gathering of people for whom relatedness itself is the very stuff of life. This mind-frame connects with others around establishing orderly life routines shared as a tradition. Traditions are changes that are allowed without disrupting social forms and norms. They can get locked into caste systems, the practices of religious sects, political dogmas generating disconnected and unimaginative movements, and so on. Within those 'tradition limits', people can do more or less what they want to outsiders (them) who do not connect with us. But grace...

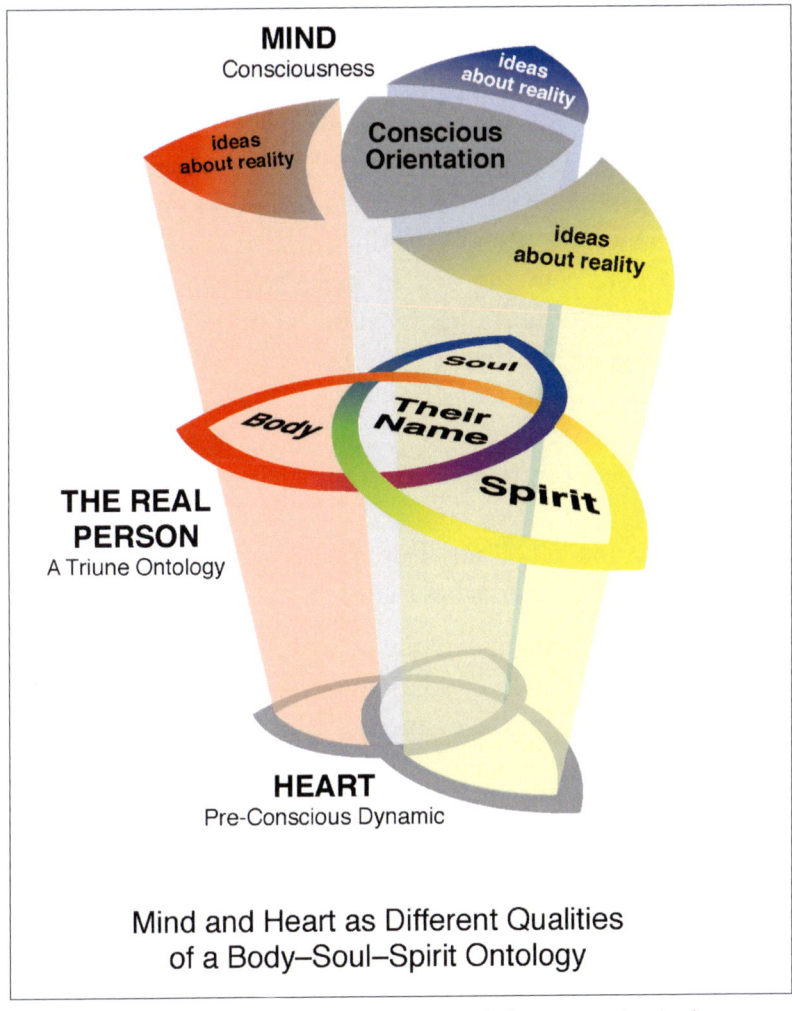

MIND
Consciousness

Conscious Orientation
ideas about reality
ideas about reality
ideas about reality

Soul
Body
Their Name
Spirit

THE REAL PERSON
A Triune Ontology

HEART
Pre-Conscious Dynamic

Mind and Heart as Different Qualities
of a Body–Soul–Spirit Ontology

Figure 16. A triune person with heart and mind

To bring this all together, as an image of a whole person in community, Figure 16 shows how the ongoing triune dynamic, invisibly at the heart of a person, is captured in the person's story, which goes by their *name*. It is 'my story', or yours. A person's story is that which he or she writes as if their signature in waves across grace and Creation, read by others in the traces of how he or she chooses to live.

The conscious mind flames with fleeting moments of illumination on an ongoing scene, digital ideas superimposed on the emotive, analogue dynamic of this inter-personal story. Brain waves repeatedly bundle senses, memories and analyses together many times a second. They thus orientate awareness, allowing rapid changes of mind-frame when attention gets distracted to new features of life. These digitally bundled 'cognits' of awareness repeatedly construct the 'self in the world' that is painted on a deeper canvas of e-motional movements in grace. Grace holds an analogue flow of life that is priming local chemistry in different people and the world for action or withdrawal. This is the heart-level core, the source of calling, the source at which grace-borne movements between people wash up against individual values of resistance for survival, or for togetherness to thrive, and in so doing generate personal reactions. This is the level at which people might want to make a name for themselves.

We can be given a new name by God. In this we become a new creation, telling a higher order story, and developing as a person one step more up into the likeness of Christ by grace.

Stepping up to join the Family

I had one hour to present all this at Płosk. That included an outline of how Emotional Logic can be used to release the traps that grief can spring on people, when they have become committed to one or another of these cognitive analytical perspectives, and a differently coloured light begins to filter in at one of its corners... Do

I shut it out, or welcome it in curiosity? It is this combined model of cognitive worldview with emotional preparations that can show how misunderstanding separates people. Grief at the risk of losing a mind-frame and a group identity can erect a defensive wall. The whole breaks into parts such as restricted groups and individual loners. Could the alternative, such as belonging in a world-wide and emotionally intelligent Church, attract people enough to face constructively those losses that must inevitably arise when letting go of cherished ideas? Could the love that people might see between disciples with all their differences enable people to risk stepping beyond their previously comfortable cliques, onto a bridge that connects up to the high platform of grace?

As it happened, people were so fascinated by the presentation that the following speaker graciously postponed her talk, and I was given a second hour to expand on the ideas and to field questions. The model became a theme for the Symposium. The Roman Catholic priests and theologians were as intrigued as the psychologists. I mentioned that a dream I had was to see this model contribute to exploring how one communion could be re-established for the entire world-wide Church, and that I would love to offer it to the Vatican for consideration.

Nothing more was said, but several months after the second EMCAPP Symposium at Płosk, Anna emailed to say they had a go-ahead from the Vatican for the Polish ACP to be presented to the Pope at a General Audience in St Peter's Square. She had been asked by the senior churchmen to invite me to join them!

I had dreamed that they might send copies of my notes to a clerk in some committee, with apologies for the challenge to centuries of theology. Instead, there was to be a large party of forty or so from ACP going on a pilgrimage to Rome first, and then on to San Giovanni Rotondo in southern Italy where Padre Pio's Friary, now St Pio, is a shrine for healing. I was invited to join a smaller party of six who would be presented to Pope John Paul II. The other five would go on, and leave me alone before him as a guest of ACP 'from the Anglican Church'.

The hope was that the party would be invited back in the following week to talk further with the Pope. Anna and the senior Roman Catholic churchmen and theologians had been very impressed with the 3+1 model, even though I had explicitly said how it supported the Eastern Orthodox view of the sacraments of Holy Mass rather than the Roman interpretation (consubstantiation, rather than transubstantiation). I think they were most deeply moved by the way those three perspectives, with their implications for incompatible beliefs, could be set within a deeper, grace-filled worldview that was Biblically rooted. They were curious. We all *needed to be different* to fully reflect God's glory in the world.

I prepared a folder containing the diagrams of the 3+1 model of personal development, and some explanation of it, to leave as a gift. The photograph shows the frame of mind I was in as I presented it.

Plate 1: Presenting the model to Pope John Paul II at a General Audience in the Vatican.

He was a marvellous man. I need to paint the picture a little to give you the context, to explain what happened. St Peter's enormous keyhole-shaped Square was packed with tens of thousands of revellers. There were parties from all over the world, some with banners and fancy dress, children's choirs, monks and nuns gently making their ways through the crowds. It was like a football World Cup crowd, well behaved with singing and celebration, and cheers raised at the announcement of each new group from all five continents. Pope John Paul II, stiff with advanced Parkinsonism, had been driven in his open-backed 'Pope-mobile 4x4' through avenues preserved among the crowd, unable to wave but still very much 'there' as a presence. As a doctor, I knew about Parkinsonism, how it affects only muscle control, leaving intact the thinking-feeling person inside a bodily cage. It needs a strong character not to become depressed under the circumstances, and *here* was a strong character before me. In the build up to the presentations—hundreds of people were being presented, including a dozen brides and grooms—the Pope had spoken firmly into his microphones, welcoming each group and making many specific responses as each announcement rolled with perfect clarity out from the banks of speakers across the Square, and the huge televised screens captured his small movements and the obvious pleasure in his eyes.

To one of the several groups of Polish children he said he would like to sing a song. He confidently set off on a popular family favourite in Poland, and reached the end of the verse without faltering. Cheers filled the square, waving of flags and banners, no horns, but laughter and smiles of amazed pleasure all around. Then he set off on the second verse, and the third, and the fourth, to ever increasing applause and cheers. He had reached the end of the song, and then mischievously he said that he had enjoyed it so much he was going to sing it again, and he did, the first verse again anyway! The crowd, myself included, loved it. It was impossible not to see that here was a world-wide family enjoying meeting its favourite grand-dad.

So this is the man I was presented to. I had had all sorts of ideas in mind to say, and when I arrived before him, kneeling, two things happened inside me. Firstly, I felt this was no place to start on a theological discussion, but I wanted to honour this father-figure who had been an inspiration for brave Poles in Solidarity to break free from their chains and oppression. Secondly, I had a sudden new and slightly shocking realisation, that the model was not yet ready to go widely public. There was more yet to do before it was safe to speak out. And *I* was not ready. I needed to work at God's pace for God to strengthen *my* heart, not at the pace a commission from the Vatican might direct. I found myself virtually silent, speaking only a generality about a hope for unity. It became a meeting of two people in which I honoured him, not the start of a project. In those moments, however, a seed was planted that grows now.

Father Benedict, before I had travelled to Rome, said he would not want to join a party going to the Vatican even if invited (as I had been discussing with him). He had been there before, and it was a place of chaos. Nothing could be organised there, he had said. After meeting the Pope, I left the folder on a table where the various gifts were being collected. A senior priest, whom the Polish ACP members knew and who had welcomed us to Rome, said he would find the folder and make sure it was seen by various people who were interested in the ecumenical movement. He went to look, but could not find it. Within just a few hours, the folder had disappeared, lost somewhere in the Vatican.

Part 2

Emotional intelligence in the challenge of unity

This is how you (plural) *should pray: Our Father...*

To build the kingdom of God here on earth, as it is in heaven, our physical and spiritual natures must meet. They must meet both within each of us, *and* where two or three diverse people gather in the Name of Jesus. As human beings our two natures meet partly in our experience of emotion, as they would have done for Jesus, our teacher and Christ Messiah. They meet not only in the feelings, however, but also in the wisdom to choose how to direct our emotional energies, which we can learn. A suitable framework for Part 2 is provided by the prayer that Jesus taught his disciples to pray.

'The Lord's Prayer' has slight variations between one Gospel and another. Do not worry about them, but hear and be moved instead by the Spirit of Truth in this prayer. Matthew 6:9-13 records:

> *Jesus said to them, "This is how you should pray:*
> *'Our Father in heaven,*
> *hallowed be your name,*
> *your will be done on earth as it is in heaven.*
> *Give us this day our daily bread.*
> *Forgive us our trespasses,*
>   *as we forgive those who trespass against us.*
> *And lead us not into temptation, but deliver us from evil.'"*

Church liturgy adds a doxology:

'For yours is the kingdom, the power and the glory,
for ever and ever.
Amen.'

Luke's Chapter 11 records Jesus teaching the disciples to pray, *"Your kingdom come,"* in place of *"Your will be done."* The traditional prayer spoken in churches includes both. Perhaps these are not different concepts, but each fills out the meaning of the other.

Chapter 7

Our Father in heaven, hallowed be your name.

The healing grief of our Father in heaven

It may be tempting to see in the world's megatrends of conflict and rejection an unspoken urge through societies to push away the Christian message, that God is a loving Father watching over all of Creation. Anyone hurt by conflict or abuse is bound to doubt that God could be love if God then withholds the power to prevent atrocities, as if this 'God' merely watches dispassionately, deistically, while people suffer. This would indeed be hateful and cruel if it were true. In personal Truth, however, people can recognise that God does not merely exist 'out there'—God *lives* and restores life everywhere now, on earth as it is in heaven, like a spring of living water surging up within eternally. If accusations of unreality then are thrown at Christians because of suffering in the world, should the living God's adopted sons react as if such doubters are the *enemies* of Christianity? No! Irritants should stimulate grace to connect and heal.

This precisely is the point of spiritual growth that is needed by a Royal Priesthood, to connect at the point of love's grief and to remain connected through to the resulting restoration of joy.

This is a spiritual megatrend that we are part of, far greater than the earthly trends that seem so overwhelming at times. Our Father in heaven is neither dispassionate, nor distant, but is present by *grace* in every moment and place where people relate, and where they do not relate well. God as living Trinity at source thus *knows* the movements of grief that tension relationships throughout Creation. Can we humans even begin to imagine how terrible it must have been for God as Father to witness a loved, firstborn Son of God torn by those whom God had created for love? The Son, in whom all Creation holds together, willingly suffered to maintain God's 'unity' for us.

Our loving Father's desire in allowing all this, we are told by the Prophets, is to recover us all into God's kingdom of ever-renewed life. The source of grace to achieve this is *our Father's grief.* God's grief pours out through grace a never-ending source of renewal for all Creation. Grace restores the patterning of love within the connections that sustain life, by calling those *who are moved by grace* into an order that restores new life potentially everywhere, for everyone. That is a true megatrend, over Millennia.

This Father, our source, restores and guides us towards this kingdom with protection, correction, example, presence and blessing. This type of love cannot protect people from grief, however, because to do so would also take away grace and renewal. This type of love cannot take away conflict either, or prevent all disagreement, because it is through these that diversity enables sustainable adjustment in changing situations. This type of love teaches the way to restoration and growth *in the midst of difficulties.* This love prophesies hope, despite pain and grief, to encourage healing, and the growth of new potential in life.

The living testimony of a Royal Priesthood

Many people nevertheless, both in and outside the major Churches, still find the notion of God as a loving Father difficult. Why?

It is an in-built feature of the human brain's workings that each of us will automatically attribute to 'God as Father' our own experience of human fathering. An extra mental step is needed to overcome the harmful effects of imperfect human parenting, or to add breadth and depth to the memories of good parenting. That mental step becomes 'real' only if there is some alternative substantive experience of the 'actions' of a pure and creative God in the world.

Those 'actions' may be known as a mystical or miraculous experience, or more commonly as an experience of being forgiven and released into personal growth—no less a miracle! Without that substantive experience of grace, evangelicals doubt the genuine conversion of heart or mind, even while other Christians in different traditions may *know* that they have been saved, are being saved, and will be saved in the traditions of their faith. Perhaps the vital mind shift that all branches of the worldwide Church have in common, rather than 'conversion', is to know an inner assurance of being a loved, adopted son of the living, awesome God, who is universally present as a loving Father of all, Abba.

St Peter describes the called-out Church of Jesus Christ to be a Royal Priesthood (1 Peter 2:9). Its role is not limited to the major Church traditions of ministering ritual, or converting minds, or mediating between the profane and the sacred as the old Levitical Priesthood did. The Church is, I believe, a priesthood of people who have experienced the mercy of God, and who therefore declare openly their praise of God, to the glory of the only living God. Through this praise the attention of others may be attracted, who are still 'far away' and who perhaps are feeling lost.

This sort of *Royal Priesthood of all believers* can speak testimony of how a relationship with the one living God has transfigured their own life. Testimony speaks realistically into other's needs, as Jesus is the testimony of our heavenly Father. This sort of Royal Priesthood can forgive and bless in the name of Jesus. It is in these encounters that new life is birthed, and spreads to others. That is spiritual adoption. Theology, right belief, and right living all come further down the line of personal development, which has to start with a Godly encounter. At some level there will be a conversational exchange that makes real in an individual's experience the feeling of pure love, and forgiving grace to heal. In that 'right feeling' of the opening encounter, the individual becomes truly a Godly, growing person, a son (non-gender) after the firstborn.

Our pure Father God lives 'in heaven'. As clarified in the first Part of this book using the triquetra diagrams, heaven is not an alternative place or a space separate from the earth. Heaven is the *presence* of one pure, loving God. It is true that the loving presence of God can seem far away at times, or even totally absent, so that to be in the presence of God can seem to be affected by space and time. But bringing those three together, to be in the presence of God in our present space and time, is the hope of the kingdom of God that Jesus taught his disciples to declare in prayer, that this kingdom will be 'on earth as it is in heaven'. The loving presence of God can be here with us as well.

In that heavenly present love is the Name of God—often unspoken—but in many tongues this name may be Almighty, Elohim, YHWH, different translations in human languages, Dieu, Gott, Iddio, Jumala, Allah to Arab Christians (Yes, Allah is Elohim in Arabic.). In the Name is personal life; life in movement relationally transforming. The Name is holy, pure, undefiled, life-giving, glorious. That's my awesome Dad, and yours.

Grief can mislead into separation

It seems obvious, but needs saying in a confused world, that natural fathering is not merely the fertilization of an egg. A fertilized ovum grows through a series of environments into a child, an adult, and a parent in its own time. Fathering, alongside mothering, is a feature of all those environments, sometimes more actively present, sometimes accessible only when needed and called upon. Both of the parent roles, mother and father, are difficult to combine in a single person, but many young adults strive to achieve that when a child unexpectedly comes along and disrupts their former hopes and relationships.

When a person's experience of being fathered falls short of that needed in response to hearing the child, disappointment follows, sometimes profoundly. Alienation becomes a risk, unless forgiveness can somehow enter the relational equation by grace.

Some disappointment in one's natural father is inevitable. Learning to adjust constructively to one's parents' humanity is a normal part of individuation into a mature adult. However, in a society where grief has become the big taboo subject, and where the skill and knowledge to talk constructively about loss has been forgotten or ignored, such grieving may be left unrecognised—left to fester. Deep within the heart, unspoken like an alien stronghold, that disappointment with earthly fathers may grow out of proportion, feeding on resentment, shame and self-doubt. It is easy to turn away, to distract oneself in the post-modern telecommunication world, and ignore the subtle messages from deep within—that something is wrong and needs addressing.

If that something wrong seems to be in 'me', and if I do not have the skills or knowledge to face or address it alone, then a natural response is to give my grief to someone else to 'see how they like it'! Maybe they can handle it better than I. Anyone will do, such as a passing stranger who doesn't know me from Adam whom I may show my displeasure at, or perhaps my father, or society at large, or perhaps to send it on up the line to an absent and disappointing God. Rejecting God may even get God's attention!

When natural fathers have shown no interest in inspiring and guiding their sons with a strong image of pure, loving fatherhood, the son will naturally separate away, and make his own way in the world with his own resources. However, this survival technique comes at a cost, the cost of separation. Existential aloneness can be bridged temporarily by joining restricted identity groups of like-minded people. But even in such a group, as in a crowd, one can be aware of the gap. That gap is nothing other than grief unrecognised and thus unresolved into personal growth.

St John the Apostle's Gospel and his three letters are a wonderful statement of how a person's relationship with God is a mirror image of the quality of their relationships with other people. People can learn to love others, and to forgive others, by learning first to love and forgive God; and vice versa, they may learn to love God by first seeing love in another human being. Love springs anew like grass even after the cold destruction of winter, so love is stronger than evil, which cannot destroy God's grace. Therefore, by learning how we grieve in our daily lives for small disappointments and setbacks first, people can next overcome the projection onto God of their powerful loss emotions from deep and distant disappointments. Hope may then break the hardened surface, faith can reconnect, and love restore grace-filled life.

Stuck in separation by whirlpools of emotion

Emotions are physical preparation states for action or withdrawal. They are God-given as part of our survival mechanisms to adjust to change. However, when several emotions are on the go simultaneously in a complex and changing situation, each cannot adequately prepare a person for one clear response. Then emotional energy builds up into tension or distress or confusion, and the entangled preparations may start to turn into a directionless swirl of emotional energy deep within the heart. Out of these 'whirlpools of emotion' (which are shallower than they may seem when first recognised as such), disturbing passions may bubble to the surface of life. Here on the surface they may be projected out, to disperse as a behavioural display of the distress or tension deep inside, producing a range of actions or withdrawals or confusions depending on the emotions involved. Emotional Logic points out practical ways to untangle the underlying emotional preparations.

New understanding and insight gives them constructive direction that leads to personal growth, self-respect, empathy, and an improved capacity to make decisions and to see them through.

A short while spent learning the whirlpools of loss emotions in relation to fatherhood will reap rewards for eternity. I am going to list the most common passions and behaviours that emerge from emotional whirlpools, so that you can see the grieving person in these—who is not a bad or a weak character, but on the contrary is a human being who has bravely taken the risk to love, and has been hurt as a consequence, perhaps badly. These people need honouring, not criticising. Eighty percent of men in prison have been sexually or physically abused by their fathers. Forgive them and read on.

Where shock disables a person and sends him or her mentally inwards, doubting their resources to cope, another emotion entangling with that can prevent the shock from fulfilling its useful purpose. Its Godly, life-giving purpose is to make you *stop* what you are doing, and find a safe place where you can mentally look inward and review your resources to handle the situation. When the other emotion that entangles with shock is also an inwardly-directing preparation state, such as guilty feelings or depressive emptiness, the person will feel an intense urge or inner behavioural drive to withdraw from life, out of proportion to the circumstances.

Guilty feelings mixed with shock generate shame. Shame includes a mistaken belief that "This guilty feeling means I must be the cause of problems (untrue!), and I doubt that I can be anything other than that." It is a lie that people tell themselves. The truth is that this is the way grief at lost values may feel as it bursts out of the relational gap that the whirlpool has made. Shock entangling with depressive emptiness, on the other hand, produces fatigue, feeling as if personal energy has been switched off all of a sudden. It may remain that way repeatedly or continuously as 'chronic fatigue syndrome', which is physical grief in a society that does not know how to handle relational grief constructively. "I am feeling empty and powerless, and I doubt my resources to be anything other than that." Shock has a powerful effect on the body chemistry through adrenaline and steroid hormones, which genuinely impairs the immune system when it goes on too long. The depressive grief reaction ensures that it does go on too long. This is physical grief.

How much does shame and fatigue arise from, and affect, creative relationships between fathers and their sons and daughters?

And what if guilty feelings get entangled with depressive emptiness? Can you work it out for yourself? What is the disturbing drive that would follow when people are thinking, "I feel empty and powerless", and at the same time "I must be the cause of feeling empty, because I feel I have done something wrong"? We have found on talking with many people that 'low self-regard' is the result; ruminating on problems, negative thoughts, hopelessness and despair. It is the guilt-depression whirlpool that makes people slip off their firmly useful Depression Stepping Stone down into the turmoil of an illness called clinical depression. Godly depressive emptiness has a noble purpose, to help people grow in wisdom to make constructive decisions having seen their limits. Conversations in grace can help to map a path of exploration on from there. But when an emotional whirlpool makes a relational gap, the readiness to explore can evaporate.

Withdrawal from life, withdrawal from fathers in distressing states of mind and heart, can thus result when two loss emotions that are both inwardly directed get mixed up together in a whirlpool. The emotional state in a whirlpool takes on a life of its own, disconnected from the events of life that have initially caused multiple hidden losses and generated all this energy to adjust, with no constructive, conversational outlet. Separated by a relational gap, people may start telling themselves lies about their own identity or character, and so further disable their hope, broken-hearted in their prison, making the best of life that they can under the circumstances. Where is the Royal Priesthood, with a realistic hope?

By contrast, there are whirlpools with another sort of behavioural effect when anger entangles with another grief emotion. Irrational actions out in the world, disrupting creative life, can result.

Anger in its pure God-given state is an outwardly directed passion for life, a constructive preparation state to engage with others despite danger to prevent the loss of something valued. If shock entangles with anger, however, an inner conflict of preparation states results. Imagine (or better make) for a moment the posture and facial expression that displays shock. Now imagine or make the posture and facial expression that displays anger. Try doing both at the same time. You can't! I know you can't, but that is exactly what your body chemistry and mental state are trying to do. This inner conflict generates confusion. People cannot think clearly when anger and shock occur at the same time. As a consequence, the person is now unsure whether "I am looking from within out into the world at danger, or I am outside myself looking in and doubting my resources to cope!" People can feel odd and 'out of it', displaced as if they are looking down on themselves and life instead. It is a state of being called 'depersonalisation'; but it is *grief*, and that grief would feel different if someone could bridge that relational gap with grace, and restore a conversational connection.

We all need a little anger to keep life in a creative order, to gather resources to create safe or nurturing environments. What might happen, however, if this drive gets entangled with guilty feelings, or with depressive thoughts? Guilt is the big weak spot in the human system, because this urge to learn involves self-questioning, and so the inner drive feels as though 'I must have done something *wrong*'? Nobody likes that feeling! It is so basic and in-built that infants naturally cry when they are first told "No!" Adults develop a wider range of ways to object or to avoid that horrible feeling. Cain murdered Abel, for example, on being told, 'Not what I want' about his offering that he hoped would bring the right of return to the blessed Garden of Eden.

One way that a whirlpool of loss emotions can get surging is when people feel angry *about having guilty feelings*. Anger and guilt are both in-built to help *prevent* loss in the world, or in relationships. Therefore, when the anger gets twisted inwards instead, and directed to prevent the inner *feeling* of guilt, its Godly useful purpose is being corrupted away from addressing some named *loss*. Neither the self-questioning, nor the passion to engage with life, can fulfil their useful purposes to improve life in the world. Instead the person takes action in some way intended to break or regulate the inner tension that has been set up by conflicting preparation states. The angry action made will seem irrational to others, because it is not connected to a recognisable loss. This whirlpool leads to compulsive and obsessional behaviour, ritualistic perhaps, such as obsessive tidiness, cleanliness, or even to bulimia and self-harming behaviour. It is not madness or bad character. It is impulsive grief, unrecognised as such and acted out, displayed to break inner tension. Perfectionism is the most common way that this whirlpool of grief emotions presents. Family carers for the disabled or ill, for example, can drive themselves to the limit for the best of intentions, because the guilt of grieving is misinterpreted as failure. Kindness to self then suffers to the point of exhaustion. The rational balance of care for others with care for self is pushed aside. It is grief emerging from the relational gap when love is bruised or disappointed. Repeatedly trying to attract attention from fathers by methods that have been unsuccessful in the past is another example of this whirlpool of grief emotions. A bit of Godly growth cycle is needed instead.

I have left the big one until last. When anger gets entangled with depression, watch out! This is the one where people most need love, and most make themselves unavailable or unattractive to receive it. Anger is the drive to go out into the world and do something to prevent the loss of something truly valued. Depression is the state of looking inward and not liking the limits of one's power and effectiveness that one sees there. A highly tensioned conflict is set up between these two emotional preparation states. Anger corrupts away from managing loss constructively despite danger, and turns instead into the energy to prevent at all costs *the feeling* of powerlessness and emptiness. Irrationally destructive behaviour results, or at least urges for this that have to be resisted. Sometimes these are brief, fleeting thoughts of taking a gun and shooting wildly or at someone blamed for the distress. Increasingly, where guns are available, it is actually happening around the world. Irrational destructive action results not only on that scale. Displays of power are made in confrontational behaviour, obstructive and argumentative disruption, vandalism, criminality, abuses of authority, excessive control. Power for its own sake may tear down the works of another, hiding at all costs in this activity the feeling inside of emptiness. And if shock then adds self-doubt into the inflammatory mixture, the destructive drive from an anger-depression whirlpool may be turned on oneself, as suicidal thoughts, to end it all—the ultimate protest—the ultimate emptiness.

Irrational destructiveness is grief emerging from the relational gap, shockingly misdirected. Our Father in heaven asks his adopted family, and his chosen people, his Royal Priesthood, to build bridges of grace across those relational gaps. People only grieve if they have loved and been frustrated or hurt, so that makes them more of a human being, not less. Join the human race! It does not absolve people from their responsibility to grieve constructively. That is where honour grows, where people grieve constructively, choosing to move onto their growth cycles to promote life and shared well-being in new ways. People grieve deeply when earthly fathering is at risk of being lost. When people do not know how to grieve constructively, an emotionally resilient Royal Priesthood is God's answer for the world God so loves, because constructive grieving requires the option to build relationships in new ways.

The more people understand their learned pattern of grieving, the more they will have choices that lead to personal growth. Life then builds around their true identity, as a son or daughter of the living God; the God who runs to meet us, your Father and mine.

Churches may see Father differently

As we look at the one worldwide Church's capacity to be a Royal Priesthood, one complication is worth remembering. In the three main branches of the Church, Christian believers may understand our Father in heaven differently, which could affect the image of true sonship (and again I say this includes male and female as a generic term).

In the Protestant tradition, the man at its very inception, Martin Luther, was a person who had suffered a very painful experience at the hands of his earthly father. He said that he found it almost impossible to say 'Our Father' at the start of the Lord's Prayer. Every time it reminded him of his natural father, which is a clear statement of the 'transference' that we all will experience to some extent.

This avoidance reaction influenced the development of Protestant theology, which is a large scale 'Butterfly Effect' within the emerging system of Christian free-thinkers. Salvation was approached down the legal road, 'justification by faith', with God as Judge over sin, and humans as lawbreakers. The alternative, triune, conversational, relational, Holy Spirit guided path to redemptive love at whatever cost was less travelled, a steeper path to healing grace for all, poured out in grief to reconnect as salvation into ever-renewed life. In this alternative route, now being much more travelled at this transition into the Third Millennium, God is our loving Father, and humans are orphans separated from the land but now adopted into Family to till and plant the Father's earth side by side with those who differ from us.

In the Protestant Reformation a view developed that grace is the unmerited favour of God. Given that sibling rivalry is such a fundamental problem in every family worldwide, this has had an unfortunate effect that individual Protestant Christians may compete with others in the hope of obtaining a special dispensation of grace, perhaps to alleviate the sentence on sin that this Judge God will impose. What does this say about the character of our Father in heaven? In the Eastern Church a vast body of believers celebrates the way God dispenses grace to *all* for the restoration of life, regardless of their moral standing. Otherwise, as the Eastern Christians say, there could be no hope for any of us! I believe that the Reformed Protestant statement was a reaction in medieval history to separate away from the Roman practice of 'selling favours' for prayers for the dead that was current at the time. Several centuries later, now in a post-Vatican II world especially, where reconciliation is high on God's renewal agenda, the purpose for that Protestant formulation about grace has perhaps evaporated; but it may have left its traces in a Protestant individual's habit of prayer of *appeal* to Father God for a special favour of grace. Can the Judge be bribed, or manipulated emotionally, or blamed as cruel for not answering? Each individual discovers that in his or her heart Adam still slips and blames someone like Eve, and Cain still resents someone like Abel. It is natural! Fortunately, the charismatic renewal that is sweeping through all three branches of the Church is powerfully enabling people to cover over with love this long history of mismanaged grief. Holy Spirit moved relations now, more than ever before, can restore the joy of unity-among-diversity that our Father God has planned for the Family.

In the Roman West a different concept of Fatherhood has faced problems at this transition into the third Millennium. The Roman Catholic hierarchical view of life had generated the 'strong Paternalism' view of a single *authority* as central provider (not as judge because Jesus is the judge), who is called God the Father. This strong but fair father figure dispenses grace by authority not to those who appeal most, but through an interconnected material chain of sacramental contacts. In this view a Father is dominant over a family, or a society, exercising power for benevolent purposes and restricting the sacramental nurture of individuals who pursue their own interests. An unmarried priesthood distributes sacraments through their marriage into a parish. In the last two centuries, the Roman Church uniquely has elevated Mary, the Mother of Jesus, to fully divine status, perhaps because this was needed to complete the picture of a family and thus to overcome the grief engendered by the medieval view of a distanced, powerful Father whose attention is difficult to attract. The godhead is thus softened by Mary, and made more approachable when a way is opened to appeal in prayer to the nurturing comfort of a Mother. However, in thus elevating Mary's status she is denied the benefit of the original sin that, for other Christians, marks their humanity out from God with *a potential for change*. The price paid for making Mary less human is a clouding of the divine-human potential in each one of us orphans, a potential that is fulfilled by God's grace at our *choice* to connect into full adoption.

Sadly, in this 21st Century and in many countries, the Roman celibate priesthood is embroiled in litigation for abuse in schools, which for society's observers brings the whole notion of benevolent single authority in Fatherhood into question. We grieve with the hurt sons, and have no answer other than to keep alive a hope of grace to heal. As a consequence, the Western Church as a *moral authority* in society has suffered enormous and possibly irreparable damage.

So, what of the Eastern Orthodox view of God as Father, the one that follows when people step back from conversational orientation in the liturgy, and try instead to analyse what is happening in its balanced mystery? As people step away from celebrating in the richly apophatic atmosphere of the mystery play about our source of ever-renewed life, a different type of Father appears in the distance thus mentally created. It is a view of Father that makes sense in the collective mind set that predominates in Eastern cultures.

Curiously, a good way to understand this angle on God as

Father is to look at how atheistic communism corrupted it. Communism, curiously, spread in the 20th Century CE over the same geographical areas that the Eastern Orthodox Church still covers. I could speculate that this happened because of the culturally prevailing mind set.

Communism was introduced in Russia and her federation of Soviet republics (the USSR) by a secular Jewish intelligentsia, who tried to make the Russian State a superior will to any father's, whether the paternalistic royal family of Russia (God's representatives on earth), or a religious Father in heaven. Stalin, a true blood Russian, removed those original revolutionaries later with a typically abrupt Russian style of dominance, and took over leadership from them. He took steps to replace the family, as the core social unit of society for personal development, with a 'soviet'. A soviet is a local committee. It was a local council that determined the corporate standards of economic behaviour and personal belief in that locality. This notion of *corporate authority* was a cultural parallel to the Eastern Orthodox Church's view that authority resides in the body of the Church family, not in a single individual.

The Father's role in the Eastern perspective on Christianity is to 'watch over all' to ensure unity, forgiveness and reconciliation among the emerging diversity. However, a Soviet under Stalin was 'watched over' not by a loving spiritual Father who was known and respected in the hearts of all his family members. It was watched over by the atheistic Communist Party representative. That 'Party' official *intruded* into individuals' lives to enforce change in accord with atheistic dogma, which did not include nurturing forgiveness and reconciliation as a loving father would. Communism forced Our Father in heaven to be an absent father. The scale of martyrdom among Eastern Orthodox priests is only now being discovered, and so those believers who were able to persevere in their hidden faith did so by believing that their loving Father watched over still from afar in heaven. Many distant or absent fathers excluded from broken families now watch over from afar, waiting and hoping for the day when their children reach the age of majority and can contact them. By the same token, many abandoned children wait in hope of finding their absent fathers.

So it was under communism, and the consequence under the atheistic, intrusive Party representative in a soviet was that loving, intelligent, equitable caring also became absent from daily life. The collective became a place of isolation for many in crowded conditions. For example, in Russian cities a dozen families could be forced to live in one huge flat sharing one toilet facility, all having to get out at the same time to their work, and deliver their children to the state nursery for a long day of indoctrination; then to collect them later and return to their 'home'...

Re-gathering in Our Father's love

So, diversity of belief about God can generate different images of a Father in heaven, all of which may appear loving, or may not.

In a Protestant view the judging father *is* approachable, perhaps even can be influenced by appeal, much as a child might cuddle into Dad to convince him that the gift of grace is deserved to dispense power and favours unequally among adults for specific purposes. For some Roman Catholics a just but distant authority called father is too busy to respond to a mere individual, but he can definitely be trusted to deliver blessing as needed. For those Eastern Orthodox who have stepped back to analyse, a father who is far distant watches over a body of people and nurtures them all with grace, to inspire them to deal as fairly with each other as he gives fairly to each of us in Christ.

Each has its merits, but alone is an incomplete view of the Father in heaven whose kingdom is to come on earth also, the source of life for us all. To each can be said a, "Yes", but qualified then by "and no-no!", because two other views are not represented. 'Yes-and-no-no' is the starting place of diversity within which, gathered in the Name of Jesus, we seek the mystery and blessing of unity. The value of starting with such clear diversity is that any one of those three fundamental perspectives may be exactly what is needed by a widow, or an orphan, to encounter a Royal Priesthood and be welcomed in to join the body, and become a new creation in Christ.

We are not intended to be orphans. When disconnected from a source of life, self-reliance and self-doubt are the two little feet that most spiritual orphans have to stand upon. Trying to stand on one or the other could easily unbalance in the slipperiness of life, leading to repeated attempts to engage and disengage from relationships. But an emotionally intelligent church could show affection and understanding safely in response. That way, belonging in adoption by grace becomes a felt reality. Adoption cannot be a preached mental belief; nor is it a behavioural practice. Adoption is intelligently emotional sensitivity, grace to respond in connection, which is as integral to the image of God in humankind on earth as it is to God in Heaven.

Source paternalism

Such a view of our Father in heaven—a balance of enormous Dad with cuddle-in room for all, who is an awesomely fair Provider, and a source of Inspirational Hope for renewed life among us all—such a view could be called 'source paternalism'. God's source of life emerges through every fleeting photon of the universe out there, and through every human heart open within to God's healing grace.

What would you be at risk of losing if you were to choose to let go of the grip you have on your present view of God as Father, and roll instead into a restful hammock from where, gently rocking, you can see God as the continuous creator and source of your life? What sort of loss reaction would that set going in you? And if currently you feed off the grief emotions that come with criticising others, to what else might you turn that energy, or status?

Distant but caring, connected but authoritarian, intimate but unpredictable—choose which you prefer—it makes no difference, because our Father in heaven *lives* and loves you before all these ideas are formed in your brains; ideas that take on a life of their own fuelled by the emotional dynamics that orphans, and even adopted sons and daughters, will experience. Hear in your heart St Paul's wholesomely passionate words again in Ephesians 3:16-19.

> *I pray that out of his glorious riches*
> *the Father may strengthen you with power*
> *through his Spirit in your inner being*
> *so that Christ may dwell in your hearts through faith.*
> *And I pray that you,*
> *being rooted and established in love,*
> *may have power together with all the Lord's holy people,*
> *to grasp how wide and long and high and deep*
> *is the love of Christ,*
> *and to know this love that surpasses knowledge,*
> *that you may be filled*
> *to the measure of all the fullness of God.*

Sibling rivalry

Such a fair Father has to manage the fact that each son (non-gender) may want all of Dad's attention. Learning to take turns is a developmental process over time, perhaps over difficult times of jealousy. Dad is a focal point when seen through human eyes. But when seen with spiritual eyes, God is also Holy Spirit connectedness everywhere, deeper in all of us than every cell of our bodies. We are each moved equally within by Holy Spirit in a vast ocean, of grace connection, of relatedness with each other, and through each other with God.

Triune prayer is a way that mature Christians can choose to overcome the sibling rivalry that is built into their human natures with its focus on individuals. It is natural, in prayer for someone else, to look with human eyes and see the individual, the recognisable form of the person. It needs spiritual eyes to be open to consider in some way the individual's network of relatedness, their 'spirit'. It is this *connectedness*, with the land, with other people, and with God that sustains that person, and adds tensions that move within the individual also. Prayer in the spirit when blessing is prayer that has a mental focus *not on the individual, but on a particular relationship of that person*. Invisible though these spiritual dynamics are to the human eye, the effects of the giving and taking in relatedness can be seen as evidence in the two relating individuals (persons) of their connection at source. It can be seen in an emotional exchange between them that simultaneously is spiritual and material.

Triune prayer is thus prayer that focuses simultaneously on **two interacting** individuals or groups. Triune prayer *in the spirit* focuses even more specifically on *the relationship between* those two individuals or groups. There may be nothing to 'see' there with human eyes, other than the fact that both individuals are emotionally in a dynamic, probably with different and even conflicting emotions. With spiritual eyes, however, it may be possible to imagine the substantial grace that lies deeper than the visible material of life, and which is connecting people at a source heart level, even when they are in conflict with each other. Prayer in the spirit, then, is prayer that Holy Spirit will blow across the substantial grace of their relationship *directly*, so influencing both individuals simultaneously. Each may then potentially be healed, transformed and delivered into liberty in unpredictable ways, seeing each other differently, at least to the extent that their human will allows.

This sort of triune prayer is non-partisan. It is fair. It does not take sides. Regardless of the human opinions that the Royal Priest may have about a situation, God knows the end from the beginning better. The Royal Priest is a gardener only, judging where prayer is needed while tilling and tending the earth with the utmost grace, not 'passing judgement'. This sort of a Royal Priest has overcome sibling rivalry, not being drawn into taking sides. Sometimes this path must be chosen despite intense emotions being stirred within him or her by choices made by one side of that relationship or the other. Overcoming that surge of grief in disappointment with Emotional Logic is vital to maintain the trinity, of priestly person and two or more people, which restores Godly life to a community.

Triune prayer is the Mind of God at source

Consider this possibility, that the living Holy Trinity behind all existence is aware… and is aware *because* the Son who sees the relationship of Holy Spirit and Father prays blessing on them, and the Holy Spirit who sees the relationship of Son and Father prays blessing on them. Without rivalry or a partisan distribution of grace, they adore, and so become one in substance, out of which we are born.

We too can have that mind of God. Protestants could pray a triune prayer in the spirit for the relationship between Eastern Orthodox and Roman Catholic believers, from whatever point of knowledge we start, which is always surpassed by love anyway. Roman Catholics could pray a triune prayer in the spirit for the relationship between Eastern Orthodox and Protestant believers. Eastern Orthodox believers could pray a triune prayer in the spirit for the relationship between Protestant and Roman Catholic believers. All could know the substance of God's grace moving through all, by which unity the Royal Priesthood may command a blessing for the world God so loves.

What am I worried I might lose if I chose to be non-partisan and pray the triune prayer? Love your enemies, and pray blessing on them. Let them bring out the best in you, not the worst. And in my neighbourhood, what am I worried I might lose if I let go of my preference for one person or another in my Spirit-filled prayers, and pray the triune prayer with the mind of God?

Am I worried I might lose something important if I let go of my Father in heaven, and work to love instead 'Our Father in heaven'?

Chapter 8
God's kingdom on earth, as in heaven

Your kingdom come, your will be done…

Jesus' wide range of parables about the kingdom of God is recorded in Matthew Chapter 13 and Mark Chapter 4. Repeatedly Jesus likens the kingdom to seed or yeast that grows and reproduces to make abundant life (or a large catch of fish pulled from the sea). Balancing against this unbounded growth is the selection of some and the rejection of others at a time of judgment *after they have lived mingling with each other*. This time of shared living is a time of heart-level testing and decisions to reveal the inner heart. It makes sense of God's creation purpose in Adam to be a gardener, observing, naming and choosing features of life that need encouraging or pruning. In the Garden of God's Creation we are all confronted with emotional temptation and the need for rational choice whether or not to magnify the value of this world's products, or to commit into the fabulous riches of the source, in the kingdom of the living God.

Jesus says to the Pharisees, recorded in Luke 17:21, "The kingdom of God will not come visibly… because the kingdom of God is within (and/or among) you". Here he addresses, among other things, the Jews' hope for the restoration of an independent kingdom of Israel, as founded by King David, throwing off the control of foreign powers. In Jesus' day this was the Roman Empire, but the same principle applies even now to this day for many Jews wherever they live. In John 18:36-37 Jesus tells Pontius Pilate, and us, that "My kingdom is not of this world." It is a clear, unambiguous statement about the kingdom of God, a *declaration of mutual inter-dependence* at a heart-level in the human community (as in Luke 17:21).

It is here, at the interface between source and product, that human choice to resist temptation and evil can open the gates of heaven to allow free movement within the kingdom of God—moving between heaven's love and earth's tumultuous growth. The kingdom is 'at hand'. All we have to do is to push any gate open where two or three are gathered in the Name of Jesus, and we are there, looking into the land of riches, flowing with milk and honey, and like Eden a garden. The gate, however, is relational; it is spiritually triune. The gate is through the quality of the relationships that a person maintains.

Some of these relationships are directly heart-to-heart before the ever-present living God, and some are triune, praying in the spirit for the relationship between two others. Relationships with God, with other people and with the land all need to be brought into this inner heart-level push to overcome the world in each and every moment *so that others can be relationally blessed*. Here is the kingdom of God.

The prophet Micah was a younger contemporary of Isaiah, and in my humble opinion as great a prophet as Isaiah, particularly for the future of the Church's triune relationship with Israel and her long-suffering neighbours. It was Micah 5:2, about Bethlehem, that the Pharisees quoted when King Herod enquired where the new King of the Jews was prophesied to be born, whom the Persian Magi had arrived to worship (Matthew 2:1-12). No wonder Herod was disturbed!

With hindsight we can understand the section Micah 5:1-5a as the context that prophesies the emergent Church from Christ's birth to this present day. 'To the ends of the earth' may refer to our Third Millennium re-gathering of Christ's flock, in Holy Spirit-led diverse unity. (But take care to read on, and to avoid triumphalism, because this does not mean that everyone will be *in* the Christian Royal

Priesthood.) This prophecy about Christ's forthcoming Church is recorded sequentially before Micah prophesies the Babylonian (Assyrian) invasion (5:5b-15). That prophecy about invasion was given a hundred years before it happened under Jeremiah's weeping gaze; but it happened six hundred years *before* the birth of Christ. So Micah's prophecies are not recorded in the time sequence of our human history on earth. They are recorded in chunked 'time-frames', which are like jigsaw pieces in an overall timeframe of eternity. Together this fits into the full picture of redemption that Micah is prophesying.

And what does Micah say, in this context, that God requires of God's People on earth? In Micah 6:1-5 God states his case against Israel (which we can extend to be against anyone who claims to be saved and adopted into God's Family). God asserts, how can people say God has burdened them, and so turn away, when from 'the everlasting foundations of the earth' God has provided so much help from heaven? Micah replies (6:6-8) on behalf of us all and of Israel as our lamp:

> With what shall I come before the Lord
>   and bow down before the exalted God?
> Shall I come before Him with burnt offerings,
>   with calves a year old?
> Will the Lord be pleased with thousands of rams,
>   with ten thousand rivers of oil?
> Shall I offer my firstborn for my transgression,
>   the fruit of my body for the sin of my soul?
> He has showed you, O Man, what is good.
>   And what does the Lord require of you?
> To act justly and to love mercy
>   and to walk humbly with your God.

Act justly, love mercy, walk humbly with your God

This is the will of God, to be done on earth as it is in heaven.

This describes the kingdom of God come on earth, as it is in heaven.

Since Pentecost, when after Jesus' resurrection the Holy Spirit was released on all flesh (as prophesied by Joel in 2:28-29), anyone who calls on the name of the Lord will be saved. This call and response is spiritual connection; it is grace. Living in grace requires an ongoing conversational orientation in life with God and equally with other people in and through the land.

Salvation cannot be put in a pocket. Salvation may be lost when its power to transform life is analysed and mentally codified, and preserved or pickled into acceptable behaviours. Salvation must be lived moment by moment as a worshipful life in the Spirit, acting justly, loving mercy, and walking humbly before your God. Life in the Spirit is movement. How people receive the Holy Spirit on whom they call, the Spirit of prophecy, will vary, depending on their backgrounds and cultures. The central theme of this book is that emotional intelligence is needed in the Church if the depth of cultural diversity among people worldwide is to be respected, even revered. Through honouring re-connection among the diverse people who call on God, God's glory is manifest to all, to the ends of the earth.

Ask yourself, "What do I stand to lose if I honour someone who understands and responds to Holy Spirit in a way that is different to mine?" "What emotions arise in me, and how do I manage these: shock, denial, anger, guilt, yearning, emptiness, sadness?" If I, as a member of Christ's Royal Priesthood, have become familiar enough with my loss reactions, then I shall know how to turn my unpleasant emotions and doubts about others into the energy to explore re-connection constructively. Part of that 'turning' is preparing the way by triune prayer, by which Holy Spirit insights and power are invited into life on earth. If so, then behavioural outcomes will be unpredictable *but Godly safe*, not bound by human rules, but innovative and appropriate in their kingdom context. Triune prayer will thus lead in time to joy—to heaven on earth.

Given this diversity, the kingdom of God can thus extend in time to the ends of the earth, through peoples' heart-level qualities of relatedness. It is about building bridges of grace through times of conflict and misunderstanding. The kingdom of God does not have to be 'spiritualised' away from earthly realities and difficulties. Its glory can be made active in a triune response, prayerfully in each and any moment of disagreement or conflict, taking life out of an analytical head-frame, and re-connecting in grace in a conversational heart-frame. Here, unpleasant grief emotions are not signs of danger or bad character or ill intent in another. They are signs of deep values being challenged. Those values can be understood and respected, even if they are not shared. That is what it means to love mercy. By mutual respect, those grief emotions may be shared as vital social messages, the recognition and acknowledgement of which *in humility with God who knows grief* then marks out a path to explore deeper than those emotions, through them even to the renewing source of life, there to work out how to act in justice together.

Now we are being practical and earthy about the coming of God's kingdom. This truly is about God's will being done. This has to happen *before* a time of judgement, before people who share through the land will separate away from each other, according to whether or not they have shared the land in justice, mercy and humility with God.

Justice

Codified law is needed to make publicly visible the boundaries of acceptable social behaviour in a defined environment. Company law, family law, criminal law, international law, these are all defined environments. Justice is easily confused with what may seem to be its conclusion, in the punishment that is awarded when transgression of the boundaries has been proven. But that, surely, is not the meaning of justice being done, or even being seen to be done. Justice, surely, IS *the equitably moving balance of life* that is established after recognition of transgression, after acknowledging 'trespasses'. Justice is a way of living.

Proof and punishment *may be* part of the path to bring insight and understanding about equitable living, but they are *not essential* if people are living aware that the kingdom of God is actively 'at hand'. Because of the vast diversity of cultural norms that co-exist around this ever-shrinking world, a visual image of justice may help to achieve equitable living with less reliance on courts, proof, conflict and punishment. Perhaps the triquetra can be used for such a visual image...

In Chapter 5, 'Unearthing the Roots of Conflict', the triquetra is introduced in Figure 3 as an image of dynamics. It is an image of the continuous creation of life, deeper than the objects of this worldly existence that so captivate our attention. Figure 6 applies this to our lived experience of being a person. It shows humankind as a triune image of the one living God, not as a tri-*partite* creature, but including relatedness as an integrally dynamic feature of our integrated humanity. Only by stepping back into an analytical perspective on life can relatedness come to seem mentally other than that. Justice is about maintaining this relational dynamic of 'public good', while somehow balancing it with the personal diversification of individuals that is essential for *adaptable* living in a changing environment. The *mutual inter-dependence* of the public good is displayed in several diagrams: conversational orientation (Figure 8—the core diagram of the 3+1 model of personal development), communion (Figure 12, Chapter 6), and the Celtic way of networking triquetra together into patterns (Figure 4, Chapter 5). By this integrating dynamic, humanity may thrive. In its perfection this is a picture of the kingdom of heaven.

In Figure 6 the central space of the triquetra is continuously created by triune interaction. It represents the 'inner heart' of a human being, pre-conscious, moved by relatedness to emotional responses, some of which preparations appear in conscious mind as intuition. The conscious mind of course is moved by many other stimuli than these three 'orientating categories' (Figure 16, Chapter 6), but order appears among the potential chaos of stimuli and memories because triune principles build *conversational orientation.* When orientating towards exploring with others the justice needed for the public good, awareness of the three orientating categories can help to keep that balance: [a] material bodily preparations for action or withdrawal (patterning the ordered form or structure of life); [b] decisions about action or withdrawal (changing responsively in mercy as the soul of community); and [c] giving out social messages in a variety of ways (being sensitive to the relational spirit that is moving others).

Now, the image of justice that I mentioned earlier maps onto the Figure 6 triquetra. Remember, each of the four spaces is a category of thoughts about life, upon which the person can reflect and also make decisions for action. By adding an ethical 'category' name-label to each of these three *orientating categories* of thoughts, plus the fourth for the central integrating space of personal wholeness (3+1 model), a balanced view of living in justice can be described. Ethical living, acting justly, will thus map onto personal wholeness. These four labels are added in Figure 17.

In the central space, the state of full integration, 'First do no harm'. This maxim is widely accepted as a balanced starting place for decisions. It is called 'non-maleficence'. Of course there will be discussions about what counts as harm, but most would agree that once people's value systems are understood it is wise to respect them.

The second ethical principle of choices is: 'Do good to others if possible'. This maxim is called, 'beneficence'. Again, extensive discussions could follow about what counts as 'good' for different individuals, but in general this ethical principle is fulfilled by forgiveness and blessing, so that all involved in a situation can set each other free to develop as human beings. This principle maps onto the relatedness aspect of human nature, the spiritual influence of one person upon another, the common good, or the public good. In some cultures the rights or standards of communities, tribes or families is considered weightier in decisions than the desires of individuals for personal development. Globalisation is bringing many challenges to such cultures, making it urgent now to explore how to keep a balance during times of change, one that honours the values of the old collectives while allowing individuals to adapt to the new technologies with their freedom of information.

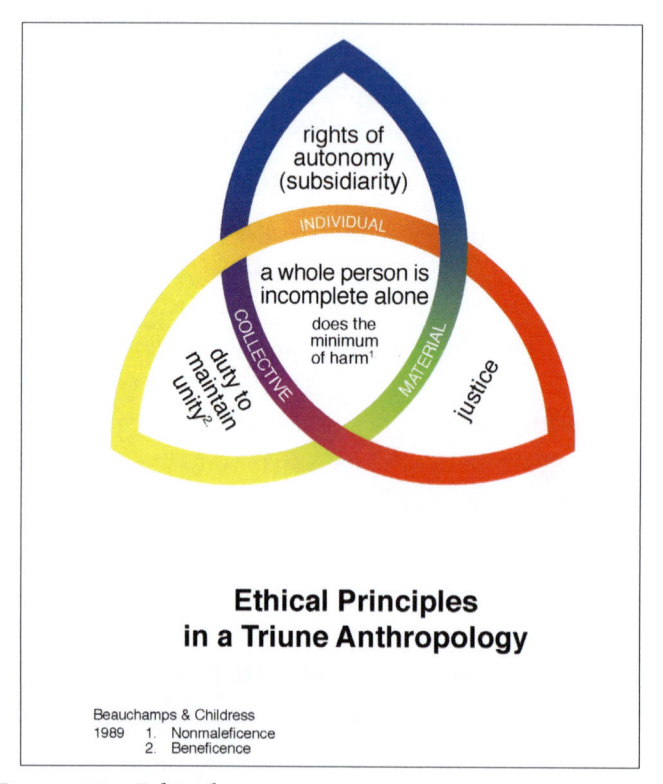

Ethical Principles in a Triune Anthropology

- rights of autonomy (subsidiarity) — INDIVIDUAL
- a whole person is incomplete alone — does the minimum of harm[1]
- duty to maintain unity[2] — COLLECTIVE
- justice — MATERIAL

Beauchamps & Childress 1989
1. Nonmaleficence
2. Beneficence

Figure 17—Ethical categories map onto triune principles

The third ethical principle is called 'respect for autonomy'. This is the principle most in tension with beneficence. Autonomy is ideally the state where a relational person is recognised to have understanding about his or her responsibilities and duties in a community or family, and simultaneously has a capacity to make informed choices about how he or she fulfils those roles. There is a concept of human will that is not always in rebellion, but which can be tuned to the common good. Individuals can make autonomous decisions how best to fulfil their roles. This ethical principle maps onto the change corner of triune wholeness, with the living soul of an adapting individual who has free will. To respect and honour that capacity for autonomy enables human diversity and culture to flourish, making a whole culture or tribe or family *adaptable* in changing life circumstances. However, the ideal is seldom lived. This principle of ethical respect for autonomy assumes that people do choose to behave reasonably for the common good. 'Individualism' has flourished in some societies, where people may separate away from each other and advance their own interests without concern for the collective, and even to its detriment. Innovative ways to fulfil duties gives way under these circumstances to individuals making a claim to have *rights* over against each other. Extensive discussions can follow. Where is the reasonable interface to be lived between human rights and social duties? The notion of 'subsidiarity' can be helpful paired with autonomy. Subsidiarity recognises the multi-layered nature of human systems, family nested in neighbourhood nested in city or state for example. Individual autonomy and rights can be granted at one level, while duties prevail at another. Extensive discussions can follow, and they will probably be highly charged emotionally.

The fourth ethical principle is called the 'principle of justice', and it concerns the equitable distribution of material resources appropriate to each person's needs for survival or development. Thus, in ethical systems language, justice is a term that maps onto the patterned structure and material form of personal wholeness. Fair opportunity to have needs met materially has to be balanced against the rationing of scarce resources. Extensive discussions can follow.

In all these discussions where different viewpoints must be

aired and compared reasonably, members of the emotionally intelligent Christian Royal Priesthood need to find (also) a non-partisan prayer stance, to invite in by triune prayer the wisdom and intelligent inspiration of Holy Spirit during conflict and disagreement. What would you stand to lose if you chose to be *non-partisan* during these extensive discussions, adopting a role to point out and name the hidden values that are moving both sides in a disagreement? What hidden losses (unnamed values) could generate sudden reactions of outrage in you, unexpectedly, that could de-rail the peace process if you could not wisely manage them? Do you value triune prayer enough to let the kingdom of God come on earth, as it is in heaven?

This fourth area, of *material justice*, is the one that I would like to focus upon now before moving on to the next line of the Disciples' Prayer. If God's kingdom is to come 'on earth', we need to have a prayerfully active understanding of the material of 'The Land'. Otherwise we shall always be frustrated if searching how to act justly, and with mercy and humility, when faced with unfair distribution of resources.

As a help to maintain ethical balance in the years to come, hear the words of poetry in prayer from King David's final place of wholeness. His last words are recorded in 2 Samuel 23:2-7. Verses 2-4:

> *The Spirit of the Lord spoke through me;*
>   *His word was on my tongue.*
> *The God of Israel spoke,*
>   *the Rock of Israel said to me:*
> *"When one rules over men in righteousness,*
>   *when he rules in the fear of God,*
> *he is like the light of morning at sunrise*
>   *on a cloudless morning,*
> *like the brightness after rain*
> *that brings grass from the earth."*

The Land
... on earth, as it is in Heaven.

We humans are made of dust. We are small clouds of dust blown up from the land that have become sufficiently organised to be consciously aware of each other. Each of us is a living, feeling, thinking, on-going, moving miracle. It is nothing short of an awesome mystery that two piles of dust, you and I via some communication technology, can converse with one another, each with our different identities knowing or feeling that we understand each other, or that perhaps that we misunderstand each other and may by conversation work out how we think differently.

The dust of land is organised into you and me. We are raised up for a season, like grass, and return to the earth in a time-frame that is our own accumulation of experiences. From there we may know resurrection at the call of one who loves us—we cannot be sure, can we, except that we have been told by one who knows us? We are raised up also from a father's loins, through a mother's womb, and yet the dust we gather on earth is God's land. We borrow it. We build with it, and we return it, and it all happens by the same *triune principles of organisation* that have generated the grace substantially in the living God out of which even that dust itself is continuously created from within.

We humans share in that capacity too, amazingly, to generate grace with others and extend it out to transform life.

Psalm 93 is a psalm of praise that sees the world as God's throne, the world for all eternity established by God's reigning majesty. The seas are mentioned, which have lifted up their pounding waves as a voice. They are a powerfully poetic picture of the waters of Genesis, the grace of God moving by the Spirit as Creation. Even as Creation heaps up, its waves cannot remove God's strength, or shake those statutes of a holy God that undergird Creation. And yet, the awesome truth is that God has set among his People the capacity to relate in the waters of grace in such a way that we can become *co-creators of life* with God. Equally awesome is that so many people reject that offer. They prefer to remain blind, and to plot and scheme in their own small huddles, as if they are invisible to God. This shows a fundamental lack of understanding about the activity and character of God's Holy Spirit.

In Chapter 5 I explain that the triquetra shown in Figures 3 and 4 can be an image also of a photon of light, a quantum of energy at a range of wavelengths, visible or not, that entangle and make moving networks as atoms, molecules, dust, land, food, human living bodies, manufactured environments, spaceships even, and so on. All of Creation is built by triune principles shaping substantial grace out of the loving inter-relatedness among eternal sub-states of one living God, who lives beyond all categories of existence.

Creation is movement in shared transformation—life. The human mind is generated from memorised patterns within the material brain that reactivate, and those patterns reintegrate repeatedly. This re-integrating process stitches together continuously a conscious and orientated picture of life in the present moment. The orientation of this picture can be disrupted by drugs, alcohol, anxiety, injury, dementia, and so on. The triune process for this, shown in Figure 6, is embedded in the material brain, as shown in Figure 7, within the three main association areas that generate impressions of space, time and real presence.

Now, the 'reality' of this mental picture of life has to be continually checked out by comparison with sensory inputs from our material environment. In Chapter 5 I introduced the double triquetra, Figure 8, as the core diagram of the 3+1 model of personal development, displaying *conversational orientation*. Consider this possibility... What if this core diagram displays not only transformational conversations between two people, and between a person and their Living God? Consider what it means if the double triquetra displays also the relationship between a person and his or her material environment. We are dust.

Extend this now to the six connected triquetra showing Communion in Chapter 6, Figure 12. That Chapter is entitled 'The Grace to Reconcile'. Here is a better picture of the wholeness of real life, of shalom. Move your finger along the lines and let your thoughts wonder with it. The communion demonstrated in these integrating movements is an ongoing conversation between God (one of those triquetra) and two people (two of the other triquetra), but all three of these connected through the other three intervening triquetra between them. These other three triquetra represent the land that has emerged from substantial grace, as quanta of energy entangling into material life. All of this, persons and land, is mutually transforming and inter-dependent on God's loving grace; all displays God's majesty enthroned in the glory of Creation.

Honour grows where people grieve constructively

Humankind is made out of dust, which God fashioned first as a manifestation of God's love. I think we should respect it, and be grateful for its fruitfulness. Humankind relates to God and to each other *through* the dust, through the land and the fruitfulness of its products. I think we should be gardeners of it, tilling and tending it with loving care—together. But humankind's minds make it more complicated than that.

Human minds may feed on heart-level jealousy and greed and ambition. Reacting to unnamed losses with unrecognised grieving twists naturally ethical behaviour into selfishness, shame and violence. The meek cower and appeal as victims. The land gets laid to waste, or is exploited and driven to exhaustion. We relate through the land, because we are the land. It reveals our hearts.

When mentally stuck in any of the three primary analytical perspectives on life (Figures 9, 10 and 11), and self-affirming the resulting human limits by associating with other like-minded people in a restricted group mentality (Figures 13, 14 and 15), the human mind separates from 'the land'. These analytical perspectives create the philosophical 'mind-body problem' by disengaging mind and matter. The problem dissipates like the morning mist on a cloudless day, however, when people rediscover truly *triune communion*.

Mind and matter are both 'triune systems', organising life using identical *principles of organisation*. The one going on with memories in the brain is constantly compared and checked out against the other going on materially in the scientifically physical and social environment of the body. In such a set of circumstances, mind and matter run in parallel exchange with each other, the one reflecting the other more or less accurately. However, when the mind drifts off into its own self-organising process of analytical organisation, the two triune systems disengage… "Hey, day-dreamer, wake up!"

I call this model of the human mind 'triune systems in parallel exchange' (or the TSIPEX model for short), which I shall explain more in the next chapter on 'daily bread'.

When stuck day-dreaming in any of the analytical perspectives, people will have to pray in hope that God's kingdom will come and 'break in', that God's will *will* be done on what seems to be the earth in this perspective, as it is in heaven. The path to overcome the fictitious divide, however, is through triune prayer, opening the door into the mystical grace and truth of material, ethical, communion.

The mental separation of heaven and earth can thus be reconciled and released into kingdom living as we choose to build bridges of grace. Honour grows where people grieve constructively as they leave behind playing with these analytical perspectives and their own self-absorbing interests. Jesus' honour grew astronomically when, from the torture and anguish of that cross, he prayed, "Father forgive, because they do no know what they are doing."

As we in communion learn to do more of that forgiving and blessing, honour will grow for those who take a risk to extend grace, breaking through previous cultural behaviours, to build a just and merciful future in humility with others around their and our named values.

Chapter 9
Give us this day our daily bread

More for myself

Many people in their preferred analytical perspectives believe that a great divide exists between the physical material bits of this earth (or the particles of matter), and the spiritual nature of inter-relating life. I have introduced the alternative idea that people's human and divine natures meet in their heart-level experience of emotion, as they prepare to interact with others physically, and with the living Word of a triune God, here in the eternal-now.

People's emotional inner preparations enter their consciousness as feelings, which make peoples' hidden values active so that they can be reasoned about. They reveal peoples' soul connections moving them with others and with treasured objects. By the same logic, to develop a soul connection with the Word of God makes emotional experience sacred. The feelings then inform and develop a human being's divine nature, by choosing to welcome spiritually the indwelling of Holy Spirit. These parallel and potentially mutually interactive conversations *enable* people to reason about God's guidance for action in and for the world God so loves.

When Jesus taught his disciples to pray regularly, 'Give us this day our daily bread', he spiritually touched the human tendency to separate the physical and the spiritual. Jesus, through this daily prayer, opens a heart-level way to mentally reconcile and heal these two separated mind-frames. As we shall see, they join in one 'kingdom living'.

Yes, of course, the bread mentioned is the material harvest from the land, which we feed upon physically in our human nature to meet our bodily needs for energy, growth and healing. Equally this bread is Jesus, as the John the Apostle tells us in his Gospel's Chapter 6. Jesus said (v35) 'I am the bread of life'. The preceding miracle of the feeding of the five thousand prophetically reveals the truth and nature of his subsequent teaching (v33), 'For the bread of God is he who comes down from heaven and gives life to the world.'

That miracle reveals the awesome integration of physical and spiritual that is the kingdom of God come on earth. Would it have been an emotional experience to have been sitting on those hills in groups, with the disciples passing between and handing out more and more and more? Did that emotion get in the way of the miracle, or was it part of the transformative power of that miracle? What do you stand to lose if you let go of the idea that emotion is only soulish and a distracting part of your physical human nature? Surely the awe and reverence with which you then might regard Jesus is sacred emotion? Are you worried that it might sully the purity of the spiritual kingdom that you might grieve on recognising how you had been taken in by the popularized view that matter comes first? Or when grief turns to joy, and celebration fills the air, can we come closer to living heaven on earth without doubting God's greater strength… as triune statutes, and holiness? We are together in this! This is Family trying to come to terms with mystery revealed.

But of course, to re-state the point made in the first Part of this book, Jesus knew that peoples' minds are often ruled by their stomachs. A full stomach feels good, just as owning and possessing a fat portion of land feels good. Security, and feelings of insecurity, then generate heart-level messages that get sent subtly, or even bluntly, to others: 'Keep away; I do not want to share this. I want more for myself.'

Sharing the land

"Give us this day our daily bread."

This transitional line of the Disciple's Prayer picks up the theme of God's will, that which is *to be done* if the kingdom of God is to come on earth. It picks up that first part of Micah's prophetic statement about God's will—you should act justly and love mercy and walk humbly before your God. Try to picture 'receiving *my* daily bread' from one of the deacons first appointed in the early Church. This mental snapshot makes a statement about what it feels like to receive from one who acts justly. However, I can only recognise the justice in the way it was done when I see others also receiving their daily bread.

I shall show in this and the next two chapters how links exist between the Disciple's Prayer and Micah's prophecy: in this chapter linking the bread of life with acting justly, in the next linking forgiveness with loving mercy, and thirdly linking temptation-evil with walking humbly before your God. Like light scattered through a diamond, Micah's prophetic utterance is visible throughout the prayer that Jesus taught his disciples to pray. We need to sell everything we think we own, and buy into this prayer to get rich!

So let's look again at acting justly in relation to the dust of the land, and the fruit of the land that God asks us to share—no, *instructs* us to share. In your mind's eye, try to recall and picture the image of communion, which is six triquetra dancing in a circle (Figure 12). Try to recall how I described selecting any one of the triquetra to represent Christ as God immanent with us. Two of the other triquetra in that dance represent you and another human being, who are separated by (or *connected through*, if you can think conversationally) a triquetra that represents a quantum of energy. Three triquetra in the ring thus represent quanta of energy. The two that arise next to the immanent God *connect* with humankind on either side. They represent how God breathed life into the earth, transforming 'it' by Word so that humankind became a living form;

male and female God made them (Genesis 1:27).

Now, let's fill out the picture a bit more. All quanta of energy transform as an entangling network in God's substantial grace. Try mentally extending the triquetra patterns out from the three that represent quanta, like the extended networks in Figure 4 on the Celtic cross. These complex patterns of interconnecting quanta and photons are the moving, visible, material universe. This is the land. This is the dust out of which you and your other have emerged as living bodies. Through this dust, through the land and its consciously wilful people, God's will and your embedded responses are revealed, prophetically, to all. God does not speak directly into the mind. God speaks through the emotionally interconnected heart, where your physical and spiritual natures meet, and from there up into your mind, translated into a language that you can understand.

Who owns the dust of your body? Is the way you shape and decorate your home an extension of you in the world? Is your body a focus of your rights as an individual, or is it the means by which you fulfil your duties to the community? What does it mean for your body to be a temple of the Holy Spirit? Perhaps you might want to do an Emotional Logic card pattern to see before your eyes the complex emotional states that will undoubtedly arise within you as you dwell on your response to these questions. That card pattern will reveal the tensioning of your inner heart that is preparing you, even now, to act and react through Creation to your neighbour and to God. It could be the starting place to learn how to turn unpleasant grief emotions into the energy of movement to adjust constructively with others. That is acting justly, while embedded in the land.

This is an 'ecological view of the human being'. Analytical mind frames may give a mental impression that we are somehow separated from the earth; or able to use it for our self-interested purposes; or that the earth is merely an illusion flaring up out of our pride and that we should let go of it and concentrate on purifying our soul. Any of these could break the connection between the two human beings in the image of communion. But all of these are partial truths only. In the triune ecological view, the dust exists embedded in the substantial grace of God who is beyond all categories of existence. Out of this dust, you, I and others are formed, and we transform this dust together, and the fruitfulness of the earth that is given each day for our shared purposes. The illusions that come with pride can be overcome, by purifying our hearts so that we act justly and love mercy and walk humbly in the land before our sustaining God.

What should we call this ecological view of the human being and the land? Each triquetra is an image of a *triune system*—with its own form, change and relatedness at any and every level of Creation. (The transcendent creator God, however, is not a system. Jesus suffered for our sakes to be born into Creation's many systems as the immanent God.) These systems of the created world interact. They exchange information with each other, changing their form (transforming) through their relatedness. In conversational orientation, shown in Figure 8, two triune systems each have their internal dynamics. They interact, however, in a 'parallel exchange' of a conversation (Latin: *con* = with; *verso* = I change). So if one triune system is a human being, and the other extended triune system is the earth of their 'field', then the parallel exchange of man and earth would look like a human being tilling the earth and preparing the ground to take seed. If the land is treated justly, and loved mercifully, and not exploited selfishly or fought across with neighbours, it will respond with increased fruitfulness. The information the land returns by its fruitfulness tells the human being whether he or she is 'getting it right'. This ecological view of the human being could therefore, as for the body-mind model, be called 'triune systems in parallel exchange'.

Each triune system has its own systemic existence running in parallel; each is self-organising, in accord with the same triune principles; each is thus *able* to interact *with* the other.

(This overcomes the philosophical problems of dualisms, and of monism.)

The powerful beauty of triune systems in parallel exchange is that this ecological approach solves the body-mind problem by establishing relational grace as the deeper spiritual reality behind both matter and mind. The solution to a mental construct problem is thus one that directly addresses the *ethical balance* needed for healthy living. The solution to the body-mind problem is found by personal development of a just, loving and humble character.

And there is more. An important door is opened for health and social welfare promotion by moving on from an atomistic way of understanding dust and matter to a triune quantum network view that is based in shared grace. Triune systems in parallel exchange can give a constructive account of how peoples' mental worlds can become *disconnected* from the material world of their shared existence with others. Figure 7 shows the three association areas of the brain that each are constructing, ordering and orientating our sensory inputs from 'the world system' (and integrating them with memories). The connections *within* each of these generate different patterns that we know as space, time and real presence. Infinitely subtle variations of brain activity can shift the balance of connections *between* these association areas, still consistent with triune principles of integration. The resulting mental pictures of self in the world can thus be vastly different, as previously explained. Two people, therefore, adopting different analytical viewpoints can each be convinced they see reality, but still have conflicting mental impressions of an identical event they have witnessed. Are they both disconnected from reality? Or are they both triune systems in parallel exchange through God's grace-filled reality of entangled quanta? Perhaps each could approach God's reality with more understanding and awe if they joined in conversation with each other, in 'parallel exchange'? They could argue about details, and disagree about facts, and their frustration and disappointment in their relationship will set grief on the move, and without wisdom this may ignite into a blaze; but approached wisely, this conversation in parallel exchange may equally well lead to mutual understanding of their inter-dependence to see truth. Out of that recognition of each other as different may arise an awareness of the balance of justice and a love of mercy and a more humble walk with God.

This disconnection of mind and matter does not mean that either one or the other must be a figment of imagination. In a 'triune systems in parallel exchange' view of an ecological human being, they are both real systems; both working according to the same triune principles; therefore there can be different levels of matching and mismatching between two triune systems that are in parallel exchange. The important feature is to return to conversation with those who see life differently having spent some time in curiosity adopting and listening to various analytical perspectives.

As I mentioned before, I call it the TSIPEX model of an ecological human being (Triune Systems in Parallel Exchange). The parallel exchange starts with God's land and our human identities; it goes on to acting justly with others to manage the fruitfulness of the land by which God, the immanent God of justice, gives us our daily bread.

Priestly farming and gardening

I am indebted here to the various authors who have contributed to an important volume called, *The Land Cries Out*. It is produced by the Jerusalem-based Musalaha reconciliation project, which brings together Messianic Jews and Arab Christians who live alongside each other in that troubled land of Israel-Palestine. The volume is a well of resources to explore, working as far as is possible towards a shared, or perhaps a diversely enriched, theology of the land.

When you next pray, "Our Father, give us this day our daily bread", think of your equivalent neighbours where *you* live. Which ones do you have difficulties building bridges of grace to share that bread with? It is so easy to go to a nearby supermarket and buy bread from the shelf, forgetting that the wheat or rye from which it is baked was grown somewhere, by someone. That loaf is in your hands through tiers of sharing. You can be part of its distribution, breaking the bread and giving it with reverence to those who are in need.

In a Zimbabwean village we visited on the edge of Lake Kariba, the poor Tonga villagers bring flour as their offering on a Sunday morning. During the church service two women bake this into the loaves that are shared during their communion celebration. Whenever you drink water purified as wine or as any other safe source, consider, what sharing process are *you* becoming a part of? And if you were to reflect so, what do you stand to lose in your enjoyment of a full stomach? Is there a spiritual reality of grace behind a prayer of thanksgiving, or is it just a form of ritual words? If you can name your hidden losses here, and try to manage them constructively, then your honour will grow, and qualify you as a part of a Royal Priesthood for others.

In that volume, *The Land Cries Out,* Phillip Ben-Shmuel brings to our attention some important words in the Hebrew Old Testament that Martin Buber saw as important for the Hebrew nation's relationship with the land. Try to make a 'gear-shift' in your reading to tease out the wonderful detail presented here. Previously pointed out is the close connection of the name Adam for humankind (male and female) and adamah, Hebrew for the earth or soil.

> ... the verbs commonly used to describe the actions of the Priests and Levites in the sanctuary ('avad and shamar) are the same verbs that describe Adam's mission in Eden—to serve it, and to keep it (Gen 2:15; Num 3:7-8; 8:26; 18:1-7). 'Avad is the verb used also to describe the tilling of the soil (adamah); and so, the Israelite who tills the soil may be described as serving the land. The 'avodah (worship) of YWHW in the sanctuary is thus deeply connected to the

'avodah (tilling) of the land: they are both a service and a divine mission. [p147]

Thus 'tilling and keeping the land' are parallel concepts to 'priestly service and guardianship' of God's People. Jesus gave his life into the land for us. At the ritual of Holy Communion we remember and reverence that. We might do so also in a moment of reflection, in grace-filled connection with Jesus by Holy Spirit, before we share a meal.

Certainly Christians need to gather to feed together on the Jesus' Words as the Body and Bread of Life. That in-gathering prepares our inner hearts, keeping in the forefront of our minds the need to build the kingdom of God justly here on earth. From that moment on, however, the Royal Priesthood turns outwards to face the wider community of the world, to serve and guard them through extending those ligands of personal 'communion'. If Christianity were to become just about feeding the priesthood, or the ritual ministration of sacraments, Christianity would fall into exactly the same problems for which the Pharisaic Priesthood was so heavily criticised by the prophets, and by Jesus. As a Royal Priesthood, 'positioned for blessing' does not mean fed enough to feel like a blessing. It means being conversationally orientated to all nations to serve and guard and bless them. It means being positioned to bless from God's House of Prayer for All Nations, which exists now in the hearts of its Royal Priesthood.

This type of human-divine love for others who cry out to receive their daily bread will almost certainly include grief and pain. Peoples' reactions and behaviour will not be the same as yours. Priestly counsel is to till and keep peoples' hearts, to break up the hardened, downtrodden and grieving earth so that the seed of the kingdom of God can find good soil to root in and flourish. For such a farming or gardening role, Godly emotional intelligence is vital. The fruitfulness of the land depends on careful input from farmers, and in just the same way the growth of the people depends on prayerful input from Priests. Otherwise the priestly counsel will go no further than the schismatic effect of belief in ideas rather than in persons, or the irrational demand for faith rather than the informed choice to love. This is, however, the setting in which triune prayer, in the Spirit for a relationship *between two other persons* in a non-partisan way, is the prayer of love that the emotionally intelligent Church can uniquely live. It is the emotional intelligence of the Christian who has come to realize that it is much more important to be in relationship than in the right.

The Shared Meal

Give us this day our daily bread.

God distributes gifts unequally but *fairly*, according to peoples' needs for the kingdom tasks set before them. Our experience of Godly justice may be obscured, however, by human jealousy and greed. But in the big system of Creation, the existence of injustice, jealously and greed feeds back into the tensions of the whole system, and re-appears as a Godly call on those who know grace. This Royal Priesthood, who can change their routines in response to a Godly call, can now act in time to distribute blessing justly according to diverse needs. This distribution of blessings, of bread even, is a service delegated to deacons in many church fellowships. It is, however, a delegated role of a Royal Priesthood that lives for *all* in their communities.

The shared meal of 'communion' in a church fellowship is intended to be preceded, as expressed in Paul's inspired 1 Corinthians 11 instructions, by a time of personal reflection and of inter-personal choice, purposefully to overcome divisions and to bring good order into the church fellowship by distributing food justly among the diversity of people found there. It is the ideal setting in which triune prayer by the deaconate could overcome the focus on individuals as they present their needs, and increase the focus on relational community. Praying in a non-partisan way for the relationship between two people who are in different factions could influence both to think, and perhaps to act differently with their bread. It is a form of prayer that does not show favour to either the poor or the rich; both have their needs for personal development, perhaps with regard to each other. It is, a form of prayer that can lead widows and orphans to find spiritual fathers and mothers in the Church, and for spiritual parents to adopt sons and daughters into Christ.

In this there is Godly justice, in collaboration for kingdom growth where there is diversity. In building these bridges of grace there is a renewable source of honour, because people can now grieve constructively, and find new ways to the joy of Godly love.

So, the prayer is not, give me my daily bread to meet my needs. It is our Father, give *us* this day our daily bread, so that like you we may act justly, with your Word growing in our hearts, to cultivate and distribute the fruitfulness of *your* land.

Chapter 10
Forgiveness

And forgive us our trespasses, as we forgive those who trespass against us

I have been shocked on some Emotional Logic training courses for the wider community at the strength of feeling, amounting to outrage, that many people seem to feel against the notion of forgiveness. It is perceived by many as weak, religious, giving in, dangerous, letting people off the hook and encouraging bad behaviour. A significantly large number of people genuinely feel that revenge is a reasonable and preferable alternative. On one course of thirty people, I asked if any of the participants would describe how they had felt on an occasion when they had been forgiven. I had anticipated an opportunity to teach about new beginnings. There was utter silence for an uncomfortably long gap, before a man said sheepishly, "Well it depends, if you have ever done anything wrong."

It seems to me now that it is extremely difficult for anyone to consider forgiving another person unless they have themselves felt the release and freedom of having been forgiven. This, of course, is what Christians call salvation, the realisation that a living God is not going to condemn out of crushing authority, but rather give good news to the poor, heal the broken hearted, release those who feel captive, open the eyes of those who are blind to life, and declare God's favour on those who do not deserve reward, but are now nevertheless given an opportunity to grow into the likeness of this loving creator God. That growth occurs not as single feed on a 'take-away' meal, but by continuously choosing to build a living relationship with the One whose love allows such liberty to grow. That connection is grace freely given. The experience of connecting into the 'freedom to grow' of the kingdom of God is called forgiveness.

Grace moved by love thus has a creative power to heal and restore life. Because the outcome is an opportunity to choose 'personal growth', the strength and resilience of this power seems deceptively gentle. Forgiveness is, in truth however, an act of spiritual war against the sucking vacuum of darkness. The choice to forgive opens the door for the glory of God to shine into peoples' lives, restoring a fullness that the darkness cannot understand. Until people have experienced what it is to be forgiven, they remain powerless, lost in darkness, incapable of themselves forgiving others. Christians need to forgive others for being lost, by extending grace. By doing so, a rolling wave of light can spread, started by Jesus while nailed to that cross, that we continue, setting people free from the traps of their destructive, shameful and confused feelings. Once set free, they have a lifetime of choices now to make. From my point of view, as a Christian, I extend an arm to the Holy Spirit and say, "Over to You!" My job is to keep the grace connection.

I find the old psychological test of 'the glass of water' useful at this point. Are you an optimist, or a pessimist? Is this glass half full of water, or half empty? The same mental attitude applies when making the choice between forgiveness and revenge. (Yes, even after all these years, and after writing about forgiveness, I still have to make that choice daily myself to actively live forgiveness!) Is the outcome that I seek a half full one, which fills the dark emptiness with a kingdom potential for new and shared growth? Or, do I seek a half empty outcome, into which my power for revenge spreads to prove that I exist, temporarily? Given the choice, I tend to go for shared growth, and for fullness of life. But it is a choice. God will never remove the fact of choice from the freedom of life.

How does forgiveness fit in the Emotional Logic of adapting?

Forgiveness is the giant leap from feeling angry about loss, to accepting that I am powerless to take action in a way that can restore every part of the situation.

Anger in its pure, Godly form is a passionate urge to engage with others or the world despite danger to *prevent* the loss of something or someone valued. When focused on self-advancement, however, anger can aggressively shape the personal energy to take *control* of situations, which is a corruption of its Godly purpose. This corruption of Godly emotion in changing situations can follow when a multitude of hidden losses each start their own loss reactions, so that one course of *action* angrily energised cannot achieve everything desired, and also prevent everything undesired. Forgiveness is needed to soften the effects of 'treading on toes' while trying to achieve what seems most important at that moment. That is why I feel that the old translation 'trespass' is better than 'sin' in the newer translations of the Disciple's Prayer. 'Forgive us our trespasses' more accurately conveys the accidental or incidental nature of treading beyond personal boundaries while trying to manage an overwhelming or distracted situation.

Forgiveness therefore involves naming one's own and other peoples' losses in a changing situation, and choosing to make amends where possible to re-make 'just relationship' with mercy and humility. This is where Emotional Logic can be so powerful to help the process of forgiving, when situations have seemed so overwhelming, and where peoples' reactions have been perhaps devastating. Emotional Logic breaks forgiveness down into small achievable steps, which can then set people free progressively to grow once again, rather than pull each other down with vengeful acts.

Each step in this forgiveness process is focused around a named, previously hidden loss or worry about possible loss. The choice to forgive is a choice to remain neither in Denial, nor in Anger about that named loss, or in any of the other grief emotions that might be used to fuel revenge, but instead to 'sling your anchor forwards' into Acceptance (or assertive Bargaining) and drag yourself there. By choosing to do so for that named loss, you can release all the potential growth energy of grief emotions for its more constructive Godly purposes.

This Emotional Logic way to understand forgiveness works when it is applied to individual named losses, one at a time, not to the whole situations that have sparked off all its multiple loss reactions. That is the key, the secret to forgiveness's power to change the quality of life. It is an open secret that you can share with others, as you help them to name what they have lost, or what they are worried they might lose, and then name the forward-looking aspect of life to which they could put that grief-adjustment energy. Forgiveness is not just letting go of revenge, and being thus diminished in power by the situation; forgiveness is a choice to grow stronger through the situation, and thus to improve the overall context of life. That is how honour grows when people choose to grieve constructively.

"But what about justice?" people might say. "You can't just leave people to blunder on through life like that. They need punishing!" Forgiveness, as described, clearly does not include approval of bad behaviour, excusing it, pardoning it, denying it, or (in fact) forgetting it. Forgiveness is moving on from a situation, by disempowering the capacity of its memory to distort your relationships now and in eternity. All of those other transactions and more can still occur *if they are wise for personal development*. And here we must clarify the purpose of Godly punishment. Is it for mere retribution (revenge to 'balance the books'), or is Godly punishment a way to publicly restore the likeness of God's fairness, mercy and humility in those who have trespassed across personal boundaries? There is no doubt in my mind that Godly justice is 'restorative justice', restoring light into the relationships of life; while humankind falls repeatedly into the darkness when using punishment to recover only an individual's or a society's sense of power, perhaps as a surprise or sneak attack for retribution.

That said, to choose to forgive does need a picture of life that is greater than the individual. The choice to accept that my own power has limits has to be matched by my belief that 'the Big System' in which I belong can in time bring a perpetrator of injustice to realise the effects of what they have done. That is the purpose of Godly punishment, to extend a blind blunderer's vision, restoring sight to the spiritually blind who have no sense of belonging, from which point of enlightenment a restorative process of learning and personal development into connection can begin.

Until a perpetrator has reached that point of understanding, however, Emotional Logic adds a fourth type of 'safe place' to its original three (physical place, state of mind, and relationship). It adds 'safe distance'. The Emotional Logic approach to forgiveness separates away reconciliation, seeing that process of re-connection as an optional step that may or may not be wise for the various people's personal development as they move on from a situation. For example, a victim of abuse does not need to reconcile with an abuser in order to set that person free psychologically into *their potential* for growth by repentance. Safe distance during that time of development can still be grace-filled, however. If the hope of the afflicted person is for the perpetrator's awareness to grow and for the personal development of a changed heart, then grace fills the darkness of the gap with the glory of God. Forgiveness based in grace thus releases oneself from the oppression of memories. It creates the conditions where reconciliation could occur, should that be wise and achievable. Lack of reconciliation, however, does not in itself negate the value of forgiveness.

Likewise, it is possible to have truly forgiven others and self and God in a situation, and then to find oneself again grieving and hateful. This simply means that another hidden loss has emerged from the memories, and it too needs submitting to the same process of getting onto the Growth Cycle for the kingdom of God. Forgiveness is a repeated choice to sling one's anchor into Acceptance and drag oneself on from the earlier Stepping Stones of grieving without dissipating your energy in worthless revenge and rumination.

The same principle applies when people feel aggrieved or let down by God. Having perceived God to have acted unfairly, through eyes that see only the overwhelming complexities of life from a limited viewpoint, you or I may come to feel we need to forgive God. Breaking this down into named losses (my values), and trying to broaden my picture of God as Father from the different viewpoints we have earlier discussed, can make even that transaction of forgiveness more achievable and humane and maturing.

Problems for Christians with forgiving

Christians of any tradition are at risk of misunderstanding and taking the spiritual power out of forgiveness. As soon as there is a hint in a Christian's thinking that Christianity is about being 'nice', or that in order not to be aggressive or angry Christians have to be passive, there is a problem. Christianity and forgiveness are far more assertive to liberate captives than that!

Christ being 'led like a lamb before his shearers' was not being passive! He had emerged from his self-review in Gethsemane and was assertively submitted to his Father's love, strongly enough to 'stand having done all' and confront evil for us and for our salvation. There is a strange movement among both Christian and secular society that says all emotion is bad, and anger in particular, and that it is good character to get rid of all emotion, anger in particular. I hope I have confronted that unhelpful attitude enough already, so here I need only point out that Christians are at risk of pretending to forgive for the sake of appearing free from unpleasant emotion, so to avoid criticism or intrusion by church leaders, or even by God.

Forgiveness is the giant leap from anger about loss to Acceptance and through that to an active Growth Cycle. It cannot be a genuine leap without first honestly engaging with and balancing on the Anger Stepping Stone, recognising with outrage the injustice of the situation. It is far more comfortable sometimes to avoid the issue, and put it instead into Denial, only saying "I have forgiven..." Of course, the way to tell whether something has been truly accepted or denied is to note what happens when the issue is recalled. In true Acceptance, the issue will be recalled with a still sadness, which may be intense, and may even recur throughout a lifetime, but the person does not have to 'live in the sadness'. It is an honest statement of enduring value. If the issue has been denied, however, then when recalled it will bring with it the more active and unpleasant emotions of shock, anger, guilt, despair, and so on. This is the situation in which whirlpools of emotion can re-activate, and vengeful aggressive thoughts take over the mind. A bit more spiritual work needs doing.

By the same mechanism, when Christians try to counteract their aggressive thoughts with a cultivated passivity, the life of the Church ebbs away. Standing in the face of adversity demands of Christians their assertive energy, their tough love, and their enduring choice for grace, from the strong platform on which we can bless those who curse us. That is the freedom that is won by forgiveness: when appropriate to frolic like released lambs while justice, mercy and humility are restored by Holy Spirit within, and then when kingdom life is threatened once again to choose firmly to stand, by Holy Spirit within, to claim God's kingdom over the land. If we do not assertively forgive others (and ourselves?) as we make our stand, then Holy Spirit cannot strengthen us adequately from within for the battle that is won only as love endures, as Christ forgave from the cross.

Standing as sons, not orphans

Trespass across 'personal boundaries' within the kingdom of God is rather like the situation in a community. Does a fence in a neighbourhood separate two peoples' gardens, or is it where their two gardens meet? As a meeting place, the owners who are responsible for the growth and maintenance of each garden can talk across the boundary and appreciate the diverse beauty that has arisen there by their influence in life's creativity. What produces a garden? Triune principles of life require that each owner *speaks life*, thus bringing order conversationally through into the changing relationships of the growing fauna that they value. That is a complicated way of saying, 'It's about planting seeds in soil and watering and tending them.' The garden that grows is not just in the mind's eye; the conversational word takes root in the physical reality of Creation. Each person's own garden thus exists within God's shared garden, where God encourages us all to talk across our fences.

Of course, in this fallen world some neighbours' gardens are disaster zones. Without the Holy Spirit to bring Godly order, all hell may break loose there. When needful orphan spirits move in next door, lacking the assurance of grace because of having been starved, forgiveness by a son of God may be their first experience of grace. It would be honouring if these neighbours experienced grace first from a humble, merciful 'son' as *their* neighbour who is confident of his or her kingdom inheritance. Ownership of a patch of land in the kingdom of God is not about its possession. Ownership rights over the land are about our ability to bless others who live alongside you.

Please ask yourself, "What do I stand to lose if I let go of the idea of ownership of my land, and see it as custodianship of God's land?" And what about sharing the land with others, with a risk that they might be disruptive? What might you stand to lose then? And as compensation in the kingdom, what might you stand to gain? You might make a list with a friend, with whom you can help each other to be honest.

Having undergone such a self-review, you can move on

assertively from your Guilt Stepping Stone to your Growth Cycle knowing your values and the values that God would have us live by. As a custodian of God's land, does forgiveness of neighbours now look more reasonable? Could you then continue to do it, if it felt as if you were being crucified by them?

A command to love your enemies and bless them

Forgiveness leads to personal development more into the likeness of Jesus. Automatically this will lead to Church development, by promoting healthy, insightful relationship among emotionally intelligent believers. Loving God, and loving your neighbour as if that neighbour were yourself, may be more achievable in an emotionally resilient church, where already forgiveness and blessing are shared as kingdom tools for 'personal gardening'.

Then Jesus raised the bar when he told his followers, "I tell you: love your enemies and pray for those who persecute you." (Matthew 5:43-48. Luke 6:27-38.) Perhaps we can just about cope with standing in the power Holy Spirit and the love of Christ to bless those who curse us, but loving enemies? Does Jesus mean by this the sort of cotton wool and comforting, try to be nice, don't upset them sort of gooey feeling of love? Or is it the opposite sort of 'lurve' that smothers them with good wishes and cake? I doubt it! I think Jesus meant spiritual warfare, reclaiming kingdom rights over the land that has been spiritually stolen, by establishing there the *loving Godly rule* of acting justly and loving mercy and walking humbly with your God, together with others mingling in the midst.

This follows from the basic theme of this book that love is made known equally as joy on gathering together, and as grief on separation, brokenness and misunderstanding. To spend time seriously listening to your enemy's story in the disputed land, and to listen with emotional intelligence for the grief hidden within and moving it, and then to mercifully explore how to get him or her onto relevant Growth Cycles together, and to spend quality time doing this *is* loving your enemy. You might still find this person unpleasant, irritating, embarrassing, even hateful and distrustful, but as you give time to listen, you are showing him or her the love of God, and opening the door to the possibility of change. Doing that with the right Godly attitude, and with emotional resilience and strength, is spiritual warfare.

When an orphan spirit feels insecure, then possessing the world's *material* may be that ailing person's only means to find comfort. Behind the displays of power and confrontation that accompany this seemingly ambitious or needful search for security, however, is grief. The mutual inter-dependence of the personal world mingles with that gathering of valued material. It appears at that meeting place of the two worlds (at the TSIPEX point of our physical and divine natures), where emotional preparations for action or withdrawal formulate as security or comfort seems threatened. Who is my enemy? Is my enemy the one who possesses land or material that I want? In the personal world illuminated by the glory of God, viewed from God's perspective on that high viewing platform of grace, a human enemy is only the person whose story I have not yet properly heard.

People often find it is more difficult to forgive themselves than to forgive others. Forgiving oneself may be the toughest of all mercy trails. Perhaps that would change if 'I' could stop making an enemy of myself, which people may do, I believe, to recover at least for the other part of 'me' a sense of moral righteousness that 'I' can correctly judge. Jesus said we should pray for those who persecute us, and that includes the other half of ourselves. Self-persecution aims to control to prevent *further* loss of self-respect or status. Punishing ourselves will probably take the form of seeking revenge rather than seeking personal growth through open confession about the painful situation and disappointment. Perhaps self-punishment explores a sense of power, at a time when I know that part of me is weak in the face of temptation.

All of these are unmerciful judgments on 'the grieving me', which do not establish justice, and which do not set moving a humble walk with my God towards greater strength and resilience.

However, you understand God to be, your God already knows. The one, living, loving God—who suffered internally as he watched his son die in the flesh, and whose grace pours out to re-connect with you—already knows and is running towards you now to welcome and restore you. Your whirlpools of loss emotions at first may surge and then calm into a growing sense of trust and mutual understanding. In time, restoration will include the Godly way to live fully your righteousness, your capacity to judge or discern rightly, your self-respect and status, your power to resist temptation, and, having done all, your power to stand. In this recovered true identity, you stand as an adopted son or daughter of God, an identity that includes the capacity to turn your grief emotions, when they next arise as they surely will if you love, to their Godly useful purposes. Then it is your turn to assertively build fellowship. In that way, honour grows.

So moving on, in a walk that includes the humility to forgive oneself, Jesus also said we should pray for those who persecute us. Here I remind you of the triune prayer that triune Christians can learn to pray, which amounts to 'prayer in the Spirit'. While continuing to honour the range of Christian traditions and the styles of prayer that are part of them, triune prayer is an additional conversational relationship with God that can happen moment by moment throughout the day. It is a prayerful attitude that Christians of all traditions can adopt in celebration of our adoption as sons and daughters of the living God. Gentiles mingling with the Jews have thus become equal inheritors of God's promise. With that status in God's kingdom, we can think more assertively about our persecutor's life circumstances. We might try to picture his or her significant relationships, at whatever level of life makes sense: with family, with members of political organisations, religious movements of believers, the populations of neighbouring countries, the whole sea of nations and peoples that the triune God surveys from that high viewing platform of grace, from which Jesus had stepped down to live among us.

So, let us be triune Christians about this, not partisan with restricted mind-frames, and not restricting ourselves into exclusive group mentality and backing one side and making enemies of the other. Triune Christians, from any church background world-wide, can know that it is most powerful to pray directly for the *relationship between any two others*. This sort of triune-centred, self-effacing prayer invites Holy Spirit into the ones for whom I am praying. Two people or organisations are thus transformed simultaneously in their relations with each other; and simultaneously 'I' praying for 'them' am placed in a triune position of divine-humanity, for now I share in Christ the restoration by grace of God's world.

In this I am forgiven. Honour grows where people grieve not by habits of mourning, but with emotional intelligence, constructively and appropriately forgiving others in different situations. Thus other people grow in strength as they mingle among God's People as a source of light for society. What do I stand to lose if the alien who loves and worships God, who lives among my people, grows stronger? Naming that will keep the forgiveness real. Then God's glory can shine through liberated and healed persons, sharing the land with insight, mercy and empathy for others.

Chapter 11

Temptation and evil

And lead us not into temptation, but deliver us from evil

Forgiveness is appropriate where people have blundered across personal boundaries, either without thinking, or as the 'collateral damage' that can follow when people have aimed for a narrow goal in a situation that is too complex for that. When human will is involved in the breaking of personal boundaries, however, the situation is spiritually different. When someone is purposefully crossing those same boundaries, it is not trespass; it is transgression.

The human psyche naturally thinks better of one's self (me) than of others (them), and so most people will automatically assume that the wilfulness talked of in this chapter refers to other people purposefully intruding or transgressing into *my space*. But pause for thought. What if Jesus in his wisdom had taught his disciples to pray first, "Lead me not into temptation"? For example, one of the 613 Commandments in the Old Testament is to forbid moving your neighbour's boundary stone. The tenth of the Ten principal Commandments (Exodus 20:1-21) is: "You shall not covet your neighbour's house. You shall not covet your neighbour's wife, or his male or female servant, his ox or donkey, or anything that belongs to your neighbour." Covetousness, greed, pride, aggressive hostility, these are the sorts of temptations that could lead 'me' into the wilfulness of *deciding* to transgress someone else's personal boundaries, which is the very nature of evil-doing.

Temptation and evil are different sides of the same coin.

Wilfully flicking that coin of personal decision into the air, we can watch for whichever side it lands in the hope of laying blame for transgressions on one side or the other—was I tempted; was it my own inner urge? However, from God's high viewing platform of grace the result looks the same. Why did this human being flick the coin and decide to provoke and transgress the personal boundaries of another? To set aright the personal injustice, God in God's loving mercy for humankind takes the punishment for precisely that human wilfulness. Astounding! The purpose of that punishment inflicted on the perfect Son is to make publicly visible even now, in God's immanent life-blood being shed and shared with others, the outrageous effects of evil choice. Only personal growth into Godly triune character of the humans involved can overcome the impact of such wilfulness on Creation.

That is why the prayerful response both to my temptation, and to being the victim of another's evil intent, is to *appeal* for God's life-blood to bring salvation, deliverance and healing by the personal growth of those involved.

I would like to tell you about a dream I had that guides my teaching about evil. I was in a celebratory feast. Three lower tables extended far into a hall from the high table away to my right. I was having a great time with nearby people, sitting on the outer side of one of the edge tables a fair way down. But an evil presence suddenly appeared behind me, having entered through a side door. The mysterious man extended his arm between my neighbour and myself and grabbed hold firmly of the table cloth. I poised to strike his arm away, and then realised that if I did so, then *my* choice and movement would achieve the evil one's purpose, disrupting the feast by pulling the cloth and meal off the table. In a dilemma, in the dream, I prayed an appeal to God to know what to do. I felt an answer that I should attract the attention of the host, who would make the evil presence go by a means that I could not understand. So I stood up and called to the host in the centre of the top table. Jesus looked at me, and walked around the outside to approach the evil presence. Jesus then looked at him, and simply, silently, the evil one let go of the cloth and went. Evil simply could not remain in the presence of the love of Christ.

I am reminded of James 4:7, 'Resist the evil one, and he will flee from you.' There is a major difference between taking action against the evil one as if that person is your enemy, and resisting the influence of another person's disruptively evil choices. Christians can offer resistance in a way that does not turn another person into an enemy. It is to stand and appeal through Christ to the Father to deliver us from evil. That triune Christian choice includes me resisting my temptation to meet power with power in my own strength. Instead I must make use of my emotional resilience, and all my spiritual strength, to make the Godly choice to meet evil power with my love for Christ and all God's Creation. Evil presence simply cannot remain in the presence of such love calling one to another. Under these circumstances, grace fills from within where grace is allowed in.

Evil choice distorts God's love wilfully

An archetype of someone bearing affliction is Job, who suffers for a higher and unseen Godly purpose. His three friends had intended to comfort him, but after a week of sitting with him they end up accusing him of sinning against God in his grief by cursing the day of his birth. Finally the wise but young Elihu presents him with the greatness of God against which to compare his life, and in Job 36:21 Elihu cautions him, "Beware of turning to evil, which you seem to prefer to affliction."

None of us knows how we shall react under severe affliction, but this caution is for us all, whether we curse ourselves or others. The curse is intended to disempower someone, to end their life even, or at least to make them vulnerable so that their personal energy can be turned to the benefit of the one who is cursing. That disempowering and turning may be construed as a wilfully evil transgression of personal boundaries. If the purpose of affliction is to restore wholeness in society by bringing into the light where personal growth is needed (in self or others), then turning to evil distorts God's greater purpose.

It is possible to take this view of evil personal choice a step further. Evil, in conversationally orientated terms, is the wilful personal choice to *magnify* someone's grief feelings *in order to* separate them from others, and thus to gain power over them.

Evil would thus have real effects in the world, but have no power or existence of its own. Evil steals its power by magnifying and distorting the grief half of Godly love. That is a nasty strategy. Because grief is unpleasant, people try to avoid it, and so grief becomes our blind spot, which evil choice can manipulate by magnifying out of proportion to the responses that are appropriate for the disappointments and setbacks concerned.

What is the Scriptural basis for this view of evil?

In Matthew 5, Jesus' Beatitudes include, "Blessed are those who mourn." It seems odd, until we recognise that mourning (the behavioural way that people grieve) is a sign that people have loved. It is the start of a painful but creative path to restoring Godly connection after separation, brokenness or misunderstanding.

But in Revelation 18:7 St John the Apostle inspirationally describes the three outrageous boasts made by spiritual Babylon, the Great Whore who tempts God's people away from kingdom living: "I sit as queen; I am not a widow; and *I will never mourn.*"

These boasts may be generalized as: "I have absolute power; I can take for myself whatever I want; and *I will never be moved by love to connect with others.*" As a consequence, Babylon becomes: 'a haunt for every evil and foul spirit'. (Rev 18:2)

The effects of these ungodly spiritual claims can be traced through the destructive lives of Jezebel and King Ahab (1 Kings 16:29-22:40; 2 Kings 8:25-9:37). These scriptural stories reveal the effects of a total absence of love or concern for 'the other', at both personal and national levels. We can say that as a consequence of *refusing to mourn*, the soul or inner heart of a person becomes a home in which evil can thrive and even take residence. That sort of a heart and mind attracts other like-minded persons. An evil-minded 'restricted group' could develop, feeding each others' thoughts and developing a pattern of behaviour that is inflicted upon others to disempower them.

I am presenting to you here a triune view of evil, not as an absolute that exists in and of itself, but as a potential consequence of choices that any one of us might make under pressured circumstances, like poor Job, when feeling disconnected from God.

As a consequence of refusing to mourn, or of not knowing how to mourn constructively, peoples' hearts may become fertile ground for evil to get a hold on their lives. Jesus knew the prince of this world had no hold on him (John 14:30), because he could self-question and effectively move on, engaging with his grieving and *turning its energies in this world* assertively to their Godly useful purposes. What is the rightful Godly purpose of loss reactions? The grief of love is there to help you and others find new ways to re-connect during times of change, thus to experience the creative joy of love again.

Ephesians 4:26-27 reads: "In your anger do not sin: do not let the sun go down while you are still angry, and do not give the devil a foothold." Anger is a Godly passion to engage with others and life to prevent the loss of something valued despite danger. However, like manna in the desert, it rots if ruminated upon overnight. This does not say, 'Do not be angry.' It means, 'Turn your anger to its Godly useful purpose *straight away*. If not, watch out! Ruminating on the situation or injustice will make your anger fester', as it did for King Saul, and for King Ahab later. Their anger and depressive feelings then entangled to create whirlpools of destructive drives acted out on others. Perhaps that was how they chose to break out of their withdrawal feelings of shamefulness that had previously been plaguing them, when their self-doubting shock and their guilty feelings had also entangled to trouble their spirits in another whirlpool of loss emotions. Could history have been different if they had been familiar enough with grief to step out of these whirlpools onto firmer emotional Stepping Stones, and adjust to the situations constructively, and with Godly courage?

James 4:7 could be interpreted thus: Resist the drive to turn to evil choices in your grief, and the evil one will flee from you. Emotional Logic makes people 'familiar with grief' enough to resist evil choice in others also, in a constructive way. As a minimum, you could learn and practise in small conversational groups: [a] to keep the Emotional Logic Turning Points diagram in mind as an overall process of adjusting to change, and [b] to recall the meanings and useful purposes of the seven emotional Stepping Stones. This minimum will set you on the path as an emotionally intelligent Christian to have conversations anywhere, anytime in which you can resist the temptation to evil choice, both in yourself, and when seeing others as they prepare to react to situations. In those conversations the glory of God can be invited in directly. God's presence through your open heart may empower people to turn grief's unpleasantness, by *their own choice*, to Godly purposes instead of evil. Then Jesus' prophesied mission, to bind up the broken-hearted, release captives, and give sight to the blind, can continue to move through you.

If anyone still doubts the scriptural basis of this view of evil, consider how our Christian hero St. Peter was rebuked by Jesus in the words "Get behind me Satan!" We have already looked at the setting in which this rebuke came. Both Matthew 16:23 and Mark 8.33 record Jesus saying a bit more: "Get behind me, Satan! You do not have in mind the concerns of God, but merely human concerns." This rather reduces the emphasis on evil (or the evil one) as a universal force or deceiver external to the person. It increases the triune possibility that evil is also a resurgent *human* characteristic by choice. The Good News is therefore that, equally by choice, people can keep in mind instead the concerns of God.

It is these distortions that create the handles on our lives by which those with evil intent can suck Godly energy from our preparations for movement in life, and so sustain their ungodly living. Anger, anxiety, fear, guilt, despair, self-doubt, all can be magnified out of proportion by a misplaced word. All can thus create handles on our lives that others can use to manipulate us, create conflict or misunderstanding, and thus disempower others further in the social system *through us*. It is not the presence of such emotional states that opens the door to evil choice, but misunderstanding the Godly purposes of these emotional preparations, and *refusing* to mourn constructively.

Analysing evil creates 'it', and thus hides human wilfulness

Evil is not a popular word in modernist and post-modern societies, where people consider they are enlightened and progressive. For such people the word 'spiritual' may be synonymous with magical, or superstitious, for which the remedy is reasoning based on faith in science and matter. However, there is a growing consensus among healthcare workers at least that spirituality does refer reasonably to a person's sense of connection to something beyond their own self, and to values held within this wider system, thus adding meaning to an otherwise random universe. Even within this view, however, the spiritual associations of the word 'evil' are disagreeable to some. This may be because of doubt arising from conflicting interpretations of the word within one or another of the three, primary *analytical perspectives* on life.

In a structuralist analytical perspective, an 'observer of life' focuses on the material forms of life that have cause-effect connections in a time-line—a linear processing model of life. Evil may seem as if 'it' is an *alternative hierarchy of disorder*, one which resists the motives of those who try to maintain good material order. In this mindset, anything that breaks up good material order might be described as evil. As such, even the random or ignorant effects of matter, or of personality, such as earthquakes or selfishness, might be described as evil if it is that which does the breaking up.

In a change-orientated analytical perspective, a 'creator of life' focuses on information-processing that is stressed to achieve some goal in a time-frame. Rich, multi-level inter-connections create a non-linear system that gets into 'states', from which reactions are primed but not exactly predictable. These states (patterns of connectivity) can be altered by introducing new information. Evil could seem to be the effects of someone else's *selfish choice* impacting on the ability of others to manage the reactivity of their own lives. In a self-centred way, anything that restricts *my* flow of information from and into a system, thus adding further unpredictability into the state, limits the processes I want to initiate, and so could be thought of as evil.

In a participator analytical perspective, impersonal life forces are coursing through shared space, influencing souls now, with implications for eternity. Evil could thus appear as an *alternative force* to the good. The evil 'it' may seem to be a dualistically different 'negative energy'. A battle thus ensues between good and evil, in which people have the choice to 'lock in' to either one of these impersonal forces, hoping in the process to be carried along socially with others by its light or darkness.

All these primary analytical views of an evil 'it' are reductions from triune conversational orientation, by a personal choice to focus attention on different *types of connection*, physical, psychological, or social. Therefore, there is no way to commend any one view over the others, or to say that any one is 'nonsense'. Each alone is commendable only in a 'yes-and-no-no' sense, true as far as it goes in *that* analytical perspective, but not true as an absolute. Flipping between one view and another is fine for entertainment (May the force be with you, while in the cinema, and when at home may other peoples' disruptive choices not limit mine!), but this mental 'flipping' cannot provide a stable base for moral society or ethical behaviour. Avoiding talk of 'evil' may seem a reasonable strategy to avoid confusion between conflicting analyses, but even that strategy breaks down when faced in the news with shockingly abusive harm that some people can wilfully perpetrate, who can very *reasonably* be described as 'evil'. In such a situation, a stable base for a morally just response *can* be provided, however, when all three analytical perspectives are integrated into a triune, whole person, balance. This balance, to be creative in God, would be needed to explore ways conversationally that would guide both the victim's, and the perpetrator's respective grief (if that is possible) to their own Growth Cycles, separated by safe distance. A triune statement about evil might look something like this:

Evil is a quality of wilful personal choice that magnifies another person's grief and prevents that grief from fulfilling its Godly creative purpose (which is for adaptive personal growth to enable re-connection with others in grace), thus to gain control over another's life.

The main point I want to emphasise here is that the wilful choice generates a sense of power over the other without a concern for that person's well-being. Such choices require getting a 'handle' somehow on someone else's life to disempower them. It is the exact opposite of a benevolent father watching over to keep good order among people by promoting strength of character for shared thriving.

Understanding how these 'handles' appear in our lives is where Emotional Logic fits within the 'spiritual social-psychology' of resisting evil, by removing the handles, and replacing them with the loving outreach of grace.

The heavenly realms

Having first established that evil choice can be made by oneself and one's human neighbours, something also needs to be said about the heavenly realms mentioned by St Paul five times in his Epistle to the Christian saints in Ephesus. By way of introduction, let me say that predestination, mentioned twice in Chapter 1 of that Epistle, is not the same as predetermination. In the extensive, multi-layered adaptive systems of life there is an infinite number of routes to get to the same destination, all of which can be influenced by someone else's choices. The route, the next step, is not predetermined. That would make us puppets. It is explored. Finding a path to the destination uses human choice and wisdom in the face of afflictions that are felt when the direct route gets blocked by someone else's trespasses and transgressions, or by one's own. How we choose to manage those obstructions *is* the kingdom of God coming on earth as it is in heaven.

As described above, evil power-seeking choices can be made by any human being, with knock-on effects to others. St Paul in the Ephesians Epistle, however, sets this affliction within a far greater picture of the greatness of God, much as Elihu did for Job. He starts, in the first three mentions of the spiritual realms (1:3; 1:19b-21; 2:6-9), by emphasising how you and I are saved into Christ in the heavenly realms, and how Christ is above all rule, authority, power and dominion, and above every other title that can be given. He then states in the whole of Chapter 3 that God's intention is that, 'through the church (and please read about the centrality of love here), the manifold wisdom of God should be made known to the rulers and authorities in the heavenly realms' (3:10). To achieve this, St Paul exhorts Christians in Chapter 6:10-20 to put on the full armour of God's truth, righteousness, readiness to spread peace, faith in salvation, spiritual advancement of the word of God, and prayer in the Spirit for all the saints (is that triune prayer?). The purpose of clothing oneself thus for conflict is, however, because making the manifold wisdom and power of God's love known in the heavenly realms is a struggle. It is not a struggle against flesh and blood (Ephesians 6:12), 'but against the rulers, against the authorities, against the powers of this dark world and against the spiritual forces of evil in the heavenly realms'.

Where grace is the substance of one living God, the heavenly realms are the fact of grace. This substantial fact of grace spiritually connects one person's choice of action to distant effects, some of which may influence all eternity. The causal sequence through this spiritual network of connections is non-linear. It influences the general context or spiritual 'atmosphere' of personal life and of the energy fields out of which particles emerge like triquetra networking into structures from within. It is not *necessary* to see rulers, authorities, powers and forces in terms of angels, demons and spirits, although it is wise to remain humble before Jesus' description of some of his actions, which were to cast out demons. Some people are gifted to discern features of life in this way, and to pray in the Spirit of God to cleanse the context of someone's life. However, no matter how much cleansing goes on, and whether or not people are inspired to recognise demons, the spiritual *atmosphere* of the heavenly realms is maintained by every single one of us, to the measure of grace that we each can attain in changing situations. Evil may thus have real effects to pre-tension reactions in different world situations, but evil has no power or existence of its own, gaining power only by distorting the grief half of Godly love. Becoming absorbed with the overwhelming experience of unpleasant emotions can make people lose faith in their role to preserve grace. This is the struggle, for Christ's presence to have dominion in the world through us also. Because grief is unpleasant, people try to avoid it, and so grief becomes our blind spot, which evil choice can manipulate by magnifying any of its unpleasant emotions out of proportion to situations with misunderstanding, brokenness and separation.

Preparation for delivering us from evil, and aftercare

Jesus taught his disciples to pray to Our Father, and in so doing to appeal to Our Father to deliver us from evil. Jesus knew for a fact that evil choice in others had no hold over him. Preparing his disciples to manage without him when he has gone, Jesus explains to them (John 14:30-31) that the Holy Spirit, the Spirit of Truth, will be released in and among them when he departs to be with His Father, and theirs. "I will not say much more to you, for the prince of this world is coming. *He has no hold over me*, but he comes so that the world may learn that I love the Father and do exactly what my Father has commanded me."

The first preparation for ministry for members of an emotionally intelligent Church is to know how to use their in-built 'Guilty self-questioning' Stepping Stones constructively, for a life review that will produce strength and resilience to face evil choice squarely, and then to stand. It requires truthfulness with others in the Church—no lone rangers here—otherwise where is the Spirit of Truth in the relational process?

Helping others to conduct that sort of life review, and to become familiar with grieving *before* they receive ministry and supportive prayer is also good preparation for the aftercare someone needs following the 'surgical intervention' of cleansing prayer. Jesus gave good advice to us when he refuted his critics who had claimed he was casting out demons by the power of Beelzebub, the prince of demons. In Luke 11:24-26 he says, "When an evil spirit comes out of a person, it goes through arid places seeking rest and does not find it. Then it says, 'I will return to the house I left. When it arrives, it finds the house swept clean and put in order. Then it goes and takes seven other spirits more wicked than itself, and they go in and live there. And the final condition of that person is worse than the first.'

Evil attracts evil, and a person's soul unprepared to resist the influences of others by emotional resilience and insight provides a staging home from which evil choice can manipulate life. The owner of that home may be totally unaware that choices that increase other people's grieving are being 'transited through' their home environment in thoughtless reactions to situations. A minimal amount of learning about Emotional Logic, and the willingness to pray for all the saints with a triune prayer in the Spirit, would make all the difference, creating a 'kingdom home'.

Prayer that specifically casts out named spiritual influences from a person's life, such as breaking ungodly soul-ties, generational curses, and curses over the land, all can cleanse the soul, the 'house'. But there is no avoiding the fact that personal choice and active insight are needed by a believer to 'keep the house clean' afterwards. More than that, those same choices to resist evil choice simultaneously alter the spiritual 'atmosphere' and environment, making it less favourable for those who do make evil choices. This becomes like a Neighbourhood Watch scheme's effect on crime rates. We never were designed to face these intrusive choices and make these preparations to resist them on our own.

Care is needed where church teaching traditions foster guilty feelings in believers to correct behaviour towards perfected goals. Such teaching about behaviour has to be balanced by equally powerful teaching about shared grace, and about individual soul cultivation to adapt in a changing community. Being aware of that need for triune balance, and striving to prevent its loss, may also keep grief about controlling behaviour from being magnified into grab handles. St Paul in Romans 14:22-23 sets the gold standard for this when writing about eating freedoms and food laws for Messianic Jews and Gentile Christians. He says: 'Everything that does not come from faith is sin'. Sin is *not* about breaking the behavioural codes prevalent in an established but restricted culture. Sin is to act out of law or habit, rather than out of a living faith.

Choosing the blessings

In closing, an example of cultural misunderstanding may further embed this triune, emotional intelligence approach to managing temptation and evil. It is not uncommon for people to believe that their enemies are evil. Closer inspection of their enemy's values might reveal that they are only human. Proverbs 25:21-22 reads:

> *If your enemy is hungry, give him food to eat;*
> *if he is thirsty, give him water to drink.*
> *In doing this, you will heap burning coals on his head,*
> *and the Lord will reward you.*

In developed societies, people do not know that carrying goods on your head is painful. Perhaps they imagine, erroneously, that practice makes the skill pain-free. To ease the pain that *is* a common feature of this practice, a kindness is to first put on the head a cushion, and the most luxurious sort of cushion is a cloth in which is wrapped some pleasantly warmed charcoal. The warmth of this cushion takes away pain when carrying heavy goods. Thus, 'heaping burning coals' on the head of your enemy is not a retributive punishment! It is an act of loving concern, and in this scripture one that is recommended for your enemy. For doing such things, the Lord will reward *you*. From God's perspective this is acting justly, because the person you have declared to be your enemy probably is behaving in ways that irritate you out of their own grief. Acknowledging *that* grief, naming the values that have become hidden losses in an overwhelmingly complex situation, and negotiating assertively shared Bargaining strategies together, can gradually remove the enemy status from the situation in a Godly, merciful way. This can happen at an international scale and in the main street of Ivybridge, over a coffee in the local café for example, bought for your enemy from a neighbouring church.

And of course this sort of reconciliatory meekness is the ideal setting for triune prayer as part of assertive peace-making. The reason is that most hidden losses occur in peoples' relationships; and the most intense loss reactions affecting behaviour tend to occur in those relationships that people do not normally talk about. So by listening to your enemy's story, and hearing the grief within it, and enquiring in loving concern about the values and relationships that underlie that grief, and the hopes frustrated in those difficult relationships, you as a Royal Priest will be enabled then to pray with insightful love, lifting that disappointing *relationship* to God, and asking the Holy Spirit to rest within that relationship and inspire both people in it to see some new possibilities for growth. Is this a practical way to love your enemies? What do you stand to lose by losing an enemy?

This path to walk in humility with God does not mean being passive and weak and hoping for God's miraculous and retributive *intervention* from a separated heavenly realm breaking into 'my world' or 'our world'. The humility God asks of his Royal Priesthood is to allow God's glory to be present 'where two or three are gathered' in conversational orientation, there to explore and agree solution strategies as ways forward from named disagreements, brokenness and misunderstanding. In this, you would be resisting evil and turning instead towards blessings shared in the midst of affliction. You will have brought the kingdom of heaven and the glory of God 'here on earth' through sharing your listening heart with someone different from you. Here is an emotionally intelligent Church building bridges of grace.

Chapter 12
Kingdom living

For yours is the Kingdom, the power and the glory, forever and ever. Amen!

This closing part of the Disciple's Prayer sets Jesus' words into Church liturgy, clasping a glittering diamond onto a ring of gold.

Kingdom, God's power, God's glory emerging for eternity to renew life everywhere—we have mentally touched on these already. All these are innate to conversational life. Not one of them is self-existent or the possession of any one person, whether a Holy Person (Father, Son or Holy Spirit of the triune living God) or one very human sinner now saved. They are all inter-personal truths.

This is the perspective offered by viewing life from the high platform of grace, where those adopted into the Holy Family are worshipping *together* in celebratory awe one living God in three Persons. Out of that sharing of worship shines glory, with movement in life, the power of which establishes the kingdom of God in peoples' hearts and in their relationships physically lived through the land. The blessing for all nations can flow when unity is restored among diverse people, all of them piles of conscious dust, embodied stardust, celebrating together by grace.

Amen means "I agree". Expressing this out loud is a choice to respond, which makes the relationship alive. That personal choice transfigures into physical waves among matter-energy—sound waves, heat waves, electro-magnetic waves in the visible and invisible spectra as photons of energy radiating from the organising dust of our living bodies. We see and we hear a serious Amen. If spoken loudly we may even feel it resonating in the thorax, where harmonies can also be felt if the Amen is sung courageously by many people together. The mental concept becomes physical information, transmitted and received—heard. There is no separation here of mind and matter when movement is included in our picture of inter-personal life.

Is 'word' the mental concept only? Or is 'word' *also* the energetic transfer of information from one expressing person to a different receiving person, who must choose to interpret and translate its movements into meaning? A living word reverberates around the double triquetra of Figure 8, and around the extending network of living communion shown in Figure 12, and through those Celtic networked patterns of material human society shown in Figure 4, echoing, calling from somewhere distant, as if from somewhere in a cathedral. Living word transforms the systems of life that we walk among. Within these human systems we can learn to 'speak life' in grace to each other. An Amen response makes spoken words then systemically *real*—if you are serious about prayer.

A church is a gathering of called-out ones

Amen is a church word, but 'church' is not a purely religious word. Does that surprise you? A 'church' is a gathering of people who are called out from the rest for a particular purpose. So, in the old Wild West stories, a posse of people called out to chase a crook, who has escaped on his horse, is a 'church' from the local community. Members of Parliament in a democracy are a church called out by votes from the constituencies. A Committee of MPs called out from the House for a special enquiry is a local church within Parliament. The difference for Christianity is that One Church has been called out from the world by God to honour the

Name of Jesus of Nazareth, the Jew born in Bethlehem as Son of Man, to be witnesses that life can be ever-renewed *from within* by the power of God's love in that Name.

The one Church of Jesus, the Messiah-Christ, is commanded to conversationally re-make grace-filled unity, having analysed life from different perspectives. In that grace-filled attitude of tensioned unity we listen wisely to the increasing diversity that has now been discovered. We are all on paths of personal growth and exploration. We are all climbing by different routes to that same high viewing platform. Not all ways lead to God, but there is no path that God will not run along to meet and guide those who truly seek. In God's grace we learn to handle with maturity the disagreements that arise on diversification. The wisdom for this has been learnt by becoming familiar enough with grief to see how to turn its unpleasant emotions to constructive purposes. Thus we can share *silently* even with others in conversation, with humility and merciful justice, and patience. Holy Spirit is the Counsellor; Jesus is the Teacher for us all; the Church is the physical evidence of this in the heavenly realms.

Indwelling word uniting the Church family may shine out as God's glory to bless the world. This is the power of the kingdom for eternity. It is the gift of Good News, which the world keeps turning its back on, preferring darkness instead of saying their Amen to the testimonies of people whose lives have been transformed in love.

The world-wide Church could be viewed as a collection of locally developing, maturing *family systems*. Local or regional traditions of 'churched' behaviour may obscure that picture, however, so that then people may imagine that Christianity means the historical traditions of those restricted groups. To overcome that misconception, I have started to call myself a 'triune Christian' when asked about my religion, which opens an opportunity to explain that I believe Jesus never wanted to start a new *religion*. Christianity is a character—the character of Jesus Christ growing in each one of his disciples as their lives transfigure. This transfiguration of the soul-life of a person, this personal growth, occurs as a constant renewal while in community (in koinonia, in fellowship as church family). It is like a spring of living water that swells up to stir the surface of a courtyard pool in the family home.

In the very early Church this notion of renewal in community was the norm, and in complete contrast to the individualism that abounds today. Local 'bishops' administered the Holy Supper, the sacrament of communion, to *every believer* in a geographical locality. This geographical family perspective was largely lost from sight over the centuries as factions separated more and more around different interpretations of right belief and right living. Perhaps it can be recovered, as people discover again by Holy Spirit the right feelings in Christ for each other, which run deeper than belief or behaviour. Perhaps it can be recovered as grace.

Imagine the nation of Israel in Exodus, set free from Egypt, migrant, camping in their hundreds of thousands in twelve tribes neatly arranged to north, east, south and west around the tent of meeting. There around that centre are the tents of the Levites, a buffer to keep the tribes from the wrath of God in their midst if they were to get too close. The Levites served the people through maintaining the tabernacle, and fulfilling various social and sacrificial tasks that assured equity, purity and unity among the diversity of the twelve tribes. They were the practical outreach, the 'arm', of the Aaronic priesthood, from whose chief Levite family came the High Priest. All Israel honoured and worshipped God, regardless of tribe, profession or status, but their spiritual needs to maintain unity among their necessary diversity were met by 1/13th of the total population of migrant Israel.

The Levites were 1/13th of the Israelites. Jesus was central to twelve apostles. These apostles had vastly different backgrounds and characters, which made them ideal (even while imperfect) to instruct and guide the early Church's growth, moving out north, east, south and west. They moved in the grace and power of the Holy Spirit, the practical outreach 'arm' of Jesus, the great high priest of the new covenant with God (Hebrews 4:14-5:10).

Could it be equally reasonable to imagine that God's one Church of Jesus Christ, called out by Holy Spirit from all the peoples of the earth, might emerge mystically as servant-priests who are about 1/13th of all local community's populations? The glory of the eternal kingdom of God come on earth will not require everyone to be in the Royal Priesthood; but in this established kingdom of God everyone, in whatever diverse role they have in the holy nation, will be able to say Amen to God's glory. Perhaps to minister Christ's unity by grace among the increasing *diversity* that will appear as all Creation is restored to kingdom life is a clear role for triune Christians worldwide. Through triune prayer in the Spirit for relationships between others, this role could be fulfilled by acting justly and loving mercy and walking humbly with God. The Jewish nation as a whole was not able to achieve this function by obedient behaviour alone, limited by Law or Guidance (as Torah means), to be 'a light for all nations'. Perhaps God is not asking Christians to *convert* all Gentiles *into look-alikes of themselves*. That would be equivalent to saying that the Levite's role was to turn all Israel into Levitical priests.

Consider what you might lose if, instead of trying to convert, God is asking his Christian Royal Priesthood to pray for and minister to the needs of all Jews and all Gentiles *in their diversity*. It is by Holy Spirit moving in them that they will honour God in everything they do. Would God be adequately honoured if there was no one standard religious traditional behaviour, but everyone around the earth showed their respect for God by acting justly and loving mercy and walking humbly before *their* God, whatever their tribe, profession or status, and whatever their understanding of God is at this stage in their personal development. Could God be adequately honoured if each person in his or her heart could be open to Holy Spirit and therefore say their own sincere Amen to God's power and glory forever?

One thirteenth of a population is 7.7%. The process of exploration and discovery of an identity in Christ means that church attendees may number, say, 10-15% of a population, testing their calling. If so, then Christians who feel a drive to conversion fervour, and who worry about beliefs that differ in detail from theirs, can now let go of the tent rope. The Tabernacle of the new covenant will stand by the power and love of Holy Spirit, not by keeping tension on the guy rope when other Christians seem to be pulling in some other direction. Christians are not called to fill churches. Christians are called into churches, where they mature and turn outwards again, facing the world clothed in grace, ready for action, or wise withdrawal, or simply to stand, and when all is done, to stand. Christians are called to pray in Holy Spirit, calling to Christ at the head table of the feast, praying impartially for the relationship between two other persons or organisations or principalities or powers, while the power of Christ's love is at work.

To respond to a call from God to mature into a royal priesthood there will have to be loss—letting go associated with grief. This does not mean letting go of our humanity to become holy. It means becoming as fully human as Christ Jesus. The joy is restored on that high viewing platform. For those who are curious to know if they have been called to triune prayer in the Spirit, we could make out a Loss Reaction Worksheet as a start to work out how to turn the grief half of love's letting go into that joy of growing into a wider Family. It starts with naming the situation and writing that at the top of the Worksheet—'Letting go of old habits of praying'. Then ask yourself questions in a self-review such as, 'What do I enjoy about praying in that habitual way? What does it say about who I am? How does it fit into my daily routine?' You may think of other relevant questions, the answers to which are your values, which you could lose if you were to explore some new way of praying. You might then move on to 'How does the way I pray maintain a safe distance? How do I get to know the values that are moving the person I am praying for God's Spirit to influence? What would I lose if I drew closer? What would I lose if I heard their story, or understood their situation?' What is the price of increasing in compassion? What is the price of acting justly between two people or groups who I do not know well? What is the price of humility? At some point you might look down that deepening list one by one, and put one, two, three or more ticks across each row as you reflect on how you feel 'right now' about the possibility (or reality) of losing that valued aspect of your present way of praying, and the next, and so on down the list. The resulting pattern of loss emotions shows the depth of your humanity, and how complex we human creatures are. Perhaps you could show it to someone trusted, to God even in prayer, and seek guidance for which one named loss to try to recover as you start to pray also in a new triune way anytime and anywhere for the relationship between two others. Knowing now the emotional pattern of your grieving that may tension your experiments with this new way of praying, you could prepare yourself to react constructively if there were any setbacks or disappointments, rather than letting that pattern drive a 'kneejerk reaction'. It is this willingness to choose to grieve constructively at such times that draws honour from God and from others. As Christ grieved constructively for us in new ways, and so Jesus' honour grew in time among humankind, so your honour in time would grow.

Emotional turbulence may distract people from living a passionate life for God. It may, however, also be part of it! Grief emotions do not mean there is anything wrong with the calling. Restoring and building community wisely with others is a passionate life, in which overcoming difficulties in grace together is a vital part. So also is building the Church, as a Family of Godly-wise people. God metaphorically spits out the lukewarm, distracted, complaining church. God is present, however, as people hover over the choice to put their emotional energy into building life with others 'on the rock' of Godly values and grace. Holy Spirit hovers beside you. Grace is warmly washing up against your feet as you hesitate over that choice. The emotional turbulence that may come with that sort of *overcoming* is not a distraction from the Kingdom of God; it is part of it!

This relates to: Letting go of my previous habit of praying

NAMED LOSSES	SHOCK	DENIAL	ANGER	GUILT	BARG'N	DEPR'N	ACCEPT
Approval of others							
Being part of something							
Knowing what to do next							
Predictability							
Safety							
Salvation							
Continuing a tradition							
Familiarity							
Knowing when to stop							
Being right							
Pleasing God							

Figure 18 – A Loss Reaction Worksheet – developing triune prayer

King David was not perfect, but he was anointed. Jacob's youngest son Joseph was not wise when he was young as he boasted to his brothers, but he was anointed. The Pharisee Saul was not teaching grace when he persecuted the early Christians, but he was anointed. The Church is not and never will be perfect, but Christians are anointed...

Chapter 12 Kingdom living

Imagine glory shining from Jew and Gentile reconciled in Christ. What might you worry about losing if that were to happen? What could prevent you praying in love, impartially, for that reconciliation?

Overcoming sibling rivalry in humanistic terms is impossible; but in the grace of God, with Godly forgiveness, a blessing from a Royal Priesthood may inspire people to try more mature management of their competitive feelings. The anointed role of a Royal Priesthood is to minister grace impartially, and to hover prayerfully.

Arab descendants of Ishmael can proudly stand among Gentiles as descendants of Abraham. Ishmael and his Egyptian mother Hagar were blessed by God and survived the desert to thrive as a great nation, but at loggerheads with his younger half-brothers. Reconciliation between the descendants of Ishmael and the descendants of promise through Isaac is vital nevertheless to the blessing of all nations that is prophesied to come through Abraham's seed. Conversationally-minded triune Christians may discover they have a role to minister grace for that reconciliation in the kingdom, praying the power and glory of grace in a non-partisan way, and praying to bless the *relationship between* these two great 'nations'. Present day Jews and Arabs are not the clearly defined descendant groups of those original half-brothers, the vast majority of whom have dispersed; but praying for the mutual forgiveness between Arab and Jew and reconciliation is a good place to start. We could pray for the peace of Jerusalem. What sort of curiosity and constructive grieving do we need to start that process in ever greater depth?

Of course, if we Christians need practice at this sort of prayer we could start by praying nearer to home, for our own families, or what about our neighbours? Do you know how your brother or sister's values have changed during the last year? Do you know anything at all about your neighbour's values and hurts that move his or her connections with others who are significant for them? Neighbourliness is not about just good behaviour, or about believing the same things are important.

The kingdom of God is *at hand* for all. Just beyond the fingertips is a gap, however. It is filled with more value-driven emotions than you had ever imagined. Now you know that there are ways to map them, and to move them on constructively. All of them are God-given for the same useful purpose, to help people to re-connect, to bridge that gap with grace. It might happen, if our neighbours had someone to show them the way.

Appendix

A simple look at triune neuroscience

This Appendix details how the triquetra diagram, showing triune principles of organisation, can be incarnate in the human brain's structure, in such a way that *three different pairings* of three fundamental features of sensory experience (form, change and relatedness) could be mixed variably in the three main association areas of the brain to generate the conscious impressions of being a person orientated in space, time and real presence.

The description that follows is NOT a proven fact. It is a *speculative summary* that is induced from experimental scientific observations. It is a *hypothesis* that could inspire further experiments that might refute it. Nevertheless, this summary does show how known facts fit with triune principles. These triune principles of organisation could enable the brain to self-organise a picture of life that approximates to that which is actually happening in a person's physical and social environment (the TSIPEX model of consciousness: Triune Systems in Parallel Exchange).

I differentiate *orientating* sensory input (vision, hearing, touch, joint position, joint movement, and inner ear balance), from other senses such as smell, taste or blood sugar detection as examples among other chemical sensors and immune system detectors. These are *alerting* senses that activate the orientating senses to localise behavioural responses. Orientating sensory input is broken into its significant component features in the 'primary sensory cortex' for that sense modality. Vision, for example, separates into colour, edges, angles, movement at different speeds, off and on changes, and so on. Each is 'clarified' along different pathways of the primary visual cortex (which is at the back of your brain). Among this range of features *in all orientating sense modalities* are pathways that clarify features of form, change and relatedness, the three 'fundamentals for orientation'. Touch senses in the parietal cortex (above your ears) have pathways, for example, clarifying changes that get focused onto single points, with 'two point discrimination' that helps to recognise relatedness; and so on for hearing, and joint positions.

Patterns of simultaneous stimulation, such as edges, angles, curves and so on stimulate nerve cells in the *secondary* sensory cortex, closely arranged adjacent to the primary sensory cortex, that begin to re-integrate these isolated features into clarified 'form' or shape complexes. Changes and synchronicity (relatedness) are likewise clarified into patterned complexes, which the TSIPEX model calls 'fundamental features for orientation'.

Here is the unique proposal of the TSIPEX model. Each of these identified fundamental features of the orientating senses may then be 'forwarded' in three directions simultaneously from the secondary sensory cortex towards the three main association areas shown in Figure 7. Neural pathways exist to do this. There in the association cortices the same fundamental features *from different orientating senses* could be mixed with their equivalent features from other secondary sensory cortex areas to make poly-sensory fundamental 'complex patterns' of form, and of change, and of relatedness information ongoing in sensory experience. (This should be experimentally testable.) That is what an 'association cortex' does. It gathers together information from different senses (and memories). Among this gathering process, that which relates to form, change and relatedness could be used to 'orientate' all the other features (for example the colour red gets orientated within a bus shape that is moving towards you fast). Here, orientation means constructing a mental picture that enables sensible *interaction with other organisms* or with other features of the person's physical environment, such as rivers, clearings in forests for a team to hunt in, buses on busy roads, and so on.

The brain's surface 'cortex' is structured in closely-packed columns perpendicular to the surface like honeycomb. Each column is a hollow, lattice-like tube made of small nerve cells. Into the middle of each tube there are up-and-down inputs, and also outputs from it. These input-outputs from the centre are *modulated by* the electrical activity that can be set up in the surrounding wall of the tube. The TSIPEX model will focus your attention on what happens in the walls of the tubes to modulate the inputs, thus putting extra information into the outputs from that tube.

Outputs from any cortical column tube fast-forward to hundreds or thousands of other places in the brain simultaneously, all of which join into reverberating feedback circuits. The complexity is fabulous! I am tempted to compare this with a jazz or orchestral vibraphone, which has tubular 'bells' suspended below the percussion plates. The difference is that in the brain's cortex each tubular 'bell' can ring a note that is *determined by the electrical activity mixing in its tube...* and the output sets a whole pattern of other tubular bells also ringing as if with harmonics. So when the musician strikes a single percussion plate (an input), a whole symphony can be set rippling off through the cortex... (This is quite literally true! This happened during a brain operation on a conscious patient who had a life-threatening disease that needed a very precisely located intervention. Stimulating an individual nerve cell had this effect, reported by the patient as 'hearing a whole symphony' to everyone's amazement!)

Now, the point is (I must not lose my way in the excitement generated by these findings of high-tech neuropsychology!) that the *pairing of sensory fundamentals* we are so interested in can and may occur in Layer III of these six-layered, electrically-active, columnar cortical tubes. One pair of sensory fundamentals, for example *relatedness* and *forms*, could gather in parietal lobe association area of the brain from various orientating sensory areas of the brain into the activity of the lattice-like Layers III of its cortical columns. If so, then the up-and-down inputs into the middles of the columns of that parietal association area would be *modulated at their Layers III* by a representation of *space*. (Space = the relatedness of forms.) The columns would then fast-forward their outputs, now modulated to be 'in a context of space', to adjacent strips of the association cortex (the cortex is organised in parallel strips of cortical columns, across which electrical activity spreads over the surface of the brain, and deeper in, in waves) and to wherever else more distantly in the brain these outputs will further mix and compare.

These receiving areas all *feed-back* through their reverberating loops to the forwarding association area. It is called 'boot-lacing', and it happens everywhere in the brain, which is a massive network of feedback loops. The complexity is awesome! The activity within any and all of these feedback loops can thus reverberate at a 'brain wave' frequency. This feature of feedback may be important to bundle together inputs from different parts of the brain into coherent but rapidly evolving patterns, like an old-fashioned film projector. This iterative, boot-lacing frequency involving the association area (and other significant areas) may thus create a reverberating 'attractor state', which is an impression of consistent space around the original sensory inputs going up into the centres of the columns. If it endures over several seconds, then the thinking observing person may generate an impression that space has some objective reality! The TSIPEX model says that it certainly does have a parallel reality, but that the parallelism could diverge under the influence of alcohol, anxiety, mental overload, brain injury, etc.

To be sure that you are clear about this process, I shall repeat this description of how a concept of space may be constructed in the parietal lobe association area, repeating it twice (in outline only!) applying its triune principles to the other two 'primary constructs' that are necessary and sufficient to orientate one's experience as a self-in-world… time and presence.

So, similarly, another large set of parallel strips of cortical columns in the ventro-medial prefrontal association area of the brain will simultaneously be receiving sensory inputs into their lattice-like Layers III that carry *form* and *change* information (which has been filtered as fundamentals from a number of senses and memory inputs). That association area will modulate its inputs in a way that its outputs are embedded in a context of *time*. The inputs fast-forwarded on will be *understood* in the rest of the brain as being 'in time'. This will feed-back to create an attractor state impression within that association cortex that time exists in some objective sense around the original sensory inputs.

Again, when yet another large set of strips of columns in the temporal lobe association area of the brain receives into its Layers III sensory inputs that have been filtered into fundamental *relatedness* and *change* content, then that association area of the brain will pass on its inputs-outputs modulated in a context that can be understood as *matter*, or graspable substance, or essence, or energy, or if it is a person then their *presence* as the reality of their human being.

So bringing this all together, to repeat the same example, 'red' may have been detected in the primary visual cortex, and is being processed as a *new sensory input* up into to the centres of cortical columns in all three association areas simultaneously. The input 'red' is surrounded in all three association areas Layers III with various pairings of 'forms changing in their relatedness'. The 'red' thus emerges from the association areas now modulated and forwarded to higher association areas as 'something red transforming in space and time and real presence'.

This resulting mixture is *also* fast-forwarded into the upper frontal brain cortex. Here muscular (motor) reactions are primed and co-ordinated. This mixing of sensory input with muscular priming of posture and action generates a sense of 'me'. It is the ongoing source of the 'I', or ego, renewed each morning on waking up. So, from now on in this story I shall have to introduce 'self' into this neuropsychology description, which means this ongoing mixture of forwarding *orientated* sensory information with preparations of muscular posture for action.

My self's memories becomes activated as well. This adds an interpretation to this impression of 'something red transforming'. From past experience, suddenly, I find myself jumping backwards! A solid London bus lumbers by me with heavy momentum. It is *really* happening, here, now—not in my un-orientated dreams! I feel the warmth of the engine, the wind as it passes, smell the diesel, hear the shouts of passers by, and it all makes sense.

And so I can build up a composite picture of life's events. They are coloured by my memories and hopes. Reverberating feedback loops add three dimensions to that bi-focal (two-eyes) and bi-lateral (two ears) space; and ongoing mental comparisons add a sense of progress to the changes of form that I notice. I now have a choice, how do I respond to those passers by who have expressed their concern for me?

A small abnormality (a 'lesion') in the inferior temporal cortex can, as an example of the disruption of this system, produce strange mental states in which people feel that life and one's self has become unreal or odd. Our impression of reality, and the real presence of time and space, is an ongoing mental construct. Underlying it is the fact of *connection*. Relatedness information is fundamentally detected at the first levels of brain activity. Belonging in something bigger *is* our spirituality, whether secular or religious. Human beings are not physical creatures with some mysterious optional component called spirit; we are spiritual creatures exploring how to become more human. That fundamental connectedness information becomes organised into a potentially wide range of impression of my self and of others, or of me and it (I-thou, or I-it) by triune principles of organisation. These principles of organisation are conversational—there must be an other if I am to be an orientated person.

* * *

What might happen to this sense of orientation, I wonder, when I become curious *about* one of those three sensory fundamentals (form, change and relatedness) that get paired for the mutual interdependence of dialogue? What if I want to *understand* form itself, or change, or relatedness? To analyse 'it' I would need to focus my attention on one or other of these features that orientate my life for conversations with my other. To do this *while remaining orientated as a conscious person* I would need to construct a new mental context out of the remaining two fundamentals for orientation, as a context in which I can simultaneously orientate both me and it!

Let's say I became curious about, or even fascinated by, the *forms* of life… What might the world begin to look like as I focus my attention on the nature of forms? I might, for example, be hoping to develop my understanding of the legal or political *structures* that give shape to life in a society. Or I might, for example, just be attracted to and fascinated by the physical appearance of another individual; or I might simply want to understand atomic structure.

To mentally *analyse* forms, for example, in an orientated way my brain would have to project that fundamentally filtered information about forms up *into the centres* of the cortical columns in the inferior temporal association cortex, where *the other two fundamentals* are mingling in Layer III to construct a context of *presence* (Presence = changing relatedness.). Real presence thus becomes the context in which to 'understand' *whatever* is being analysed in the centre of the column. In this situation, when 'form' information is being projected up into the centres of these cortical columns, it will then spread all across the brain as an output of 'forms modulated by a sense of their own real presence'. The forms fast-forwarded will thus seem to have *an objective existence of their own*.

The price for this is that while I am thus analysing forms the person I converse with will become less of a real presence, and simultaneously I become less of a whole person and more of a disembodied, observing mind.

Notions of space and time would, however, continue to be constructed in the cortical columns of the other two orientating association areas. They no longer would be able to orientate the whole *conversational me* in dialogue, because 'I' will have become 'formless'. 'I' would have become a real 'presence of mind' observing the objectified forms I have mentally constructed that now fill my mind. Space and time orientating information being forwarded now to the motor planning areas would instead orientate not my conversation with my other, but those imagined *external objectified forms* that have been spread all over my brain. That spread of an analytical idea will reverberate by feedback loops, and so may continue to occupy my attention for an ever extending period of time—unless I 'snap out of it', leave behind the day-dream, and restore my fully human conversational orientation with the grace to re-connect with others who have been seeing life differently to me.

When stuck in a frame of mind that analyses forms in this way, life comes to look like objects moving with momentum in space-time. There seems to be an externally self-existent universe, and these personally orientating concepts of space and time are no longer available to orientate the observing *mind*. The person, in this Observer mind-frame, becomes a non-spatial, non-temporal presence of mind that in its human nature is nothing more that the power of observation and analysis.

Exactly the same triune principles of the re-distribution of outputs from the three association areas apply to constructing the Creator and Participator analytical mind-frames. Herein is the source of much misunderstanding, with grief that then separates and breaks humanity.

Glossary of triune terms

Analogue	A continuous variable such as time or volume, in contrast to a stepped or digital variable such as numbers of marbles.
Analytical mind frame	A mental 'step back' from conversational engagement with some person or thing in which features of 'it' can be examined and compared.
Anthropology	The study of mankind, especially of its societies and customs, to understand human nature.
Apophatic theology	The study to understand God as totally other than human nature, so that human words can only say what God is not, leaving God as mystery revealed in life.
Association areas of the brain	Areas of cerebral cortex where analysed sensory input, memories, and 'motor' preparation states all feed back to be integrated into orientated and responsive human behaviour.
Big Picture	The most inclusive mental picture that a person can make as a context in which to make sense of their present and memorised experiences.
Calling	An inner sense of motivation that a person may feel generated from their emotional

	attachments, which may be reasoned and/or intuitive.
Cataphatic theology	The study to understand God by making assertive statements of the knowable attributes of God.
Chaos theory	A 'catch all' term for a science that studies how order can emerge from systems where there are interactions between large numbers of elements.
Church	A 'called out' body of people from a larger population for a particular purpose. The Church of Jesus shows the resurrected life of Christ.
Cognits of awareness	A 3+1 conscious orientation theory term referring to the digital 'pictures' in which people may think, like an acetate film reel, that allows rapid change of attention. This digital cognition contrasts with the analogue biochemistry of emotion.
Collectivist	A primary analytical perspective focusing on relatedness in life, in which people sense they are participators in the flow of something greater.
Communion	A quality of group relatedness that welcomes diversity in its unity, requiring a sense of mystery to sustain forgiveness and humility.
Complex adaptive system	A feedback process within an extended interacting system that continues to self organise in response to changes of its environment.

Continuous creation	The theological view that triune principles of organisation emerge from grace as quanta of energy moving in relation to each other in ways that continuously re-entangle as energy-matter.
Conversational orientation	The interactive engagement of two self-organising entities that are mutually inter-dependent for their lives to continue and thrive.
Creator	The identity that emerges when a person is in an Individualist analytical mind-frame focused on the changes of life. This is a reflection in humanity of the Father sub-state of God.
Digital	The notion that information or energy-matter is parcelled into small, discrete 'particles' that somehow interact and 'split'. This is in contrast to analogue transformations of energy-matter.
Emotion	The inner physical re-organisation of the living body in reflex response to environmental change (local and distant) that prepares the individual for survival or thriving.
Emotional chaos theory	The view that when emotional preparation states become turbulent or chaotic, physical and mental health, and social and spiritual well-being, suffer.
Emotional intelligence (EQ)	The original work of Daniel Goleman that awareness of emotions in self and others provides vital information for social interactions.

Emotional Logic (EL)	The in-built capacity for one emotion to evolve constructively into another as a person prepares in different ways to adjust constructively to changing circumstances.
Entanglement	The mutual interaction of two entities that are each self-organising and transforming according to triune principles. This may or may not be helpful for specific life purposes.
Epi-genetic	Environmental factors that influence a genetically guided process, such as laying down nerve fibre tracts in the developing brain, leaving a long-term impact.
Eternal now	The quality that 'time' adopts in a Collectivist analytical perspective, which is contrasted with time sequence and time frame in the other two. Each present moment is a window into eternity.
Ever-renewed life	A triune statement about the dynamic nature of eternity in continuous creation, to be contrasted with a never-ending time-sequence when understood in an Observer analytical perspective.
Evil	The quality of wilful personal choice that magnifies another person's grief and prevents that grief from fulfilling its Godly creative purpose (which is for adaptive personal growth to enable re-connection with others in grace), thus to gain control over another's life..
Feeling	Information entering consciousness that an emotion is re-organising body chemistry

	and posture to prepare for action or withdrawal.
Forgiveness	The giant leap from anger about loss to creative acceptance of one's powerlessness to resolve every aspect by forcing power over another, thus releasing the gentle power of grace to heal.
Fundamental for orientation	Selected features of sensory inputs to the brain, separated out from others, which are re-mixed in association areas to generate the orientating impressions of space, time and real presence.
Gentile	Any person who is not a Jew. Not all descendants of Patriarch Abraham's son Isaac or grandson Jacob are present-day Jews. The term Jew refers to genetic descendants of the former residents in the divided kingdom land of Judah.
Gnosticism	The belief that possessing special, esoteric spiritual knowledge can lead to an individual's salvation.
Grief	The wide range of unpleasant emotions activated on separation, brokenness or misunderstanding that has a Godly purpose to move people to re-connect with others when change has pushed them out of their comfort zone. Grief and joy are both features of love, in its widest sense of connection.
Harmonics	The parallel activation of some form at a distance from a source of kinetic (movement) energy.

Heaven	The presence of God's love.
Hologram	A static, three-dimensional image that seems suspended in space, created by the interaction of two laser beams (co-ordinated light waves).
Individualist	A primary analytical perspective focusing on change in life, in which people sense they are creators of the activity that is life.
Information	In triune conversational orientation, the transformative process of giving and receiving exchanges. In an Individualist mind frame this becomes reified as 'data', the essence or real stuff of life, which a Creator of life 'handles'.
Intelligence	The activity of one component of a shared system is modified by the changing activity of another component with different connections. Where a component's activity and memory varies with the output of an interactive pair of other components, triune principles may potentially generate intelligent awareness.
Linear time	The view of time that results as a single linear sequence of cause-effects with a direction only from past to future.
Materialist	Another name for the Structuralist primary analytical perspective, one which emphasises a focus on the physical world rather than on the worlds of constructed mental ideas or structured hierarchies of relationships within organisations.
Matter	In triune conversational orientation, the

	patterned form resulting (at different levels as body and mind) and transforming during the process of giving and receiving exchanges. In a Structuralist mind frame this becomes reified as particles, the essence or real stuff of life, which an Observer of life uses experimentally to build.
Mercy	The sensitivity to hear another person's story or plea and to respond with grace, which enables re-connection, but does not necessarily mean leniency where retribution is needed for justice.
Nested system	Where one set of complex interactions creates an adapting form that is embedded within a larger set of complex interactions, each system will mutually influence the dynamics of the other.
Observer	The identity that emerges when a person is in a Structuralist analytical mind-frame focused on the forms of life. This is a reflection in humanity of the Son sub-state of God.
Paradox	A seemingly absurd or contradictory statement that on further investigation turns out to be well-founded, though its propositions may be difficult to reconcile.
Participator	The identity that emerges when a person is in a Collectivist analytical mind-frame focused on the relatedness of life. This is a reflection in humanity of the Holy Spirit sub-state of God.
Particle	The appearance (or feeling) of a

	transformation of entangled energy during an analogue process of mutual triune transformation. The analogue process may be pictured as a physics equation, for example $E = mc^2$. [E, m and c are forms; the multiplication of m and c, and the power ^{2} are the changes; the = is the relatedness. Together they are triune principles of life – a living word.]
Person	An individual of a people, innately relational, and mutually inter-dependent with others for life to be creative. Originally a hypo-stasis, a 'sub-state' of one living God, all three sub-states being of one sub-stance (under-standing). Three mutually aware persons can be of one mind in agreement.
Positivism	A philosophical stance that claims real existence (ontology) of only those features of life that can be measured or observed. Associated mentally with cataphatic theology.
Phenomenology	A philosophical stance that claims features of life perceptible to the senses are the only 'objects' of knowledge, and that we can have no direct perception of any other reality (ontology).
Photon	A quantum of energy in the visible light spectrum.
Pre-conscious	Triune activity patterning networks of electrically active cells, not only in the brain, which primes sensitivity and reaction but does not enter consciousness. This

Glossary of triune terms

	term is different to the psychotherapy use of terms such as subconscious and unconscious.
Primary analytical perspective	The worldview that results when people take a mental step away from conversational orientation in order to analyse some feature of life that is normally used to construct orientation.
Quantum	The smallest package of energy that can relate with others in different forms and changes, such as cyclically in matter, transmitted change as in light, and potential as is gravity in space.
Restricted group mentality	The group identity that results when people choose to relate around the worldview that results from one of the three primary analytical perspectives on life, excluding others who see life differently.
Sin	Any way of living that is not based on faith in one living God who sustains all. Those of strong faith may tolerate the sin of others by covering in love.
Sozo	Redemption into wholeness and peaceful living by salvation (transfiguration), healing (transformation) and deliverance (liberation).
Spirit	The emergence of transformation within as an effect of wider systemic change in which the person is embedded. It can be likened to a spring of water welling up out of dry earth. Likewise the human spirit is that which induces changes in someone else's life as a

	consequence of one's own choices
Spirit, Holy	The emergence of transformation within as an effect of God's living word inducing change and movement that connects a person who is uniquely diversifying into the wholeness of life..
Structuralist	A primary analytical perspective focusing on forms in life, in which people sense they are observers, as minds with pure reason able to act experimentally on inanimate matter.
Subsidiarity	Where one nested system is embedded within a larger one, the larger system can agree to allow subsidiary freedoms of self-regulation to the smaller, within limits that do not de-stabilise the larger system.
Substantial grace	The effect of agreement for unity among three Holy Persons of one living God, being the one substance (mutual understanding) upon which the spoken word moves all Three to create waves, as if over waters, out of which energy-matter forms.
Sub-state	Where eternal life is in God, the movement with reconciliation that is life appears to us to have been a Big Bang at the core of the universe, the pre-conditions for which are that living unity has three independent states between which movement creates space, time and real energy.
System	Any collection of a large number of independent elements that richly

	communicate among themselves and so generate a state of tension that predisposes the elements to behave as if a whole, such as a flock of starlings in the autumn.
Tao (vitalist life force)	In triune conversational orientation, the fact of relatedness in the giving and receiving exchanges. In a Collectivist mind frame this becomes reified as a pre-material energy or vital force, the essence or real stuff of life, which a Participator in life submits to.
Time frame	The quality that 'time' adopts in an Individualist analytical perspective, where time is a 'real presence' within which a certain number of changes have to be created if the person is to be alive.
3+1 model of personal development	The model that shows how triune principles of organisation can demonstrate ways to reconcile through constructive grieving, when misunderstanding between people who have adopted different analytical perspectives on life has produced separation and brokenness of relationship.
Triquetra	A three-cornered shape that is not a triangle. It is the Celtic symbol for the eternal dynamic underlying apparent stillness.
Triune prayer	A type of prayer in which an individual increases his or her awareness of the relationship between two others, and chooses to be a presence of grace for them to promote the life between them, as Jesus Christ is praying for us.

Triune principles of organisation	The active life of the theology of dust (land, body and mind), which equates living Word with the continuous creation of matter, transforming into bodies that have the potential in their social interactions for awareness, orientated consciousness, and informed communication.
Yes-and-no-no analysis	A way to analyse a claim about life or a worldview statement that a person makes, identifying from which of the three primary analytical perspectives it derives (yes), and then showing how it does not fit the truth criteria for the other two (no-no), so that it falls short of creative triune conversational balance.

Bibliography

Bannister, D. & Fransella, F. *Inquiring Man: The Psychology of Personal Constructs*. 2nd Edition. 1980. Penguin.

Barbour, I. *When Science Meets Religion*. 2000. SPCK.

Barbour, J. *The End of Time: The Next Revolution in Physics*. 2000. Oxford University Press.

Bateson, G. *Steps to an Ecology of Mind*. 1972. University of Chicago Press, Chicago and London.

Bateson, G & Bateson, M.C. *Angels Fear: Towards an Epistemology of the Sacred (Advances in Systems Theory, Complexity and the Human Sciences)*. 2004. Hampton Press, NJ.

Beauchamp, T & Childress, J. *Principles of Biomedical Ethics*. 2001. New York, Oxford. Oxford University Press

Bentall, R. *Madness Explained: Psychosis and Human Nature*. 2004. Penguin Books.

Brothers, L. *Friday's Footprint: How Society Shapes the Human Mind*. 1997. Oxford University Press.

Brown, C. *Christianity and Western Thought: A History of Philosophers, Ideas and Movements. Volume 1, From the Ancient World to the Age of Enlightenment*. 1990. Apollos, Leicester.

Burnham, J.B. *Family Therapy: First Steps Towards a Systemic Approach*. 1986. Routledge, London & NY.

Cilliers, P. *Complexity and Postmodernism: Understanding Complex Systems*. 1998. Routledge.

Cohen, J. and Stewart, I. *The Collapse of Chaos: Discovering Simplicity in a Complex World.* 1995. Penguin Science.

Crabb, L. *Inside Out.* 1988. Scripture Press.

Crabb, L. *Connecting: Healing for Ourselves and our Relationships.* 2005. W Publishing Group.

Damasio, A.R. *Descartes' Error: Emotion, Reason and the Human Brain.* 1996. Papermac.

Damasio, A.R. *The Feeling of What Happens: Body, Emotion and the Making of Consciousness.* 2000. Vintage.

Damasio, A.R. *Self Comes to Mind: Constructing the Conscious Brain.* 2010. William Heinemann, London.

Davies, P. *About Time: Einstein's Unfinished Revolution.* 1995. Penguin.

Day, J. T*he Secret to Letting Go and Moving on.* 2009. Newlandscape Books.

Documents of the Christian Church. 2nd Ed. Editor Bettenson, H. 1963. Oxford University Press.

Evans, P., Hucklebridge, F. and Clow A. *Mind, Immunity and Health: The Science of Psychoneuroimmunology.* 2000. Free Association Books

Fisher, J. *Meet Me at the Olive Tree: Stories of Jews and Arabs reconciling to the Messiah.* 2012. Monarch Books, Oxford, UK and Grand Rapids, Michigan, USA.

Gazzaniga, M.S., Ivry, R.B. & Mangun, G.R. *Cognitive Neuroscience: The Biology of the Mind.* 1998. W.W. Norton & Co., New York & London.

Gleick, J. *Chaos: Making a New Science.* 1988. Penguin

Godwin, R & Roberts, D. *The Grace Outpouring: Blessing Others Through Prayer.* 2008. David C. Cook Publishing, Kingsway

Communications, Eastbourne, UK and Colorado Springs, CO, USA.

Goleman, D. *Emotional Intelligence: Why it can Matter More Than IQ*. 1996. Bloomsbury, London.

Griffiths, T. *Lost and Then Found: Turning Life's Disappointments into Hidden Treasures*. 1999. Paternoster.

Gunton, C.E. *Christ and Creation*. 1992. Paternoster.

Gunton, C.E. *The One, The Three and The Many: God, Creation and the Culture of Modernity*. 1993. Cambridge University Press.

Harold, G. Koenig, H.G. and Cohen, H.J. *The Link between Religion and Health: Psychoneuroimmunology and the Faith Factor*. 2002. Oxford University Press.

Hawkins, S.W. *A Brief History of Time: From the Big Bang to Black Holes*. 1988. Bantam Press.

Holmes, J. *John Bowlby & Attachment Theory*. 1993. Brunner-Routledge.

Jones, E. *Family Systems Therapy: Developments in the Milan-Systemic Therapies*. 1993. John Wiley & Sons.

Kelly, J.N.D. *Early Christian Doctrines*. 5th Ed. 1977. A & C Black, London.

Lewis, C.S. *Mere Christianity*. 1952. Fount Paperbacks.

Meadows, D.H. *Thinking in Systems: A Primer*. 2009. Earthscan.

Munayer, S. & Loden, L. *Through My Enemy's Eyes: Envisioning Reconciliation in Israel-Palestine*. 2013. Paternoster.

Pascal Pensées. Eds. Rieu, Baldwick, Radice & Jones.1966. Penguin.

Rebiai, M. *Islam, Israel and the Church*. 2006. Sovereign World, Lancaster.

Richards, J. *But Deliver Us From Evil: An Introduction to the Demonic Dimension in Pastoral Care*. 1974. Darton, Longman & Todd, London.

Stacey, R. *Complex Responsive Processes in Organizations: Learning and Knowledge Creation.* 2001. Routledge, London & New York.

Talbot, M. *The Holographic Universe.* 1991. Grafton Books.

Tarazi, P.N. *Land and Covenant.* 2009. St. Paul, Minnesota. OCABS Press.

The Land Cries Out: Theology of the land in the Israeli-Palestinian context. Eds: Munayer, S. & Loden, L. 2012. Cascade Books, Wipf & Stock. Eugene, OR.

Thunberg, L. *Microcosm and Mediator: The Theological Anthropology of Maximus the Confessor.* 2nd Ed. 1995. Open Court. Illinois.

Torrance, J.B. *Worship, Community, and the Triune God of Grace.* 1996. Paternoster Press.

Ward, K. *God, Chance and Necessity.* 1996. Oneworld, Oxford.

Ware, K. *The Orthodox Way.* 1979. Mowbray, London & Oxford.

Ware T. *The Orthodox Church.* 1993. Penguin

White, A. *Father, Forgive: Reflections on Peacemaking.* 2013. Monarch Books, Oxford, UK and Grand Rapids, Michigan, USA.

Young, P.W. *The Shack: Where Tragedy Confronts Eternity.* 2007. Hodder.

Zizioulas, J.D. *Being as Communion: Studies in Personhood and the Church.* 1997. St Vladimir's Seminary Press. Crestwood, NY.